THE ROYAL HISTORICAL SOCIETY
ANNUAL BIBLIOGRAPHY OF BRITISH
AND IRISH HISTORY
Publications of 1976

ROYAL HISTORICAL SOCIETY

ANNUAL BIBLIOGRAPHY OF BRITISH AND IRISH HISTORY

Publications of 1976

General Editor: G.R. Elton

R. Barker	D.A.L. Morgan
A. Bennett	J.S. Morrill
N. Brooks	G. Mac Niocaill
R.A. Griffiths	T.I. Rae
M.W.C. Hassall	A.T.Q. Stewart
J.A. Woods	

HARVESTER PRESS LIMITED
HUMANITIES PRESS INC

For the Royal Historical Society

First published in 1977 for
The Royal Historical Society by
THE HARVESTER PRESS LIMITED
Publisher: John Spiers
2 Stanford Terrace, Hassocks,
Sussex, England
and in the USA in 1977 by
HUMANITIES PRESS INC.,
Atlantic Highlands,
N.J.07716

The Harvester Press
ISBN 0 85527 819 6
ISSN 0308-4558

Humanities Press Inc
ISBN 0-391-00753

Printed in Great Britain by
Redwood Burn Limited,
Trowbridge and Esher

CONTENTS

PREFACE

The Bibliography is meant in the first place to serve the urgent needs of scholars, which has meant subordinating absolutely total coverage and refinements of arrangement to speed of production. Nevertheless, it is comprehensive and arranged for easy use. Errors have no doubt occurred; omissions are sure to have done so; there may well be some strangely placed items. There were obvious problems in covering the publications of the last part of the year, but gaps will be filled in the next volume. The general editor would welcome any information about errors and omissions.

Because the sectional headings are those approved by section editors they are not uniform. Searchers are advised to use the subdivisions in conjunction with the Subject Index which, apart from covering all place and personal names, is designed to facilitate a thematic and conceptual analysis.

Pieces contained in collective works (under Bc and sometimes in a chronological section) are individually listed in the appropriate place and there referred to the number the volume bears in the Bibliography.

Items covering more than two sections are listed in B; any that extend over two sections appear as a rule in the first and are cross-referenced at the head of the second.

The editors wish to express their gratitude to the assistance received from the Institute of Historical Research (London), the International Medieval Bibliography (Leeds) and especially Professor P.H. Sawyer and Mr R.J. Walsh, and Mr S.J. Hills (Cambridge University Library).

Abbreviations

Arch. — Archaeological
B.   — Bulletin
HMSO — Her Majesty's Stationery Office
J.   — Journal
P.   — Proceedings
Q.   — Quarterly
R.   — Review
Soc.   — Society
T.   — Transactions
UP   — University Press

A. AUXILIARY

(a) *Bibliography and Archives*

1. Cook, C. *Sources in British History 1900–1951, compiled for the British Library of Political and Economic Science; vol. 2: A guide to the private papers of selected public servants.* London; Macmillan; 1975. Pp xiii, 297.
2. Scottish Record Office. *Index to register of deeds preserved in H.M. General Register House;* vol. 36: 1696. Edinburgh; HMSO; 1975. Pp 163.
3. Craven, N. *A Bibliography of the county of Angus.* [Forfar; E. Mann] ; 1975. Pp xv, 296.
4. Bishopsgate Institute. *George Howell Collection: index to the correspondence* (revised ed.). London; the Institute; 1975. Pp 29.
5. Stockport Public Library. *Local material on microfilm.* Metropolitan Borough of Stockport, Dept of Culture; 1975. Pp 13. — With supplement no. 1; pp. 8.
6. Ibid. *Marple and district local history: a brief guide to printed works and other sources.* The Same; 1975. Pp 13.
7. Idem. *Unpublished works on Stockport and neighbourhood.* The Same; 1975. Pp 6.
8. Boswell, J.C. *Milton's Library: a catalogue of the remains of John Milton's library and an annotated reconstruction of Milton's library and ancillary readings.* New York etc.; distributed by George Prior Ltd.; 1975. Pp xv, 264.
9. Royle, E. *The Bradlaugh papers: letters, papers and printed items relating to the life of Charles Bradlaugh (1833–1891), arranged from the collection assembled by his daughter, Hypatia Bradlaugh Bonner (1858–1935), and now in the possession of the National Secular Library* [an index]. Wakefield; EP Microform; 1975. Pp xiv, 184.
10. Burchall, M.J. (ed.). *Index of East Sussex parish records, 1275–1870.* Brighton; Sussex Family History Group; 1975. 95 leaves.
11. Chalones, W.H.; Richardson, R.C. (ed.). *British economic and social history: a bibliographical guide.* Manchester UP; 1976. Pp xiv, 130.
12. Pybus, S.M. (ed.). *Basic books on Sheffield history* (6th ed.). Sheffield City Libraries; 1976. Pp 16.
13. Hunt, C.J. *The book trade in Northumberland and Durham to 1860: a biographical dictionary of printers, engravers, lithographers, booksellers, stationers, publishers, mapsellers, printsellers, musicsellers, bookbinders, newsagents and owners of circulating*

libraries. Newcastle/Tyne; Thorne's Students Bookshop Ltd; 1975. Pp xviii, 116.

14. British Library of Political and Economic Science. *A London bibliography of the social sciences, vols. 29–31 (1972–73)* – 8th supplement. London; Mansell Information Publishing; 1975. Pp 649.

15. The Same. *Vol. 32 (1974)* – 9th supplement. The Same; 1975. Pp 451.

16. Morgan, F.C. and P.E. *Hereford Cathedral libraries (including the Chained Library and the Vicars Choral Library) and muniments* (2nd ed., revised). Hereford Cathedral Library; 1975. Pp 40.

17. Thurley, C.A. and D. *Index of the probate records of the court of the archdeacon of Ely, 1513–1857.* London; Phillimore for British Record Soc.; 1976. Pp xii, 228.

18. Rath, T., 'Business records in the Public Record Office in the age of the Industrial Revolution,' *Business History* 17 (1975), 189–200.

19. 'York Minster chamberlain accounts of St Peter's: a summary list,' *Borthwick Institute B.* 1 (1975), 43–8.

20. 'Chancery court probate index 1825–1857,' ibid. 39–42.

21. Rae, T.I., 'A list of articles on Scottish history published during the year 1974,' *Scottish Historical R.* 54 (1975), 207–14.

22. McClaren, C.A.; Stephen, M.A., 'Reports and surveys of archives in northern Scotland,' *Northern Scotland* 2 (1975), 85–93.

23. Biddle, M., 'Excavations at Winchester, 1971: tenth and final interim report: Part I,' *Antiquaries J.* 55 (1975), 96–126.

24. Lewis, C.R., 'Trade directories – a data source in urban analysis,' *National Library of Wales J.* 19 (1975), 181–93.

25. Morgan, R., 'Annual list and brief review of articles on agrarian history, 1974,' *Agricultural History R.* 24 (1976), 51–62.

26. 'First supplement to the *Guide to the Archive Collections, 1973–75,*' *Borthwick Institute B.* 1 (1975), 11–15.

27. Snell, L.S., 'Accessions to archives 1972 [Midlands material],' *Midland History* 3 (1975), 42–58.

28. Taylor, F. (ed.). *Handlist of charters, deeds and similar documents in the possession of the John Rylands University Library of Manchester; 4: Miscellaneous documents acquired by gift or purchase.* Manchester; The Library; 1975. Pp 139.

29. Royal Commission on Historical Manuscripts. *Accessions to repositories and reports added to the National Register of Archives, 1974.* London; HMSO; 1976. Pp vii, 97.

30. Yeats-Edwards, P. *English church music: a bibliography.* London; White Lion Publishers; 1975. Pp xviii, 217.

31. Loomes, B. *Lancashire clocks and clockmakers.* Newton Abbot; David & Charles; 1975. Pp 184.

32. Krummel, D.W. *English music printing, 1553–1700.* London; Bibliographical Soc.; 1975. Pp xi, 188.

33. Batts, J.S. *British manuscript diaries of the 19th century: an annotated listing.* Fontwell; Centaur Press; 1976. Pp xi, 345.
34. Revell, P. *Fifteenth century English prayers and Meditations: a descriptive list of manuscripts in the British Library.* New York; Garland; 1975. Pp xiv, 137.
35. Henrey, B. *British botanical and horticultural literature before 1800: comprising a history and bibliography of botanical and horticultural books printed in England, Scotland and Ireland from the earliest times until 1800.* London; Oxford UP; 1975. 3 vols: pp xxvi, 290; xvi, 748; xvii, 142.
36. Cherry, J.; Coad, J., 'Post-medieval Britain in periodical literature,' *Post-Medieval Archaeology* 9 (1975), 261—4.
37. King, V.J.; Wright, D. (ed.). *Parish registers in the Birmingham Reference Library.* Birmingham Public Libraries; 1975. Pp vii, 115.
38. *Scottish Material Culture: a bibliography, vol. 1.* Edinburgh; National Museum of Antiquities of Scotland; 1976. Pp 51. [Published at irregular intervals].
39. Higson, C.W.J. (ed.). *Sources for the history of education; Supplement: a list of material added to the libraries of the Institutes and Schools of Education 1965—1974, together with works from certain university libraries.* London; Library Association; 1976. Pp x, 221.
40. Gilbert, V.F.; Holmes, C. *Theses and dissertations in economic and social history in Yorkshire universities, 1920—74.* [Sheffield University Library] ; 1975. Pp 154.
41. Graves, E.B. (ed.). *A Bibliography of English history to 1485.* Oxford; Clarendon; 1975. Pp xxiv, 1103.
42. Keynes, Sir G. *A bibliography of George Berkeley, bishop of Cloyne: his works and critics in the eighteenth century.* Oxford; Clarendon; 1976. Pp xxvii, 285.
43. Gurney, N.K.M. *A handlist of parish register transcripts in the Borthwick Institute of Historical Research.* [York] ; The Institute; 1976. Pp v, 115.
44. Meyer, J., 'Bibliographie de l'histoire anglaise: histoire moderne,' *Revue historique* 517 (1976), 109—57.
45. Druker, J., 'The builders' history [list of archives],' *B. of the Soc. for the Study of Labour History* 32 (1976), 33—7.
46. Clark, C.O., 'A list of books and important articles on the technology of textile printing,' *Textile History* 6 (1975), 89—118.
47. *The Labour Party: a select reading list excluding Labour Party publications.* 2nd ed. London; Labour Party; 1975. Pp 24.
48. Schuler, R.M., 'English scientific poetry 1500—1700: prolegomena and preliminary check list,' *Papers of the Bibliographical Soc. of America* 69 (1975), 482—502.
49. Guth, D.J. *Late-medieval England* (bibliographical handbook). Cambridge UP; 1976. Pp xi, 143

50. Havighurst, A.F. *Modern England, 1901–1970* (bibliographical handbook). Cambridge UP; 1976. Pp x, 109.

51. Hargreaves, G.D. *A catalogue of medical incunabula in Edinburgh libraries.* Edinburgh; Royal Medical Soc.; 1976. Pp xiv, 54.

52. Turley, R.V. (ed.). *Hampshire and Isle of Wight bibliographies: selected nineteenth century sources.* Winchester; Sturlock; 1976. Pp xx, 432.

53. University of Durham, Department of Palaeography and Diplomatic. *List of the Shafto (Beamish) papers.* Durham; the Department; 1976. Pp 647.

54. Morgan, A. *The South Wales valleys in history: a guide to literature.* Aberfan; Ty Toronto; [1975]. Pp 47.

55. Jackson, W.A.; Ferguson, F.S.; Pantzer, K.F. (ed.). *A short-title catalogue of books printed in England, Scotland and Ireland and of English books printed abroad, 1475–1640*; vol. 2: I–Z [2nd ed. of Pollard and Redgrave's *STC*]. London; Bibliographical Soc.; 1976. Pp xi, 494.

56. Wilson, D.B. (ed.). *Catalogue of the manuscript collection of Sir Gabriel Stokes and Sir William Thomson, baron Kelvin of Largs, in Cambridge University Library.* Cambridge; the Library; 1976. Pp iii, 589.

57. Farrant, H.J. (ed.). *Sussex bibliography, 1973.* Lewes; Sussex Arch. Soc.; 1975. Pp 12.

58. Scottish Record Office. *List of American documents.* Edinburgh; HMSO; 1976. Pp viii, 167.

59. Farrington, A. (ed.). *The records of the East India College, Haileybury, and other institutions.* London; HMSO; 1976. Pp ix, 172.

60. Renford, R.K. *Archival and library sources for the study of the activities of the non-official British community in India: a brief survey.* London School of Oriental and African Studies; 1976. Pp 25.

61. 'Writings on Irish history, 1974,' *Irish Historical Studies* 19 (1975), 417–39.

62. 'Bibliography of recent books and articles dealing with the history of the Royal Society,' *Notes and Records of the Royal Society of London* 31 (1976), 169–73.

63. Campbell, R.H., 'Scottish economic history,' [review article] *Scottish J. of Political Economy* 23 (1976), 183–92.

64. Field, C.D., 'Bibliography of Methodist historical literature,' *P. of the Wesley Historical Soc.* 40 (1976), 145–9.

65. Deutsch, R. *Northern Ireland, 1921–1974: a select bibliography.* New York/London; Garland; 1975. Pp ix, 142.

66. Nicholls, D., 'Nineteenth-century English history: materials for teaching and study (Great Britain),' *Victorian Studies* 19 (1976), 345–77.

67. Public Record Office: *Exchequer K.R., sheriffs' accounts — class list.* London; List & Index Soc. (vol. 127).

68. Public Record Office: *Air Ministry, class list, part 3*. London; List & Index Soc. (vol. 128).
69. Public Record Office: *Descriptive list of state papers supplementary, part 6*. London; List & Index Soc. (vol. 129).
70. Public Record Office: *Chancery files, class list*. London; List & Index Soc. (vol. 130).
71. Public Record Office: *Cabinet office, class list, part 1*. London; List & Index Soc. (vol. 131).
72. Connolly, S.J.; Greenlees, S.R., 'Select bibliography of writings on Irish economic and social history published in 1975,' *Irish Economic and Social History* 3 (1976), 83–7.
73. Pryce-Jones, J.E. *Accounting in Scotland: a historical bibliography*, sec. ed. annotated R.H. Parker. Edinburgh; Institute of Chartered Accountants of Scotland; 1976. Pp 107, xviii.
74. Matheson, G.A.; Taylor, F. *Hand-list of personal papers from the muniments of the earl of Crawford and Balcarres deposited in the John Rylands University Library of Manchester*. Manchester; The Library; 1976. Pp 138.
75. British Library: *Catalogue of the Newspaper Library, Colindale*. London; British Museum Publications Ltd; 1975.
76. Merrington, M.; Golden, J. *A list of the papers and correspondence of Sir Francis Galton (1822–1911) held in . . . the Library, University College, London*. London; The College; 1976. Pp vi, 89.
77. Doe, V.; Sinar, J.; Strange, P. *Derbyshire's architectural heritage: a bibliographical guide*. Matlock; Derbyshire County Council; 1975. Pp 25.
78. Frankforter, A.D., 'The episcopal registers of medieval England: an inventory,' *British Studies Monitor* 6/2 (1976), 3–22.
79. Rae, T.I., 'A list of articles on Scottish history published during the year 1975,' *Scottish Historical R.* 55 (1976), 212–20.
80. Owen, D., 'The muniments of Ely Cathedral Priory,' Bc14, 157–76.
81. Sundstrom, R.A., 'Some original sources relating to Huguenot refugees in England, 1680–1727,' *British Studies Monitor* 6/3 (1976), 3–9.
82. E.G.W. Bill. *A catalogue of manuscripts in Lambeth Palace Library, MSS 1907–2340*. Oxford; Clarendon; 1976. Pp xi, 379.
83. Public Record Office: *Annual Report of the keeper of the public records on the work of the Public Record Office*. London; HMSO; 1976. Pp iii, 42.
84. State Papers: *General index to vols. 139 (1935) to 164 (1960) . . . compiled and edited in the Library and Records Department of the Foreign and Commonwealth Office*. London; HMSO; 1976. Pp 1427.
85. Elton, G.R. (ed.). *Annual Bibliography of British and Irish History: Publications of 1975*. Hassocks; Harvester Press; for Royal Historical Soc.; 1976. Pp x, 155.

86. Hanham, H.J. (ed.). *Bibliography of British History: 1851—1914.* Oxford; Clarendon; 1976. Pp xxvii, 1606.

(b) *Works of Reference*

1. Freshwater, P.B. (ed.). *Working papers for an historical directory of the West Midlands book trade to 1850; no. 1, to 1779.* Birmingham Bibliographical Soc.; 1975. Pp 18.
2. *Selden Society: publications, list of members and rules.* London; the Society; [1975]. Pp 84.
3. Mitchell, J.F. and S. *Monumental inscriptions (pre-1855) in North Perthshire.* [Edinburgh]; Scottish Genealogical Soc.; 1975. Pp v, 636.
4. Bell, S.P. *A biographical index of British engineers in the 19th century.* New York etc.; distributed by George Prior Ltd.; 1975. Pp x, 246.
5. *Wellington College Register, January 1859—December 1973*; 9th ed. [Crowthorne], Old Wellingtonian Soc.; 1975. Pp xvi, 431.
6. Ellis, M. (ed.). *Hampshire industrial archaeology: a guide.* Southampton Univ. Industrial Archaeology Group; 1975. Pp 53.
7. Chester Central Library. *The gentle reader's guide to 19th century Chester; 1: General sources.* [1976]. Pp ii, 18.
8. Bolton, P. (ed.). *The destroyed buildings of Warwickshire; a list.* Historical Association, Mid-Warwickshire Branch; [1975]. Pp 21.
9. Steer, F. *et al.* (compilers). *Dictionary of land surveyors and local cartographers of Great Britain and Ireland, 1550—1850* (ed. P. Eden); 2 parts. Folkestone; Dawson; 1975 and 1976. Pp 108; 221.
10. Bennet, J.D. *Who was who in Leicestershire, 1500—1970.* Loughborough; The Book House; 1975. Pp ix, 94.
11. Grimwade, A.G. *London goldsmiths, 1697—1837: their marks and lives.* London; Faber; 1976. Pp x, 728.
12. Wakeman, G.; Bridson, G.D.R. *A guide to nineteenth century colour printers.* Loughborough; Plough Press; 1975. Pp xii, 127.
13. Harris, P. *A concise dictionary of Scottish painters.* Edinburgh; Paul Harris Publishing; 1976. Pp 80.
14. Douglas, J. *Scottish banknotes* [list 1645 to present]. London; Gibbons; 1975. Pp xiv, 257.
15. *Cartographic treasures in the Bodleian Library: catalogue of an exhibition . . . held at the National Maritime Museum, Greenwich, 7—11 September 1975.* Oxford; The Library; 1975. Pp 35.
16. Metcalf, D.M. *Sylloge of coins of the British Isles, 23: Ashmolean Museum, Oxford; part 3: coins of Henry VII*; London; Oxford UP; 1976. Pp xlix, 106; liii leaves of plates.
17. Harvard University Library. *British History.* Cambridge, Mass.; The Library; 1975. 2 vols.
18. Farrant, J.H. *Sussex directories, 1784—1940* (2nd ed.). Brighton;

distributed by author for Sussex Family History Group; [1975].
Pp 13.

19. Cherry, J., 'Post-medieval Britain in 1974,' *Post-Medieval Archaeology* 9 (1975), 240–60.

20. Royal Commission on Historical Monuments. *An inventory of historical monuments in the county of Dorset, vol. 5: East Dorset.* London; HMSO; 1975 [i.e. 1976]. Pp xlviii, 155.

21. Parker, A.G. *Isle of Wight local history: a guide to sources.* Newport, I.o.W.; I.o.W. Teachers' Centre; 1975. Pp xi, 235.

22. Leslie, K.C.; McCann, T.J. *Local history in West Sussex: a guide to sources* (2nd revd. ed.). Chichester; West Sussex County Council; 1975. Pp v, 61.

23. Camp, A.J. (ed.). *An index to the wills proved in the Prerogative Court of Canterbury, 1750–1800*; vol. 1: A–Bh. London; Soc. of Genealogists; 1976. Pp 414.

24. Callard, J. *A catalogue of printed books (pre-1751) in the library of St George's Chapel, Windsor Castle.* Windsor; Dean and Canons; 1976. Pp xxxvi, 282.

25. Royal Commission on Historical Monuments (England). *An inventory of the historical monuments in the city of York; vol. 4: outside the city walls east of the Ouse.* London; HMSO; 1975. Pp lx, 111.

26. Reaney, P.H. *A dictionary of British surnames* (2nd ed. revised by R.M. Wilson). London; Routledge; 1976. Pp lxv, 398.

27. Oswald, A. *Clay pipes for the archaeologist.* Oxford; British Arch. Reports; 1975. Pp 207.

28. Smith, B.S. *Gloucestershire local history handbook* (2nd ed.). Gloucestershire Community Council; 1975. Pp 48.

29. Allison, A.F.; Goldsmith, V.F. *Titles of English books and of foreign books printed in English: an alphabetical finding list by titles of books published under the author's name, pseudonym or initials*; vol. 1: 1475–1640. Folkestone; Dawson; 1976. Pp 176.

30. Clinker, C.R. *Railway history sources: a handlist of the principal sources of original material with notes and guidance on its use* (revised ed.). Bristol; Avon-Anglia Publications; 1976. Pp 20.

31. Browne. D.M. *Readers' guide to books on British archaeology.* [Bury St Edmunds Library Association; 1975]. Pp 40.

32. Hart, R.E. *Victorian Britain* (3rd ed.). Bury St Edmunds; Library Association; 1976. Pp 80.

33. Gilbert, V.F. *Historical and archaeological journals: an annotated guide to the holdings of Sheffield University Main Library, January 1976.* Sheffield University Library; 1976. Pp i, 120.

34. Thomson, T.R. *A catalogue of British family histories* (3rd ed.). London; Research Publishing Co.; 1976. Pp 184.

35. Standing Conference for Local History. *Directory of national organisations.* London; the Conference; 1975. Pp 10.

36. Royal Commission on Historical Manuscripts. *Report on the papers of James Saumarez, 1st baron de Saumarez (1757–1836): Baltic naval papers, 1808–1827.* [Ipswich] ; Suffolk Record Office; 1975. 2 vols; 211, 241 leaves.

37. Brown, A.E. *Archaeological sites and finds in Rutland: a preliminary list.* University of Leicester, Dept. of Adult Education; 1975. Pp 28.

38. Clayton, P. *Archaeological sites of Britain.* London; Weidenfeld & Nicolson; 1976. Pp 239.

39. University of Birmingham Library. *Periodical articles in the social sciences and humanities: a guide to abstracts, indexes and current bibliographies* (2nd ed.). Birmingham; the Library; 1976. Pp 31.

40. Jacobs, P.M. (ed.). *History theses, 1901–70: historical research for higher degrees in the universities of the United Kingdom.* London; Institute of Historical Research; 1976. Pp viii, 456.

41. Edwards, L.W.L. *Index to Cornish nonconformist registers deposited at the Public Record Office.* London; the compiler; 1976. Pp xv, 138.

42. Temple, E. (ed.). *A survey of manuscripts illuminated in the British Isles; vol. 2: Anglo-Saxon manuscripts, 900–1066.* London; Harvey Miller; 1976. Pp 243.

43. Bindoff, S.T.; Boulton, J.T. (ed.). *Research in progress in English and history in Britain, Ireland, Canada, Australia and New Zealand* (2nd ed.). London; St James Press; 1976. Pp 284.

44. Chalmers-Hunt, J.M. *Natural history auctions, 1700–1972: a register of sales in the British Isles.* London; Sotheby Parke Bernet Publications; 1976. Pp xii, 189.

45. Insurance Institute of London (Historical Records Committee). *Developments of mercantile fire insurance in the city of London: report.* London; the Institute; [1976]. Pp 66.

46. McCollum, M.S. *Durham diocesan records, bishops' transcripts of parish registers: summary list of outside dates of transcripts.* Durham Dept. of Palaeography; 1976. Pp iv, 18.

47. Freshwater, P.B. (ed.). *Working papers for an historical directory of the West Midlands book trade to 1850*; no. 2: 1780–1789. Birmingham Bibliographical Soc.; 1976. Pp iv, 10.

48. Steer, F. *et al.*; ed. Eden, P. *Dictionary of land surveyors and local cartographers of Great Britain and Ireland, 1550–1850*; part 3. Folkestone; Dawson; 1976. Pp 222–377.

49. McRoberts, D., 'The Catholic directory for Scotland 1829–1925,' *Innes R.* 26 (1975), 93–120.

50. Feather, J.P. *Book prospectuses before 1801 in the John Johnson Collection: a catalogue with microfiches.* Oxford; Bodleian Library; 1976.

51. Thoday, A.G. *A list of the apparatus of Sir Francis Galton (1822–1911) held in the Galton Laboratory, University College, London.* London; The College; 1976. Pp 10.

52. Wallis, P.J. *An index of British mathematicians: a check list; part 2 – 1701–1760.* University of Newcastle; Project for Historical Bibliography; 1976. Pp xxvii, 136.
53. Driver, J.P., 'Worcestershire knights of the shire; part 3, Biographies F–W,' *T. of the Worcestershire Arch. Soc.* 3rd ser. 5 (1976), 7–22.
54. Chaplin, R., 'Ordinary men: recent work in social history,' *Local Historian* 12 (1976), 131–5.

(c) *Historiography*

1. Warren, W.L. *Undergraduate history* [inaugural lecture]. Queen's University of Belfast; 1975. Pp 18.
2. Daniel, G. *Cambridge and the back-looking curiosity* [inaugural lecture]. Cambridge UP; 1976. Pp 32.
3. Bedarida, F., 'Elie Halévy et le socialisme anglais,' *Revue historique* 254 (1975), 371–98.
4. Douglas, D.C., 'John Le Patourel, 1975,' *Northern History* 10 (1975), 1–27.
5. Garside, P.D., 'Scott and the "philosophical" historians,' *J. of the History of Ideas* 36 (1975), 497–512.
6. Pocock, J.G.A., 'British history: a plea for a new subject,' *J. of Modern History* 47 (1975), 601–28.
7. Gransden, A., 'Propaganda in English medieval historiography,' *J. of Medieval History* 1 (1975), 363–81.
8. Stones, E.L.G. (ed.). *F.W. Maitland: Letters to George Neilson.* University of Glasgow Press; 1976. Pp xxvi, 56.
9. Phythian-Adams, C. *Local history and folklore: a new framework.* London; Bedford Square Press; 1975. Pp 39.
10. Earl, D.W.L., 'Procrustean feudalism: an interpretative dilemma in English historical narration, 1700–1725,' *Historical J.* 19 (1976), 33–51.
11. Hernon, J.M., 'The last whig historian and consensus history: George Macaulay Trevelyan, 1876–1962,' *American Historical R.* 81 (1976), 66–97.
12. Masters, B.R., 'Local archivist 1876–1914: Dr Reginald R. Sharpe,' *J. of the Soc. of Archivists* 5 (1976), 275–82.
13. Hopkins, A.G., 'Imperial business in Africa; part II: interpretations,' *J. of African History* 17 (1976), 267–90.
14. Cullen, M., 'Some recent writings on the history of Great Britain from 1832 to 1868,' *New Zealand J. of History* 10 (1976), 63–74.
15. Huxley, G., 'The historical scholarship of John Bagnell Bury,' *Greek, Roman and Byzantine Studies* 17 (1976), 81–104.
16. Hudson, K. *Industrial archaeology: a new introduction* (3rd ed., revised). London; J. Baker; 1976. Pp 240.

17. Richardson, R.C., 'The English Revolution and the historians,' *Literature and History* 1 (1975), 28—48.
18. Rogers, A., 'The study of local history — opinion and practice; 3: new horizons in local history,' *Local Historian* 12 (1976), 67—73.
19. Gant, R., 'The topography as a resource for Welsh urban studies,' *National Library of Wales J.* 19 (1976), 217—26.
20. Samuel, R., 'Local history and oral history,' *History Workshop* 1 (1976), 191—208.
21. Le Patourel, J., 'Is northern history a subject?,' *Northern History* 12 (1976), 1—15.
22. Allison, A.F.; Rogers, D.M., 'Twenty-five years of *Recusant History*,' *Recusant History* 13 (1976), 153—6.
23. Jones, G.R.J., 'Historical geography and our landed heritage,' *University of Leeds R.* 19 (1976), 53—78.
24. Hancock, K., 'The historian and his evidence,' *J. of the Soc. of Archivists* 5 (1976), 337—45.
25. Watt, D.C., 'The historiography of appeasement,' Bc8, 110—29.
26. Brooke, C.N.L., 'Geoffrey of Monmouth as a historian,' Bc14, 77—91.
27. Chibnall, M., 'Charter and chronicle: the use of archive sources by Norman historians,' Bc14, 1—17.
28. Chapman, J.K.; Littlejohn, C.J., 'Home Rule revisited: an essay in historiography,' *Historical Reflections/Réflexions historiques* 3 (1976), 27—47.
29. Biggs, B.J., 'J.S. Piercy, Retford historian,' *T. of the Thoroton Soc.* 79 (1976 for 1975), 60—71.
30. Farrant, S., 'Some records of the old poor law as sources of local history,' *Local Historian* 12 (1976), 136—9.
31. Le Patourel, H.E.J., 'Pottery as evidence for social and economic change,' Bc15, 169—79.
32. Gelling, H.; Watts, U.E., 'The evidence of place names,' Bc15, 200—22.
33. Roberts, B.K., 'The anatomy of settlement,' Bc15, 295—326.
34. Bartley, D.D., 'Palaeobotanical evidence,' Bc15, 226—35.

B. GENERAL

(a) *Long Periods: national*

1. Pridmore, F. *The coins of the British Commonwealth of Nations to the end of the reign of George VI, 1952*; part 4: India; vol. 1: East India Company Presidency Series c. 1642—1835. London; Spink; 1975. Pp xv, 275.
2. Davies, R. *Women and work.* London; Hutchinson; 1975. Pp 191.
3. Ashwin, C. (ed.). *Art education: documents and policies, 1768—*

1975. London; Soc. for Research into Higher Education; 1975. Pp x, 158.

4. Faber, R. *French and English.* London; Faber; 1975. Pp 211.
5. Kelly, A. *The story of Wedgwood* (revd. ed.). London; Faber; 1975. Pp 91.
6. Starsmore, I. *English fairs* [i.e. fun-fairs]. London; Thames and Hudson; 1975. Pp 128.
7. Masters, B. *The dukes: the origins, ennoblement and history of 26 families.* London; Blond and Briggs; 1975. Pp 432.
8. Nicholas, H.G. *The United States and Britain.* Chicago/London; Univ. of Chicago Press; 1975. Pp viii, 195.
9. Daniell, D.S. *Cap of honour: the story of the Gloucestershire Regiment (the 28th/61st Foot), 1694–1975* (new ed.). London; White Lion Publishers; 1975. Pp 410.
10. Packett, C.N. *The county lieutenancy in the United Kingdom (1547–1975): a brief history and 'A to Z'* (revd. ed.). [Bradford; the author; 1975]. Pp 138.
11. Middleton, N.; Weitzmann, S. *A place for everyone: a history of state education from the end of the 18th century to the 1970s.* London; Gollancz; 1976. Pp 506.
12. Beckett, J.V., 'Local taxation in England from the sixteenth century to the nineteenth,' *Local Historian* 12 (1976), 7–12.
13. Griffiths, D.N., 'Four centuries of the Welsh prayer book,' *T. of the Honourable Soc. of Cymmrodorion* 1975, 162–90.
14. Howell, C., 'Stability and change 1300–1700: the socio-economic context of change of the self-perpetuating family farm in England,' *J. of Peasant Studies* 2 (1975), 468–82.
15. Mercer, E. *English vernacular houses: a study of traditional farm-houses and cottages* [for Royal Commission on Historical Monuments]. London; HMSO; 1975. Pp xxii, 246.
16. Smith, P. *Houses of the Welsh countryside: a study in historical geography* [for Royal Commission on Ancient and Historical Monuments in Wales]. London; HMSO; 1975. Pp xxv, 604.
17. Kerridge, E., 'British field systems (review article),' *Agricultural History R.* 24 (1976), 48–50.
18. Warner, O. *The British Navy: a concise history.* London; Thames & Hudson; 1975. Pp 191.
19. Allen, D.E. *The naturalist in Britain: a social history.* London; Allen Lane; 1976. Pp xii, 292.
20. West, T. *The fireplace in the home.* Newton Abbot; David & Charles; 1976. Pp 160.
21. Clarkson, L.A. *Death, disease and famine in pre-industrial England.* Dublin; Gill & Macmillan; 1975. Pp 188.
22. Wilkinson-Latham, C. *The Royal Green Jackets.* London; Osprey Publishing; 1975. Pp 40.
23. Carr, R. *English fox hunting: a history.* London; Weidenfeld & Nicolson; 1976. Pp xxi, 273.

24. Brander, A.M. *The Royal Scots (The Royal Regiment)*. London; Cooper; 1976. Pp x, 111.
25. Birrell, T.A., 'English catholic mystics in non-catholic circles,' *Downside R.* 93 (1976), 60–81, 99–115, 213–31.
26. Osborne, K. *Boat racing in England, 1715–1975*. London; Amateur Rowing Association; 1975. Pp 71.
27. Kennedy, P.M. *The rise and fall of British naval mastery*. London; Allen Lane; 1976. Pp xviii, 405.
28. Seymour, W. *Battles in Britain, and their political background*; 2 vols (1066–1547; 1642–1746). London; Sidgwick & Jackson; 1975 [i.e. 1976]. Pp 232; 231.
29. Havins, P.J.N. *The spas of England*. London; Hale; 1976. Pp 192.
30. McWilliam, C. *Scottish townscape*. London; Collins; 1975. Pp 256.
31. Bossy, J.A. *The English catholic community, 1570–1850*. London; Darton, Longman & Todd; 1975. Pp xv, 446.
32. Blake, R. (Lord Blake). *The office of prime minister*. London; Oxford UP; 1975. Pp 74.
33. Taylor, C. *Fields in the English landscape*. London; Dent; 1975. Pp 174.
34. Williams, M. *The making of the South Wales landscape*. London; Hodder & Stoughton; 1975. Pp 271.
35. Jewell, C.A., 'The impact of America on English agriculture,' *Agricultural History* 50 (1976), 125–36.
36. Fussell, G.E., 'Countrywomen in old England,' ibid. 175–8.
37. Borer, M.C. *Willingly to school: a history of women's education*. Guildford; Lutterworth Press; 1976. Pp 319.
38. Sparkes, I.G. *Stagecoaches and carriages: an illustrated history of coaches and coaching*. Bourne End; Spurbooks; 1975. Pp 160.
39. Boyd, D. *Royal Engineers*. London; Cooper; 1975. Pp xxii, 162.
40. Clifton-Taylor, A.; *et al*. *Spirit of the age*. London; BBC; 1975. Pp 240.
41. Bunch, A.J. *Hospital and medical libraries in Scotland: an historical and sociological study*. Glasgow; Scottish Library Association; 1975. Pp xii, 186.
42. Jurow, K., 'Untimely thoughts: a reconsideration of the origins of due process of law,' *American J. of Legal History* 19 (1975), 280–312.
43. Darley, G. *Villages of vision*. London; Architectural Press; 1975. Pp viii, 152.
44. Havins, P.J.N. *The forests of England*. London; Hale; 1975. Pp 208.
45. Buchanan, R.A.; Watkins, G. *The industrial archaeology of the stationary steam engine*. London; Allen Lane; 1976. Pp xiv, 199.
46. Gregg, P. *Black death to Industrial Revolution: a social and economic history of England*. London; Harrap; 1976. Pp 344.
47. Fawcett, J. (ed.). *The future of the past: attitudes to conservation, 1174–1974*. London; Thames & Hudson; 1976. Pp 160.

48. Norman, E.R. *Church and Society in England, 1770–1970: a historical study*. Oxford; Clarendon; 1976. Pp 507.
49. Webb, W. *Coastguard: an official history of HM Coastguard*. London; HMSO; 1976. Pp xvii, 196.
50. Wilson, D. *The people and the Book: the revolutionary impact of the English Bible, 1380–1611*. London; Barrie & Jenkins; 1976. Pp x, 182.
51. Gurnham, R. *A history of the trade union movement in the hosiery and knitwear industry, 1776–1976: the history of the National Union of Hosiery and Knitwear Workers, its evolution and its predecessors*. Leicester; the Union; 1976. Pp xiii, 197.
52. *The English sermon: an anthology*; 3 vols. Vol. 1: 1550–1650, ed. M. Seymour-Smith; vol. 2: 1650–1750, ed. C.H. Sisson; vol. 3: 1750–1850, ed. R. Nye. Cheadle; Carcanet Press; 1976. Pp xiii, 491; 358; 325.
53. Apps, M. *The four 'Ark Royals'*. London; Kimber; 1976. Pp 256.
54. Gill, J. *Racecourses of Great Britain*. London; Barrie & Jenkins; 1975. Pp 256.
55. Hardy, R. *Longbow: a social and military history*. Cambridge; Stephens; 1976. Pp 216.
56. Yarwood, D. *The architecture of Britain*. London; Batsford; 1976. Pp 276.
57. Wardle, D. *English popular education, 1780–1975*; 2nd ed. Cambridge UP; 1976. Pp viii, 197.
58. Chivers, K. *The Shire horse: a history of the breed, the Society and the men*. London; J.A. Allen; 1976. Pp xxix, 834.
59. Sharpe, R.J. *The law of habeas corpus*. Oxford; Clarendon; 1976. Pp xii, 254.
60. Rackham, O. *Trees and woodland in the British landscape*. London; Dent; 1976. Pp 204.
61. Taylor, G. *History of the amateur theatre*. Melksham; Venton; 1976. Pp 196.
62. Parry, N. *The rise of the medical profession: a study of collective social mobility*. London; Croom Helm; 1976. Pp 282.
63. Cockerell, H.A.L.; Green, E. *The British insurance business, 1547–1970: an introduction and guide to historical records in the United Kingdom*. London; Heinemann Educational; 1976. Pp xiii, 142.
64. Port, M.H. (ed.). *The Houses of Parliament*. New Haven/London; Yale UP; 1976. Pp xxi, 347.
65. Machin, R., 'The Unit system: some historical explanations,' *Archaeological J.* 132 (1976 for 1975), 187–94.
66. Allen. H.C., 'The American revolution and the Anglo-American relationship in historical perspective,' Bc5, 149–77.
67. Campbell, D., 'Trees in the changing English landscape,' *J. of the Royal Agricultural Soc.* 137 (1976), 34–41.

68. Sunderland, J. *Painting in Britain, 1525 to 1975*. Oxford; Phaidon Press; 1976. Pp 256.
69. Lofts, N. *Domestic life in England*. London; Weidenfeld & Nicolson; 1976. Pp 254.
70. Taylor, J.S., 'The impact of pauper settlement 1691–1834,' *Past & Present* 73 (1976), 42–74.
71. Potts, W.T.W.; Sunderland, E., 'History and blood groups in the British Isles,' Bc15, 236–61.

(b) *Long periods: local*

1. Awdry, W. (ed.). *Industrial archaeology in Gloucestershire*. (2nd ed.). Cheltenham; Glos. Soc. for Industrial Archaeology; 1975. Pp 34.
2. McGrath, P. *The merchant venturers of Bristol: a history of the Society of Merchant Venturers of the City of Bristol from its origin to the present day*. Bristol; the Society; 1975. Pp xviii, 613.
3. Grant, N. *The Campbells of Argyle*. London; Watts; 1975. Pp 96.
4. Jones, G.P., 'Some sources of loans and credit in Cumbria before the use of banks,' *T. of the Cumberland and Westmorland Antiquarian and Arch. Soc.* new ser. 75 (1975), 275–92.
5. Hall, D.J. (intr.). *The ADC, the first 120 years: an exhibition at the University Library, Cambridge, July–November 1975*. [Cambridge; the Library; 1975]. Pp 8.
6. Turnbull, L. *The history of leadmining in the north east of England*. Newcastle/Tyne; Hill; 1975. Pp 80.
7. Wills, N.T. *Woad in the Fens* (2nd ed.). Lincoln; Industrial Archaeology Subcommittee of the Soc. for Lincolnshire History and Archaeology; 1975. Pp iv, 29.
8. Walton, M.; Meredith, R. *Beauchief Abbey past and present* (2nd ed.). Sheffield City Libraries; 1975.
9. Stapledon, H.E.C. (ed. G.G. Pace and J.E. Day). *A skilful master-builder: the continuing story of a Yorkshire family business, craftsmen for seven generations*. York; Wm. Anelay; 1975. Pp viii, 72.
10. Jones, E. *Senedd Stiniog: hanes Cyngor Dinesig Ffestiniog, 1895–1974*. Y Bala; Gwasg y Sir; [1975]. Pp 114.
11. Glover, J. *The place names of Kent*. London; Batsford; 1976. Pp viii, 215.
12. Lemprière, R. *Portrait of the Channel Islands* (2nd ed.). London; Hale; 1975. Pp 224.
13. Meadows, A.J. *The Royal Observatory at Greenwich and Herstmonceux, 1675–1975*; vol. 2: recent history (1836–1975). London; Taylor & Francis; 1975. Pp xi, 135.
14. Sherlock, R. *The industrial archaeology of Staffordshire*. Newton Abbot; David & Charles; 1976. Pp 216.

14

15. Ehmann, D.; Marshall, M. *The constitution of Guernsey*. St Peter Port; Toucan Press; 1976. Pp 18.
16. Sharpe, F. *The church bells of Herefordshire, their inscriptions and founders*; vol. 5: summarised accounts of the bells at the Reformation and the present day and details of bellfounders. [Launton]; the author; 1975.
17. Hinings, E. *History, people and places of the Cinque Ports*. Bourne End; Spurbooks; 1975 [i.e. 1976]. Pp 144.
18. Waters, I. *A list of vicars of Chepstow*. Chepstow; the author; 1975. Pp 15.
19. Weaver, L.T. *The Harwich packets: the story of the service between Harwich and Holland since 1661*. Seaford; Lindel Organisation Ltd; [1975]. Pp 53.
20. Young, J.R. *The inns and taverns of old Norwich*. Norwich; Wensum Books; 1975. Pp 102.
21. Wright, N.R. *Spalding: an industrial history* (2nd ed.). Lincoln; Industrial Archaeology Subcommittee of the Soc. for Lincolnshire History and Archaeology; 1975. Pp 87.
22. Borer, M.C. *Mayfair: the years of grandeur*. London; Allen; 1975. Pp 308.
23. Turnock, D., 'Small farms in north Scotland: an exploration in historical geography,' *Scottish Geographical Magazine* 91 (1975), 164–81.
24. Andrews, C.T. *The first Cornish hospital*. [Truro; the author]; 1975. Pp 225.
25. Saunders-Jacobs, S. *West Chiltington in West Sussex*. [Pulborough; the author; 1975]. Pp 47.
26. Agnew, J. *The story of the Vale of Leven*. [Alexandria, Dunbartonshire; the author; 1976]. Pp 79.
27. Seymour, W., 'Cranborne Chase,' *History Today* 26 (1976), 48–55, 68–9.
28. Greenslade, M.W. (ed.). *A history of the county of Stafford*, vol. 17 (Victoria County History). Oxford UP for Institute of Historical Research; 1976. Pp xxiv, 310.
29. Allison, K.J. (ed.). *A history of the county of York, East Riding*, vol. 3 (Victoria County History). Ibid.; 1976. Pp xvi, 220.
30. Scott-Giles, C.W. *Sidney Sussex College: a short history*. Cambridge; The College; 1975. Pp xiii, 144.
31. Tonkin, J. and M. *The book of Hereford: the story of the city's past*. Chesham; Barracuda Books; 1975. Pp 148.
32. Robinson, C.; Birtchnell, P. *The book of Hemel Hempstead and Berkhamstead: the illustrated record of both towns' past*. The Same; 1975. Pp 140.
33. Savidge, A. *Royal Tunbridge Wells*. [Tunbridge Wells]; Midas Books; [1975]. Pp 216.
34. Brotchie, A.W. *The tramways of Falkirk*. [Dundee]; New Traction Group; 1975. Pp 35.

35. Western, H.G. *A history of Ickleford.* Ickleford; D.W. Morgan; 1975. Pp xi, 82.

36. Burford, E.J. *Bawds and lodgings: a history of London Bankside brothels, c. 100–1675.* London; Owen; 1976. Pp 206.

37. Cox, M.; Hopkins, L.A. *A history of Sir John Deane's Grammar School Northwich, 1557–1908.* Manchester UP; 1975. Pp xvi, 317.

38. Weaver, L.T. *The Harwich story.* [Dovercourt; Harwich Printing Co.]; 1975. Pp 176.

39. Sutermeister, H., 'Excavations on the site of the Tudor manor house at Micheldever, Hampshire,' *Post-Medieval Archaeology* 9 (1975), 117–36.

40. Maddams, J.E. (ed.). *Unvanquished: a history of the Baptists of Saffron Walden and their antecedents, 1550–1975.* [Saffron Walden Baptist Church; 1975]. Pp 32.

41. Hair, P.E.H., 'Family and locality: an encouraging exercise in Herefordshire records,' *Local Historian* 12 (1976), 3–6.

42. Crossley, D. *The Bewl Valley ironworks, Kent, c. 1300–1730.* London; Royal Arch. Institute; 1975. Pp x, 98.

43. Burnby, J.G.L.; Whittet, T.D. *Plague, pills and surgery: the story of the Bromfields.* [Enfield; Edmonton Hundred Historical Soc.]; 1975. Pp 13.

44. Nelson, J.P. *Chipping Campden: some aspects of the past and present of a North Cotswold country town and its surrounding district.* [Broad Campden]; the author; 1975. Pp xi, 120.

45. Nuttgens, P. *York, the continuing city.* London; Faber; 1976. Pp 130.

46. Verity, T.E.A. *A brief history of the church and parish of Stapleton in Cumberland.* Newcastle/Tyne; Mrs C.M. Hall; 1976. Pp 16.

47. Hobley, B., 'The archaeological heritage of the City of London: a progress report for the Department of Urban Archaeology, Museum of London,' *London J.* 2 (1976), 67–84.

48. Bick, D.E. *The old metal mines of mid-Wales*; part 3: Cardiganshire—North of Goginan. Newent; The Pound House; 1976. Pp 72.

49. Watson, R., 'A study of surname distribution in a group of Cambridgeshire parishes 1538–1840,' *Local Population Studies* 15 (1975), 23–32.

50. Brunskill, R.W., 'Vernacular architecture of the northern Pennines,' *Northern History* 11 (1976 for 1975), 107–42.

51. Speake, R., 'Under-registration in the Warton (Lancs.) registers,' *Local Population Studies* 15 (1975), 45–6.

52. Dunning, R.W., 'Ilchester: a study in continuity,' *Somerset Archaeology and Natural History* 119 (1974–5), 44–50.

53. Raistrick, A. *The lead industry of Wensleydale and Swaledale*; vol. 2: The smelting mills. Buxton; Moorland Publishing Co.; 1975. Pp 120.

54. Percy, G.H.G. *History of Whitgift School.* London; Batsford; 1976. Pp xii, 388.
55. Hartley, W.C.E. *Banking in Yorkshire.* Clapham, Yorks.; Dalesman; 1975. Pp 168.
56. *A history of Blaydon* [Winlaton and District Local History Soc.] Gateshead Metropolitan Borough Council; 1975. Pp xxi, 182.
57. Hughes, M. *The small towns of Hampshire: the archaeological and historical implications of development.* Southampton; Hampshire Arch. Committee; 1976. Pp 148.
58. Brown. W.E. *The history of Bolton School.* Bolton; The School; 1976. Pp 266.
59. Cochrane, H. *Glasgow: the first 800 years.* City of Glasgow District Council; 1975. Pp 64.
60. Langley, M. *The Loyal Regiment (North Lancashire: the 47th and 81st Regiments of Foot).* London; Cooper; 1976. Pp xvi, 118.
61. Williams, S. (ed.). *South Glamorgan: a county history.* Barry; S. Williams Publishers; 1975. Pp 246.
62. Ashmore, O. *The industrial archaeology of Stockport.* Univ. of Manchester, Dept. of Extra Mural Studies; 1975. Pp 100.
63. Wade, C. (ed.). *The streets of West Hampstead: an historical survey of streets, houses and residents* (compiled by the Camden History Society's Street History Group). London; High Hill Press; 1975. Pp 72.
64. Courtney, T. *Chesterfield: the recent archaeological discoveries.* Chesterfield Arch. Research Committee; 1975. Pp 24.
65. Spaul, J.E.H. *A short history of Andover.* Andover Local Archives Committee; 1976. Pp 40.
66. Ashmall, H.A. *The High School of Glasgow.* [Edinburgh] ; Scottish Academic Press; 1976. Pp viii, 204.
67. Patterson. A.T. *Portsmouth: a history.* Bradford-on-Avon; Moonraker Press; 1976. Pp 164.
68. Forbes, E.G. *The Royal Observatory at Greenwich and Herstmonceux, 1675–1975*; vol. 1: origins and early history (1675–1835). London; Taylor & Francis; 1975. Pp xv, 204.
69. Fallon, G.A. *The Roman Catholics in Standish.* Standish Local History Group; 1976. Pp 35.
70. Harris, G. and F.L. (ed.). *The making of a Cornish town: Torpoint and neighbourhood through two hundred years.* Redruth; Institute of Cornish Studies; 1976. Pp 192.
71. Lane Poole, E.H. *Damerham and Martin: a study in local history.* Tisbury; Compton Russell; 1976. Pp x, 230.
72. Baker, T.F.T. *A history of the county of Middlesex*, vol. 5. (Victoria County Histories). London; Oxford UP; 1976. Pp xix, 424.
73. Tomkinson, K.; Hall, G. *Kidderminster since 1800.* Kidderminster; the authors; 1975. Pp 262.
74. *Rugby: aspects of the past.* Rugby Local History Group; [1975]. Pp 71.

75. Pevsner, N.; Simpson, D. *Wiltshire* (2nd ed. revised by B. Cherry and D. Bonney). Harmondsworth; Penguin; 1975 [i.e. 1976]. Pp 651.

76. Dunning, R.W. *Christianity in Somerset*. Somerset County Council; 1976. Pp xii, 132.

77. Koop, H.V. *Broughton in Furness: a history*. Beckermet; Michael Moon; 1975. Pp 71.

78. Portergill, J., 'The Banbury Bluecoat Foundation,' *Cake & Cockhorse* 7 (1976), 19—22.

79. Bailey, J.L.H. *Finedon otherwise Thingdon*. Finedon; the author; 1975. Pp ix, 225.

80. Eason, R.E.; Snoxall, R.A. *The last of their line: the bible clerks of All Souls College, Oxford: some notes and reminiscences*. Oxford; the College; 1976. Pp vii, 24.

81. Wilshere, J. *The town halls of Leicester*. Leicester Research Dept of Chamberlain Music and Books; [1976]. Pp 16.

82. Hughes, S.J.S. *Cardiganshire, its mines and miners*. Ceredigion; the author; [1976]. Pp 49.

83. Ogley, R. (ed.). *Lady Boswell's School, 1675—1975*. Sevenoaks; Lady Boswell's School Parent-Teacher Ass.; 1976. Pp 92.

84. Arkinstall, M.J.; Baird, P.C. *Erdington past and present*. Birmingham Public Libraries; 1976. Pp vii, 71.

85. Smith, V. (ed.). *The town book of Lewes, 1837—1901*. Lewes; Sussex Record Soc.; 1976. Pp xiv, 469.

86. Legg, E. *The clock and watchmakers of Buckinghamshire*. Milton Keynes; Bradwell Abbey Field Centre; 1976. Pp 39.

87. Cowie, L.W., 'The London Greyfriars,' *History Today* 26 (1976), 462—7, 484—5.

88. Jones. R.E., 'Infant mortality in rural north Shropshire, 1561—1810,' *Population Studies* 29 (1975), 305—17.

89. Eden, P., 'Land surveyors in Norfolk 1550—1850, Part II,' *Norfolk Archaeology* 36 (1975), 119—48.

90. Salmon, J.E. (ed.). *The Surrey countryside: the interplay of land and people*. Guildford; Univ. of Surrey; 1975. Pp 217.

91. Armstrong, P. *The changing landscape: the history and ecology of man's impact on the face of East Anglia*. Lavenham; T. Dalton; 1975. Pp 144.

92. Bartle, G.F. *A history of Borough Road College*. [Isleworth; the College]; 1976. Pp 114.

93. Taylor, A.W. (ed.). *The history of Beaconsfield*. Beaconsfield and District Historical Soc.; 1976. Pp viii, 112.

94. Bushell, T.A. *Kent*. Chesham; Barracuda Books; 1976. Pp 134.

95. Chapman, V. *Rural Darlington: farm, mansion and suburb*. Durham County Council; 1975. Pp vi, 64.

96. Clarke, D. *Otford in Kent: a history*. Otford and District Historical Soc.; 1975. Pp xiv, 297.

97. Latham, F.A. (ed.). *Cuddington and Sandiway: the history of*

two Cheshire villages. Cuddington Local History Soc.; 1975. Pp 111.

98. Elliott, D.J. *Buckingham: the loyal and ancient borough.* London; Phillimore; 1975. Pp x, 262.

99. Geddes, R.S. *Burlington blue-grey: a history of the slate quarries, Kirby-in-Furness.* Kirby-in-Furness; the author; 1975. Pp 320.

100. Godber, J. *Friends in Bedfordshire and west Hertfordshire.* Bedford; the author; 1975. Pp 100.

101. Hudson, K. *The Bath and West: a bicentenary history.* Bradford-on-Avon; Moonraker Press; 1976. Pp xiii, 251.

102. Jessup, M. *A history of Oxfordshire.* London; Phillimore; 1975. Pp 136.

103. Kissack, K.E. *Monmouth: the making of a county town.* London; Phillimore; 1975. Pp 345.

104. Lang, J. *Pride without prejudice: the story of London's guilds and livery companies.* London; Perpetua Press; 1975. Pp 192.

105. Middleton, T. *The book of Maidenhead: the story of the town.* Chesham; Barracuda Books; 1975. Pp 148.

106. Miners, H. *The story of the Bristol Cornish.* Bristol; the author; 1975. Pp 122.

107. Morris, J.A. *A history of the Latymer School of Edmonton.* Edmonton; Latymer Foundation; 1975. Pp 314.

108. *Staffordshire population since 1660.* [Staffordshire Education Department; 1975]. Pp 49.

109. Wood, E.A. *A history of Thorpe-le-Soken to the year 1890.* Thorpe-le-Soken; T.C. Webb; 1975. Pp 173.

110. Mills, D. *The place names of Lancashire.* London; Batsford; 1976. Pp 154.

111. Henderson, M.; Lascelles, L. (ed.). *Catholic registers in the county of Worcestershire.* [Malvern] ; Worcestershire Catholic History Soc.; 1975. Pp 21.

112. Morgan, V., 'A case study of population change over two centuries: Blaris, Lisburn 1661—1848,' *Irish Economic and Social History* 3 (1976), 5—16.

113. *The archaeology of Warrington's past.* Warrington Development Corporation; 1976. Pp 100.

114. Page, R. *Census of Norwich, 1851;* part 1: St Martin at Palace, St Martin at Oak. [Norwich; Norfolk and Norwich Genealogical Soc.] ; 1975. Pp 165.

115. Bennett, T.R. (ed.). *Investigating Penn: a brief history of a Staffordshire village now part of Wolverhampton.* Wolverhampton; Workers' Educational Association; 1975. Pp 113.

116. Not used.

117. Kolbert, J.M. *The Sneyds: squires of Keele.* University of Keele; 1976. Pp 32.

118. Addyman, P.V.; Hood, J.S.R.; Kenward, H.K.; MacGregor, A.; Williams, D., 'Palaeoclimate in urban environmental archaeology

at York, England: problems and potential,' *World Archaeology* 8 (1976), 220–33.

119. Lynch, L.G. *The changing face of Ellesmere Port.* [Ellesmere Port; the author; 1976]. Pp 119.

120. Popham, F.W. *A west country family: the Pophams from 1150.* Sevenoaks; the author; 1976. Pp 138.

121. Evinson, D. *St Thomas's, Fulham: a history of the church and mission.* London; Fulham and Hammersmith Historical Soc.; 1976. Pp vi, 66.

122. Buck, K.S. *Provincial Grand Lodge of Essex, 1776–1976.* [Ilford; The Lodge] ; 1976. Pp 90.

123. Sandall, K.L., 'The Unit system in Essex,' *Archaeological J.* 132 (1976 for 1975), 195–201.

124. Davies, J.B., 'The Mathew family of Llandaff, Radyr and Castell-y-Mynach,' Bc6, 171–87.

125. Jones, H.C., 'A mountain community — Watford, Caerphilly,' Bc6, 9–21.

126. Bickford, J.A.R. and M.E. *The private lunatic asylums of the East Riding.* Beverley; East Yorkshire Local History Soc.; 1976. Pp 58.

127. Johnston, J.A., 'Developments in Worcester and Worcestershire 1563–1851,' *T. of the Worcestershire Arch. Soc.* 3rd ser. 5 (1976), 51–62.

128. Wilde, P., 'The use of business directories in comparing the industrial structure of towns: an example from the south-west Pennines,' *Local Historian* 12 (1976), 152–6.

129. Hill, R., 'Some parish boundaries in Hampshire,' Bc15, 61–5.

130. Beresford, M.W.; Hurst, J.G., 'Wharram Percy: a case study in microtopography,' Bc15, 114–44.

(c) *Collective Volumes*

1. Clogan, P.M. (ed.). *Medievalia et Humanistica: Studies in medieval and Renaissance culture.* New Series 6. Cambridge UP; 1975. Pp xiv, 223.

2. Taylor, A.J.P. *Essays in English history.* London; Hamilton; 1976. Pp 335.

3. Bromley, J.S.; Kossmann, E.H. (ed.). *Britain and the Netherlands*; vol. V: some political mythologies. The Hague; Nijhoff; 1975. Pp viii, 212.

4. Baker, D. (ed.). *The Orthodox Churches and the West.* Studies in Church History 13. Oxford; Blackwell; 1976. Pp xii, 336.

5. Allen, H.C.; Thompson, R. (ed.). *Contrast and connection: bicentennial essays in Anglo-American history.* London; Bell; 1976. Pp ix, 373.

6. Williams, S. (ed.). *Stewart Williams' Glamorgan historian*, vol. 11. Barry; S. Williams; 1975. Pp 254.

7. Hunt, R.W.; Philip, I.G.; Roberts, R.J. (ed.). *Studies in the book trade: in honor of Graham Pollard*. Oxford Bibliographical Soc.; 1975. Pp vii, 403.
8. Sked, A.; Cook, C. (ed.). *Crisis and controversy: essays in honour of A.J.P. Taylor*. London; Macmillan; 1976. Pp ix, 198.
9. Coleman, D.C.; John, A.H. (ed.). *Trade, government and economy in pre-industrial England: essays presented to F.J. Fisher*. London; Weidenfeld & Nicolson; 1976. Pp x, 302.
10. Best, G.A.; Wheatcroft, A. (ed.). *War, economy and the military mind*. London; Croom Helm; 1976. Pp 136.
11. Bond, B.; Roy, I. (ed.). *War and society: a yearbook of military history*. London; Croom Helm; 1975. Pp 254.
12. Wilson, C.H. *et al. The Anglo-Dutch contribution to the civilization of early modern society*. London; Oxford UP for British Academy; 1976. Pp 72.
13. Rosbottom, R.C. (ed.). *Studies in eighteenth-century culture*, vol. 5. Madison, Wisc.; University of Wisconsin Press; 1976.
14. Brooke, C.N.L.; Luscombe, D.E.; Martin, G.H.; Owen, D. (ed.). *Church and government in the middle ages: essays presented to C.R. Cheney*. Cambridge UP; 1976. Pp xvi, 312.
15. Sawyer, P.H. (ed.). *Medieval settlement: continuity and change*. London; Arnold; 1976. Pp 357.
16. Barley, M.W. (ed.). *The plans and topography of medieval towns in England and Wales*. London; Council for British Archaeology, Research Report 4; 1976. Pp vi, 92.

(d) Genealogy and Heraldry

1. Sadler, A.G. *The indents of lost monumental brasses in southern England*. Ferring-on-Sea; the author; 1976. Pp 40.
2. The Same. *The indents of lost monumental brasses in Kent*; 2 vols. Ibid.; 1975 and 1976. Pp viii, 88; iv, 88.
3. The Same. *The indents of lost monumental brasses in Wiltshire: being a record of the remaining indents or matrices*. Worthing; the author; 1975. Pp vii, 37.
4. The Same. *The indents of lost monumental brasses in West Sussex: being a record of the remaining indents or matrices*. Ibid.; 1975. Pp vi, 53.
5. Budge, E.M. *The history and genealogy of the Budge Family of Trotternish, Skye*. Dunvegan; [the author; 1975]. Pp 53.
6. Mackinnon, D.; Morrison, A. *The MacLeods, the genealogy of a clan*; sections 2, 3, 4. Edinburgh: Clan MacLeod Soc.; 1975. Pp xxiv, 131; viii, 294; viii, 195.
7. Summers, P.; Corder, J. (ed.). *Hatchments in Britain*; 2: Norfolk and Suffolk. London; Phillimore; 1976. Pp xiv, 157.
8. Filmer, J.L. *Filmer: seven centuries of a Kent family*. London; Research Publishing Company; 1975. Pp 32.

9. Chitty, E. *Chitty of London.* Harrow; the author; 1975. Pp 34.
10. Graham, N.H. *The genealogist's consolidated guide to parish registers in the inner London area, 1538 to 1837.* Orpington; the compiler; 1976. Pp 87.
11. Borg, A., 'Two studies in the history of the Tower Armouries,' *Archaeologia* 105 (1976), 317—52.
12. Valentine, D.C. *Church brasses of Leicestershire.* University of Leicester, Dept of Adult Education; 1975. Pp 28.
13. Humphery-Smith, C.R. *An introduction to medieval genealogy;* part 2: Bibliography and glossary. [Canterbury; Institute of Heraldic and Genealogical Studies; 1976]. Pp 93.
14. Boumphrey, R.S.; Hudleston, C.R.; Hughes, J. *An armorial for Westmorland and Lonsdale.* Cumberland and Westmorland Antiquarian and Arch. Soc.; 1975. Pp xxiii, 343.
15. Wagner, A. *Pedigree and progress: essays in the genealogical interpretation of history.* London; Phillimore; 1975. Pp x, 333.

C. ROMAN BRITAIN

See also: Aa41, b31, 37, 38.

(a) *Archaeology*

1. Dool, J., 'A Romano-British pottery duck,' *Antiquity* 50 (1976), 63—4.
2. Wells, C.; Dallas, C., 'Romano-British pathology,' ibid. 53—5.
3. Graham-Campbell, J.; Laing, L., 'The Mote of Mark and Celtic interlace,' ibid. 48—53.
4. Painter, K.S., 'A Roman Christian silver treasure from Biddulph, Staffordshire,' *Antiquaries J.* 55 (1975), 62—9.
5. Walthew, C.V., 'The town house and villa house in Roman Britain,' *Britannia* 6 (1975), 189—205.
6. Munby, J., 'Some moulded face-flagons from the Oxford kilns,' ibid. 182—8.
7. Fulford, M.; Bird, J., 'Imported pottery from Germany in late Roman Britain,' ibid. 171—81.
8. Webster, P.V., 'More British samian ware by the Aldgate-Pulborough potter,' ibid. 163—70.
9. Barker, P., 'Excavations at the Baths Basilica at Wroxeter 1966—74: interim report,' ibid. 106—17.
10. Phillips, E.J., 'The gravestone of M. Favonius Facilis,' ibid. 102—5.
11. Brassington, M., 'A re-appraisal of the western enclave, Corstopitum,' ibid. 62—75.
12. Swan, V.G., 'Oare reconsidered and the origins of Savernake ware in Wiltshire,' ibid. 37—61.

13. Maxwell, G.S., 'Excavation at the Roman fort of Bothwellhaugh 1967–8,' ibid. 20–36.
14. Allen, D.F., 'Cunobelin's gold.' ibid. 1–19.
15. Wilson, D.R., 'Romano-Celtic temple architecture,' *J. of the British Arch. Association* 3rd ser. 38 (1975), 3–27.
16. Charlesworth, D. *Aldborough Roman town and museum.* London; HMSO; 1975. Pp 20.
17. Henig, M., 'A Roman lead sealing from Kirmington, Lincolnshire,' *Britannia* 6 (1975), 208–9.
18. Spratling, M., 'Fragments of a lorica segmentation in the hoard from Santon, Norfolk,' ibid. 206–7.
19. Greenway, J.; Henig, M., 'A moulded glass cameo from Silchester,' ibid. 209–20.
20. Moore, C.N., 'A Roman bronze candlestick from Branston, Lincolnshire,' ibid. 210–12.
21. Millett, M., 'Recent work on the Romano-British settlement at Neatham, Hampshire,' ibid. 213–16.
22. Munby, J., 'A figure of jet from Westmorland,' ibid. 216–18.
23. Wilson, D.R., 'Roman Britain in 1974: sites explored,' ibid. 221–83.
24. Wright, R.P.; Hassall, M.W.C.; Tomlin, R.S.O., 'Roman Britain in 1974, II: Inscriptions,' ibid. 284–94.
25. Frere, S.S., 'The Silchester church: the excavation by Sir Ian Richmond in 1961,' *Archaeologia* 105 (1976), 277–302.
26. Thompson, F.H., 'The excavation of the Roman ampitheatre at Chester,' ibid. 127–239.
27. Bradley, R., 'Maumbury Rings, Dorchester: the excavations of 1908–1913,' ibid. 1–97.
28. Lawson, A.J., 'Shale and jet objects from Silchester,' ibid. 241–75.
29. Boon, G.C.; Savory, H.N., 'A silver trumpet-brooch with relief decoration, parcel-gilt, from Carmarthen and a note on the development of the type,' *Antiquaries J.* 55 (1975), 41–61.
30. Jobey, G., 'Excavations at Boonies, Westerkirk, and the nature of Romano-British settlement in eastern Dumfriesshire,' *P. of the Soc. of Antiquaries of Scotland* 105 (1975 for 1972/4), 119–40.
31. Maxfield, V.A., 'Excavations at Eskbank, Midlothian,' ibid. 141–50.
32. Breeze, D.J. 'Excavations at the Roman fortlet on the Antonine Wall at Watling Lodge, 1972–4,' ibid. 166–75.
33. Phillips, E.J., 'The Roman distance slab from Bridgeness,' ibid. 176–82.
34. Rutherford, A.; Ritchie, G., 'The Catstane,' ibid. 183–8.
35. Laing, L.R., 'Picts, Saxons and Celtic metalwork,' ibid. 189–99.
36. Green, K.T., 'The Romano-Celtic head from the Bonmarche site, Gloucester: a reappraisal,' *Antiquaries J.* 55 (1975), 338–65.
37. Biddle, M., 'Excavations at Winchester, 1971: tenth and final interim report; part II,' ibid. 295–337.

38. Hurst, H., *et al.*, 'Excavations at Gloucester: third interim report: Kingsholm 1966—75,' ibid. 267—94.

39. Colyer, C., 'Excavations at Lincoln 1970—1972: the western defences of the lower town; an interim report,' ibid. 227—66.

40. Henig, M.; Ogden, J., 'A gold ring found near Grantham,' ibid. 382—4.

41. Stead, J., 'A Roman pottery theatrical face-mask and a bronze brooch-blank from Baldock, Herts.,' ibid. 397.

42. Boon, G., 'Two Celtic pins from Margam Beach, West Glamorgan,' ibid. 400—404.

43. Charlesworth, D., 'A Roman cut glass plate from Wroxeter,' ibid. 404—6.

44. Detsicas, A., 'A knife-handle from the Eccles (Kent) Roman villa,' ibid. 406—7.

45. Musty, J., 'A brass sheet of first century A.D. date from Colchester,' ibid. 409—11.

46. Heighway, C.M. *Ancient Gloucester: the story of the Roman and medieval city.* Gloucester City Museums; 1976. Pp 13.

47. Mowat, R.J.C., 'The Hollesley Bay Romano-British rural settlement,' *East Anglian Archaeology* 1 (1975), 17—23.

48. Royal Commission on Historical Monuments: *An inventory of the historical monuments in the county of Northampton.* Vol. 1: Archaeological sites in north-east Northamptonshire. London; HMSO; 1975. Pp iii—xiv, 133.

49. Edwards, D.E., 'The air photographs collection of the Norfolk Archaeological Unit,' *East Anglian Archaeology* 2 (1976), 251—69.

50. Swan, V.G. *Pottery in Roman Britain.* Princes Risborough; Shire Publications; 1975. Pp 56.

51. Robertson, A.S.; Scott, M.; Keppie, L. *Bar Hill: a Roman fort and its finds.* Oxford; British Arch. Reports; 1975. Pp 184.

52. Macgregor, M. *Early Celtic art in north Britain: a study of decorative metalwork from the third century B.C. to the third century A.D.* Leicester UP; 1976. Pp xix, 224.

53. Garlick, T. *Romans in the Lake Counties* (3rd ed.). Clapham; Dalesman; 1976. Pp 80.

54. Higham, N.J.; Jones, G.D.B., 'Frontiers, forts and farmers: Cumbrian Aerial Survey 1974—5,' *Archaeological J.* 132 (1976 for 1975), 16—53.

55. Green, M.J., 'Romano-British non-ceramic model objects in south-east Britain,' ibid. 54—70.

56. Todd, M.; Harman, M., 'The Romano-British rural settlement at Staunton, Nottinghamshire,' *T. of the Thoroton Soc.* 79 (1976 for 1975), 29—39.

57. Charlesworth, D., 'The hospital, Housesteads,' *Archaeologia Aeliana* 5th ser. 4 (1976), 17—30.

58. Cunliffe, B., 'The Roman baths at Bath: the excavations of 1969–75,' *Britannia* 7 (1976), 1–32.
59. Maxwell, G.S., 'A Roman timber tower at Beattock Symmit, Lanarkshire,' ibid. 33–8.
60. Jackson, D.A.; Ambrose, T.M., 'A Roman timber bridge at Aldwincle, Northants.,' ibid. 39–72.
61. Breeze, D.J.; Close-Brooks, J.; Ritchie, J.N.G., 'Soldiers' burials at Camelon, Stirlingshire, 1922 and 1975,' ibid. 73–95.
62. Davies, R.W., '*Singulares* and Roman Britain,' ibid. 134–44.
63. Blagg, T.F.C., 'Tools and techniques of the Roman stonemason in Britain,' ibid. 152–72.
64. Wright, R.P., 'Tile-stamps of the Sixth Legion found in Britain,' ibid. 224–35.
65. Jones, G.D.B., 'The western extension of Hadrian's Wall: Bowness to Cardurnock,' ibid. 236–43.
66. Goodburn, R.; Wright, R.P.; Tomlin, R.S.O.; Hassall, M.W.C., 'Roman Britain in 1975: I. Sites explored; II. Inscriptions,' ibid. 290–392.
67. Royal Commission on Ancient and Historical Monuments in Wales. *An inventory of the ancient monuments in Glamorgan; vol. 1: Pre-Norman; part 1: The stone and bronze ages; part 2: The iron age and the Roman occupation; part 3: The early Christian period*. Cardiff; HMSO; 1976. Pp xxx, 144; xxx, 135; xxx, 80.

(b) *History*

1. Hamp, E.P., 'Social gradience in British spoken Latin,' *Britannia* 6 (1975), 150–62.
2. Shiel, N., 'Vulgar Latin and the coinage of Carausius,' ibid. 146–9.
3. Miller, M., 'Stilicho's Pictish war,' ibid. 141–5.
4. Applebaum, S., 'Observations on the economy of the villa at Bignor,' ibid. 118–32.
5. Rodwell, W., 'Milestones, civic territories and ɹe Antonine Itinerary,' ibid. 76–101.
6. Dunnett, R. *The Trinovantes*. London; Duckworth; 1975. Pp ix, 165.
7. Webster, G. *The Cornovii*. London; Duckworth; 1975. Pp ix, 154.
8. Scott, J.M. *Boadicea*. London; Constable; 1975. Pp 191.
9. Keppie, L.J.F., 'The building of the Antonine Wall: archaeological and epigraphic evidence,' *P. of the Soc. of Antiquaries of Scotland* 105(1975 for 1972/4), 151–65.
10. Breeze, D.J.; Dobson, B. *Hadrian's Wall*. London; Allen Lane; 1976. Pp xii, 324.
11. Jones, G.D.B., 'British antiquity 1974–5: Romano-British and related,' *Archaeological J.* 132 (1976 for 1975), 322–31.

12. Thwaite, A. *Beyond the inhabited world: Roman Britain.* London; Deutsch; 1976. Pp 123.
13. Allen, D.F., 'Did Arminius strike coins?,' *Britannia* 7 (1976), 96–100.
14. Nash, D., 'Reconstructing Poseidonios's Celtic ethnography: some considerations,' ibid. 111–26.
15. Jarrett, M.G., 'An unnecessary war,' ibid. 145–51.
16. Thomas, C., 'Towards a definition of the term "field" in the light of prehistory,' Bc15, 145–51.

D. ENGLAND 450–1066

See also: Aa41, b42.

(a) *General*

1. Harrison, K. *The framework of Anglo-Saxon history to A.D. 900.* Cambridge UP; 1976. Pp x, 170.
2. Blair, P.H. *Northumbria in the days of Bede.* London; Gollancz; 1976. Pp 254.
3. Hart, C.J.R. *The early charters of northern England and the north Midlands.* Leicester UP; 1975. Pp 422.
4. Cameron, K. (ed.). *Place-name evidence for the Anglo-Saxon invasion and Scandinavian settlements.* [Nottingham]; English Place-Name Soc.; 1975. Pp v, 171.
5. Gelling, M. *The place-names of Berkshire*, part 3. Cambridge; English Place-Name Soc.; 1976. Pp 615–955.
6. Clemoes, P. (ed.). *Anglo-Saxon England 5.* Cambridge UP; 1976. Pp x, 320.
7. Clough, T.H.M.; Dornier, A.; Rutland, R.A. *Anglo-Saxon and Viking Leicestershire, including Rutland.* Leicestershire Museums etc. Service; 1975. Pp 92.
8. Smyth, A.P. *Scandinavian York and Dublin.* Dublin; Templekieran Press; 1975. Pp 116.

(b) *Politics and Institutions*

1. Musset, L., 'Pour l'étude comparative de deux fondations politiques des Vikings: le royaume d'York et le duché de Rouen,' *Northern History* 10 (1975), 40–54.
2. Sawyer, P.H., 'The charters of Burton Abbey and the unification of England,' ibid. 28–39.
3. Miller, M., 'Historicity and the pedigrees of northcountrymen,' *B. of the Board of Celtic Studies* 26 (1975), 255–80.

4. Sawyer, P.H., 'The charters of Burton Abbey and the unification of England,' *Northern History* 10 (1975), 28–39.
5. Petty, G.R. and S., 'Geology and *The Battle of Maldon*,' *Speculum* 51 (1976), 435–46.
6. Rutherford, A., '*Giudi* revisited,' *B. of the Board of Celtic Studies* 26 (1976), 440–4.
7. Campbell, M.W., 'The anti-Norman reaction in England in 1052: suggested origins,' *Mediaeval Studies* 38 (1976), 428–41.
8. Kristensen, A.K.G., 'Danelaw institutions and Danish society in the Viking age,' *Medieval Scandinavia* 8 (1975), 27–85.
9. Revill, S., 'King Edwin and the battle of Heathfield,' *T. of the Thoroton Soc.* 79 (1976 for 1975), 40–9.
10. Smyth, A.P., 'The *black* foreigners of York and the *white* foreigners of Dublin,' *Saga-Book of the Viking Soc. for Northern Research* 19 (1975), 101–17.
11. Dumville, D.N., 'The Anglian collection of royal genealogies and regnal lists,' Da6, 23–50.
12. Lovecy, I., 'The end of Celtic Britain: a sixth-century battle near Lindisfarne,' *Archaeologia Aeliana* 5th ser. 4 (1976), 31–45.

(c) *Religion*

1. Swanton, M.J., 'A fragmentary life of St Mildred and other Kentish royal saints,' *Archaeologia Cantiana* 91 (1975), 15–27.
2. Lanoe, G., 'Approche de quelques évêques moines en Angleterre au Xe siècle,' *Cahiers de civilisation médiévale* 19 (1976), 135–50.
3. Bonner, G. (ed.). *Famulus Christi: essays in commemoration of the thirteenth centenary of the birth of the Venerable Bede.* London; SPCK; 1976. Pp 404.
4. Sims-Williams, P., 'Cuthswith, seventh-century abbess of Inkberrow near Worcester, and the Würzburg manuscript of Jerome on Ecclesiastes,' Da6, 1–22.
5. Whitelocke, D., 'Bede and his teachers and friends,' Dc3, 19–39.
6. Ward, B., 'Miracles and history: a reconsideration of miracle stories used by Bede,' Dc3, 70–6.
7. Hill, R., 'Bede and the boors,' Dc3, 93–105.
8. Wormald, P., 'Bede and Benedict Biscop,' Dc3, 141–69.

(d) *Economic Affairs and Numismatics*

1. Johanssen, C. *Old English place-names and field-names containing lēah.* Stockholm; Almqvist & Wiksell International; 1975. Pp 170.
2. Pagan, H.E., 'The Bolton Percy board of 1967,' *British Numismatic J.* 43 (1976 for 1973), 1–44.

3. Metcalf, D.M., 'Sceattas from the territory of the Hwicce,' *Numismatic Chronicle* 7th ser. 16 (1976), 64—74.
4. Lyon, S., 'Some problems in interpreting Anglo-Saxon coinage,' Da6, 173—224.
5. Dolley, M., 'The coins,' Df11, 349—72.
6. Gill, M.A.V., 'The potteries of Tyne and Wear, and their dealings with the Beilby/Bewick workshop,' *Archaeologia Aeliana* 5th ser. 4 (1976), 151—70.

(e) *Intellectual and Cultural*

1. Dodwell, C.R.; Clemoes, P. (ed.). *The Old English illustrated Hexateuch: British Museum Cotton Claudius B. iv.* Copenhagen/London; Rosenkilde & Bagger/Allen & Unwin; 1974. Pp 73 (plus plates).
2. Eckenrode, T.R., 'The growth of the scientific mind: Bede's early and late scientific writings,' *Downside R.* 94 (1976), 197—212.
3. Gatch, M.McC., 'Beginnings continued: a decade of studies of Old English prose,' Da6, 225—43.
4. Woolf, R., 'The ideal of men dying with their lord in the *Germania* and in *The Battle of Maldon*,' Da6, 63—82.
5. Raw, B., 'The probable derivation of the illustrations in Junius 11 from an illustrated Old Saxon *Genesis*,' Da6, 133—48.
6. Parkes, M.B., 'The palaeography of the Parker manuscript of the *Chronicle*, laws and Sedulius, and historiography at Winchester in the late ninth and tenth centuries,' Da6, 149—72.
7. Meyvaert, P., 'Bede the scholar,' Dc3, 40—69.
8. Mackay, T.W., 'Bede's hagiographical method: his knowledge and use of Paulinus of Nola,' Dc3, 77—93.
9. Barnard, L.W., 'Bede and Eusebius as church historians,' Dc3, 106—24.
10. Bieler, L., 'Ireland's contribution to the culture of Northumbria,' Dc3, 210—28.
11. Blair, P.H., 'From Bede to Alcuin,' Dc3, 239—60.
12. Jones, C.W., 'Bede's place in medieval schools,' Dc3, 261—85.

(f) *Society and Archaeology*

1. Rivers, T.J., 'Widows' rights in Anglo-Saxon law,' *American J. of Legal History* 19 (1975), 208—15.
2. Evison, V.A., 'Pagan Saxon whetstones,' *Antiquaries J.* 55 (1975), 70—85.
3. Klingelhöfer, E., 'Evidence of town planning in late Saxon Warwick,' *Midland History* 3 (1975), 1—10.
4. Welch, M.G.; Myres, J.N.L., 'Mitcham Grave 205 and the chronology of applied brooches with floriate cross decoration,' *Antiquaries J.* 55 (1975), 86—95.

5. Dubuison, D., 'L'Irlande et la theorie medievale des "trois ordres",' *Revue de l'histoire des religions* 188 (1975), 35—63.
6. Bruce-Mitford, R. (with Ashbee, P.). *The Sutton Hoo ship-burial*; vol. 1: excavations, background, the ship, dating and inventory. London; British Museum Publications; 1975. Pp xl, 792.
7. Radford, C.A.R.; Swanton, M.J. *Arthurian sites in the west.* University of Exeter; 1975. Pp 62.
8. Evison, V.I., 'Sword rings and beads,' *Archaeologia* 105 (1976), 303—15.
9. Batt, M., 'The burghal hidage: Axbridge,' *Somerset Archaeology and Natural History* 119 (1974/5), 22—5.
10. Cunliffe, B. *Excavations at Portchester Castle; vol. 2: Saxon.* London; Thames & Hudson (for Soc. of Antiquaries); 1975. Pp ix, 323.
11. Wilson, D.M. (ed.). *The archaeology of Anglo-Saxon England.* London; Methuen; 1976. Pp xvi, 532.
12. Jones, G.R.J., 'Early territorial organization in Gwynnedd and Elmet,' *Northern History* 10 (1975), 3—27.
13. Cramp, R.J., 'Monkwearmouth and Jarrow: the archaeological evidence,' Dc3, 5—18.
14. Clutton-Brook, J., 'The animal resources,' Df11, 373—92.
15. Hurst, J.G., 'The pottery,' Df11, 283—348.
16. Cramp, R.J., 'Monastic sites,' Df11, 201—52.
17. Cherry, B., 'Ecclesiastical architecture,' Df11, 151—200.
18. Biddle, M., 'Towns,' Df11, 99—150.
19. Rahtz, P., 'Buildings and rural settlement,' Df11, 49—98.
20. Fowler, P.J., 'Agriculture and rural settlement,' Df11, 23—48.
21. Wilson, D.M., 'Craft and industry,' Df11, 253—82.
22. Jones, G.R.J., 'Multiple estates and early settlement,' Bc15, 15—40.
23. Wilson, D.M., 'The Scandinavians in England,' Df11, 393—403.
24. Bonney, D., 'Early boundaries and estates in southern England,' Bc15, 72—82.
25. Charles-Edwards, T.M., 'The distinction between land and moveable wealth in southern England,' Bc15, 180—7.
26. Bailey, R.N., 'The Anglo-Saxon church at Hexham,' *Archaeologia Aeliana* 5th ser. 4 (1976), 47—67.
27. Lund, N., '*Thorp*-names,' Bc15, 223—5.
28. Ford, W.J., 'Some settlement patterns in the central region of the Warwickshire Avon,' Bc15, 274—94.
29. Biddle, M., 'The evolution of towns: planned towns before 1066,' Bc16, 19—31.
30. Austin, D., 'Fieldwork and excavation at Hart, Co. Durham, 1965—1975,' *Archaeologia Aeliana* 5th ser. 4 (1976), 69—132.

E. ENGLAND 1066–1500

See also: Aa23, 34, 41, 49

(a) *General*

1. Davies, C.S.L. *Peace, print and Protestantism, 1450–1558.*
London; Hart Davis MacGibbon; 1976. Pp 365.
2. Kibler, W.W. (ed.). *Symposium on the court of Eleanor of Aquitaine* (University of Texas, 1973). Austin; University of Texas
Press; 1976. Pp xv, 183.
3. Allmand, C.T. (ed.). *War, literature and politics in the late middle
ages: essays in honour of G.W. Coopland.* Liverpool UP; 1976.
Pp xii, 202.
4. Morris, J. (ed.). *Domesday Book, 12: Hertfordshire.* Chichester;
Phillimore; 1976. n.p.
5. Morris, J. (ed.). *Domesday Book, 24: Staffordshire.* Ibid.; 1976.
n.p.
6. La Patourel, J. *The Norman Empire.* Oxford; Clarendon; 1976.
Pp 416.
7. Hilton, R.H. (ed.). *Peasants, knights and heretics: studies in
medieval English social history* [essays reprinted from *Past &
Present*]. Cambridge UP; 1976. Pp 328.

(b) *Politics*

1. Potter, K.R. (ed. and trs.). *Geste Stephani* (2nd ed. with new
introd. and notes by R.H.C. Davis). Oxford; Clarendon; 1976.
Pp 288.
2. Kirby, J.L., 'Henvy V and the city of London,' *History Today*,
26 (1976), 223–31 and 278.
3. Pollard, A.J., 'The northern retainers of Richard Nevill, earl of
Salisbury,' *Northern History* 11 (1976 for 1975), 52–69.
4. White, G., 'King Stephen, duke Henry and Ranulf de Gernons,
earl of Chester,' *English Historical R.* 91 (1976), 555–65.
5. Schnith, K., '*Regni et pacis inquietatrix*: Zur Rolle der Kaiserin
Mathilde in der "Anarchie",' *J. of Medieval History* 2 (1976),
135–57.
6. Johnston, R.C., 'The historicity of Jordan Fantosme's *Chronicle*,'
ibid. 159–68.
7. Harvey, J. *The Black Prince and his age.* London; Batsford; 1976.
Pp 184.
8. Ross, C.D. *The wars of the Roses: a concise history.* London;
Thames & Hudson; 1976. Pp 190.
9. Lander, J.R. *Crown and nobility, 1450–1509.* London; Arnold;
1976. Pp x, 340.
10. Lander, J.R., 'The wars of the Roses,' Eb9, 57–73.

11. Lander, J.R., 'Henry VI and the duke of York's second protectorate, 1455–6,' Eb9, 74–93.
12. Lander, J.R., 'Marriage and politics in the fifteenth century: the Nevilles and the Wydevilles,' Eb9, 94–126.
13. Lander, J.R., 'Attainder and forfeiture, 1453–1509,' Eb9, 127–58.
14. Lander, J.R., 'Edward IV: the modern legend and a revision,' Eb9, 159–70.
15. Lander, J.R., 'The treason and death of the duke of Clarence: a reinterpretation,' Eb9, 242–66.
16. Lander, J.R., 'Bonds, coercion and fear: Henry VII and the peerage,' Eb9, 267–300.
17. Brown, E.A.R., 'Eleanor of Aquitaine: parent, queen and duchess,' Ea2, 9–34.
18. Haahr, J.G., 'The concept of kingship in William of Malmesbury's Gesta Regum and Historia novella,' Mediaeval Studies 38 (1976), 351–71.
19. Callahan, T., 'The notion of anarchy in England, 1135–1154: a bibliographical survey,' British Studies Monitor 6/2 (1976), 23–35.
20. Schnith, K., 'Zur Vorgeschichte der "Anarchie" in England, 1135–1154,' Historisches Jahrbuch 95 (1975), 68–87.
21. Callahan, T., 'Sinners and saintly retribution: the timely death of King Stephen's son Eustace, 1153,' Studia Monastica 18 (1976), 109–17.
22. Weiss, M., 'The castellan: the early career of Hubert de Burgh,' Viator 5 (1976 for 1974), 235–52.
23. Safford, E.W. Itinerary of Edward I; part 2: 1291–1307. London; Swift; 1976 (List & Index Soc. vol. 132). Pp 286.
24. Emerson, B. The Black Prince. London; Weidenfeld & Nicolson; 1976. Pp xi, 298.
25. Theilmann, J.M., 'Stubbs, Shakespeare and recent historians of Richard II,' Albion 8 (1976), 107–24.
26. Haines, R., ' "Our master mariner, our sovereign lord": a contemporary preacher's view of King Henry V,' Mediaeval Studies 38 (1976), 85–96.
27. Weiss, M., 'A power in the North? The Percies in the fifteenth century,' Historical J. 19 (1976), 501–9.
28. Griffith, R.R., 'The political bias of Malory's Morte d'Arthur,' Viator 5 (1976 for 1974), 365–86.
29. Wolffe, B.P., 'Hastings reinterred,' English Historical R. 91 (1976), 813–24.
30. Wood, C.T., 'The deposition of Edward V,' Traditio 31 (1975), 247–86.
31. Dunham, W.H.; Wood, C.T., 'The right to rule in England: depositions and the kingdom's authority, 1327–1485,' American Historical R. 81 (1976), 738–61.

32. Wood, C.T., 'Queens, queans and kingship: an enquiry into the theories of royal legitimacy in late medieval England and France,' *Order and Innovation in the Middle Ages: essays in honor of Joseph R. Strayer* (ed. W.C. Jordan, B. McNab, T.F. Ruiz; Princeton UP; 1976), 385—400.

33. Lally, J.E., 'Secular patronage at the court of king Henry II,' *B. of the Institute of Historical Research* 49 (1976), 159—84.

34. Hollister, C.W., 'The taming of the turbulent earl: Henry I and William of Warenne,' *Historical Reflections/Réflexions historiques* 3 (1976), 83—91.

35. Stones, E.L.G.; Keil, I.J.E., 'Edward II and the abbot of Glastonbury,' *Archives* 12 (1976), 176—82.

(c) *Constitution, Administration and Law*

1. Turner, R.V., 'Roman law in England before the time of Bracton,' *J. of British Studies* 15 (1975), 1—25.

2. Carpenter, D.A., 'The decline of the curial sheriff in England, 1194—1258,' *English Historical R.* 91 (1976), 1—32.

3. Prestwich, M., 'York civil ordinances, 1301,' *Northwick Papers* 49 (1975); 28pp.

4. Harriss, G.L., 'War and the emergence of the English Parliament, 1297—1360,' *J. of Medieval History* 2 (1976), 35—56.

5. Jones, W.R., 'Purveyance for war and the community of the realm in late medieval England,' *Albion* 7 (1975), 300—16.

6. Runyan, T.J., 'The rolls of Oleron and the Admiralty Court in fourteenth-century England,' *American J. of Legal History* 19 (1975), 95—111.

7. Post, J.B., 'The peace commissions of 1382,' *English Historical R.* 91 (1976), 98—101.

8. May, P. *A fifteenth century market court.* [Newmarket; the author] ; 1976. Pp 21.

9. Jalland, P., 'The "revolution" in northern borough representation in mid-fifteenth-century England,' *Northern History* 11 (1976 for 1975), 27—51.

10. Madison, K.G., 'The seating of the barons in Parliament, December 1461,' *Mediaeval Studies* 37 (1975), 494—503.

11. Weinbaum, M. (ed.). *The London eyre of 1276.* [Leicester] ; London Record Soc.; 1976. Pp xli, 188.

12. Pugh, R.B. (ed.). *Calendar of London trailbaston trials under commissions of 1305 and 1306.* London; HMSO; 1975. Pp v, 167.

13. Lander, J.R., 'The Yorkist council and administration,' Eb9, 171—90.

14. Lander, J.R., 'Council, administration and councillors, 1461—85,' Eb9, 191—219.

15. Milsom, S.F.C. *The legal framework of English feudalism.* Cambridge UP; 1976. Pp xi, 201.

16. Barton, J.L., 'The rise of the fee simple,' *Law Q.R.* 92 (1976), 108—21.

17. Pugh, R.B., 'The writ de bono et malo,' ibid. 258—67.

18. Mason, E., '*Maritagium* and the changing law,' *B. of the Institute of Historical Research* 49 (1976), 286—9.

19. Turner, R.V., 'The judges of king John: their background and training,' *Speculum* 51 (1976), 447—61.

20. English, B.A., 'Additional records of the Yorkshire eyre of 1218—1219,' *Yorkshire Arch. J.* 48 (1976), 95—6.

21. Van Caenegen, R.C., 'Public prosecution of crime in twelfth-century England,' Bc14, 41—76.

22. Westman, B.A. [Hanawalt] , 'The female felon in fourteenth-century England,' *Viator* 5 (1976 for 1974), 253—68.

23. Hanawalt, B.A., 'Violent death in fourteenth and early fifteenth-century England,' *Comparative Studies in Society and History* 18 (1976), 297—320.

24. Piper, A.J., 'Writs of summons in 1246, 1247 and 1255,' *B. of the Institute of Historical Research* 49 (1976), 284—6.

25. Illsley, J.S., 'Parliamentary elections in the reign of Edward I,' ibid. 24—40.

26. Green, T.A., 'The jury and the English law of homicide, 1200—1600,' *Michigan Law R.* 74 (1976), 413—99.

27. Mason, E., 'The Mauduits and their chamberlainship of the exchequer,' *B. of the Institute of Historical Research* 49 (1976), 1—23.

28. Walker, M., 'Indexes to introductions to pipe rolls and other financial records [i.e. volumes published by the Pipe Roll Soc.] ,' *Liber Memorialis Doris Stenton* (Pipe Roll Soc. new ser. 41; 1976 for 1967/8); 35—212.

29. Kreisler, F.F., 'Domesday Book and the Anglo-Norman synthesis,' *Order and Innovation in the Middle Ages: essays in honor of Joseph R. Strayer* (ed. W.C. Jordan, B. McNab, R.F. Ruiz; Princeton UP; 1976), 3—16.

30. Kaeuper, R.W., 'Royal finance and the crisis of 1297,' ibid. 103—10.

31. Booth, P.H.W., 'Taxation and public order: Cheshire in 1353,' *Northern History* 12 (1976), 16—31.

32. Palmer, R.C., 'County Year Book reports: the professional lawyer in the medieval county court,' *English Historical R.* 91 (1976), 776—801.

33. Arnold, M.S. (ed.). *Year Books of Richard II: 2 Richard II, 1378—1379*. London; Ames Foundation; 1975. Pp 151.

34. Borrie, M., 'What became of Magna Carta?,' *British Library J.* 2 (1976), 1—7.

35. Dunham, W.H., ' "The Books of the Parliament" and "The Old Record",' *Speculum* 51 (1976), 694—712.

(d) *External Affairs*

1. Hollister, C.W., 'Normandy, France and the Anglo-Norman *regnum*,' *Speculum* 51 (1976), 202–42.
2. Holt, J.C. *The end of the Anglo-Norman realm* [Raleigh lecture]. London; Oxford UP; 1975 (i.e. 1976). Pp 45.
3. Peña, N., 'Vassaux gascons au service du roi d'Angleterre dans la première moitié du XIVe siècle: fidelité ou esprit de profit?,' *Annales du Midi* 88 (1976), 5–21.
4. Capra, P., 'Les bases sociales du pouvoir anglo-gascon au milieu du XIVe siècle (suite et fin),' *Le Moyen Age* 81 (1975), 447–73.
5. Runyan, T., 'The Constabulary of Bordeaux: the accounts of John Ludham (1372–73) and Robert de Wykford (1373–75); part II,' *Mediaeval Studies* 37 (1975), 42–84.
6. Mezières, P. de. *Letter to King Richard II: a plea made in 1395 for peace between England and France*. Original and trs. (G.W. Coopland). Liverpool UP; 1975. Pp xxxiv, 152.
7. Alban, J.R.; Allmand, C.T., 'Spies and spying in the fourteenth century,' Ea3, 73–101.
8. Palmer, J.J.N.; Wells, A.P., 'Ecclesiastical reform and the politics of the Hundred Years' War during the pontificate of Urban V (1362–1370),' Ea 3, 169–89.
9. Cuttino, G.P. *Gascon Register A (series of 1318–19)*, vol. 3: Index of persons and places. Oxford UP for British Academy; 1976. Pp 160.
10. Stevenson, W.B., 'England, France and the Channel Islands, 1204–1259,' *La Société Guernesiaise: Report and T.* 19 (1976), 569–76.
11. Baker, R.L., 'The government of Calais in 1363,' *Order and Innovation in the Middle Ages: essays in honor of Joseph R. Strayer* (ed. W.C. Jordan, B. McNab, T.F. Ruiz; Princeton UP; 1976), 207–14.
12. Palmer, J.J.N., 'England, France, the papacy and the Flemish succession, 1361–9,' *J. of Medieval History* 2 (1976), 339–64.
13. Pistono, S.P., 'Henry IV and the *Vier Leden*: conflict in Anglo-Flemish relations, 1402–1403,' *Revue Belge de philologie et d'histoire* 54 (1976), 458–73.
14. Pistono, S.P., 'Flanders and the Hundred Years War: the quest for the *trève marchande*,' *B. of the Institute of Historical Research* 49 (1976), 185–97.

(e) *Religion*

1. Jones, W.R., 'The heavenly letter in medieval England,' *Medievalia et Humanistica new series*, 6 (1975), 163–78.
2. Mason, E., 'The role of the English parishioner, 1100–1500,' *J. of Ecclesiastical History* 27 (1976), 17–29.

3. Callahan, T., jr., 'King Stephen and the Black Monks: abbatial elections during "The Anarchy",' *Revue bénédictine* 85 (1975), 348—57.

4. Rees, U. (ed.). *The cartulary of Shrewsbury Abbey*. Aberystwyth; National Library of Wales; 1975. Pp xxxi, 514.

5. Smith, D.M., 'Lost archiepiscopal registers of York: the evidence of medieval inventories,' *Borthwick Institute B.* 1 (1975), 31—7.

6. Compton-Reeves, A., 'William Booth, bishop of Coventry and Lichfield (1447—52),' *Midland History* 3 (1975), 11—29.

7. Pantin, W.A., 'Instructions for a devout and literate layman,' Eil, 398—422.

8. Foreville, R. (ed.). *Thomas Becket: actes du colloque international de Sédières, 19—24 aout 1973*. Paris; Beauchesne; 1975. Pp xviii, 297.

9. Desmond, L.A., 'The appropriation of churches by the Cistercians in England to 1400,' *Analecta Cisterciensia* 31 (1976 for 1975), 246—66.

10. Jennings, M., 'Monks and the *Artes praedicandi* in the time of Ranulph Higden,' *Revue Bénédictine* 86 (1976), 119—28.

11. Robertson, C.A., 'The tithe-heresy of friar William Russell,' *Albion* 8 (1976), 1—16.

12. Barker, E.E. (ed.). *The register of Thomas Rotherham, archbishop of York, 1480—1500*, vol. 1. Canterbury and York Soc. 69; 1976. Pp vii, 252.

13. Lutgens, C., 'The case of Waghen vs. Sutton: conflict over burial rights in late medieval England,' *Mediaeval Studies* 38 (1976), 145—84.

14. Johnston, A.F., 'The Guild of Corpus Christi and the procession of Corpus Christi in York,' ibid. 372—84.

15. Sheerin, D., 'Gervase of Chichester and Thomas Becket,' ibid. 468—82.

16. Saunders, P.C., 'The "royal free chapel" of Bowes,' *Yorkshire Arch. J.* 48 (1976), 97—106.

17. McCann, A.M., 'The chapel of St Cyriac, Chichester,' *Sussex Arch. Collections* 113 (1976 for 1975), 197—99.

18. Rahtz, P.; Hirst, S., *Bordesley Abbey, Redditch, Hereford-Worcestershire: First report on excavations 1969—73*. Oxford; British Arch. Reports 23; 1976. Pp 295.

19. Ingram Hill, D., 'Edward the Black Prince and Canterbury cathedral,' *Canterbury Cathedral Chronicle* 70 (1976), 10—13.

20. Turner, D.H., 'The customary of the shrine of St Thomas Becket,' ibid. 16—22.

21. Woodman, F., 'The Holland family and Canterbury cathedral,' ibid. 23—8.

22. Dodwell, B., 'William Bauchun and his connection with the cathedral priory of Norwich,' *Norfolk Archaeology* 36 (1975), 111—18.

23. Erskine, A.M., 'Bishop Briwere and the reoganization of the chapter of Exeter cathedral,' *Devonshire Association Report and T.* 108 (1976), 159—71.

24. Oakley, A.M., 'The cathedral priory of St Andrew, Rochester,' *Archaeologia Cantiana* 91 (1976 for 1975), 47—60.

25. Conlee, J.W., 'The *Abbey of the Holy Ghost* and the *Eight Ghostly Dwelling Places* of Huntington Library HM 744,' *Medium Aevum* 44 (1975), 137—44.

26. Sayers, J.E., 'Monastic archdeacons,' Bc14, 177—203.

27. Ullmann, W., 'John Baconthorpe as a canonist,' Bc14, 223—46.

28. Denton, J., 'Walter Reynolds and ecclesiastical politics 1313—1316: a postscript to "Councils and Synods, II",' Bc14, 247—74.

29. Davies, R.G., 'After the execution of Archbishop Scrope: Henry IV, the papacy and the English episcopate, 1405—8,' *B. of the John Rylands Library* 56 (1976—7), 40—74.

30. McNab, B., 'Obligations of the Church in English society: military arrays of the clergy, 1369—1418,' *Order and Innovation in the Middle Ages: essays in honor of Joseph R. Strayer* (ed. W.C. Jordan, B. McNab, T.F. Ruiz; Princeton UP; 1976), 293—314.

31. Sayers, J.E., 'The earliest original letter of Pope Innocent III for an English recipient,' *B. of the Institute of Historical Research* 49 (1976), 132—5.

32. Barnum, P.H. (ed.). *Dives and Pauper, vol. 1, part 1.* London; Oxford UP for Early English Text Soc.; 1976. Pp 359.

33. Zettersten, A. (ed.). *English text of the Ancrene Riwle: Magdalene College, Cambridge, MS Pepys 2498.* Idem; 1976. Pp 208.

34. Colledge, E.; Walsh, J., 'Editing Julian of Norwich's *Revelations*: a progress report,' *Mediaeval Studies* 38 (1976), 404—27.

(f) *Economic Affairs*

1. Fenoaltea, S., 'Authority, efficiency and agricultural organization in medieval England and beyond: a hypothesis,' *J. of Economic History* 35 (1975), 693—718.

2. Wightman, W.E., 'The significance of "waste" in the Yorkshire Domesday,' *Northern History* 10 (1975), 55—71.

3. Miller, E., 'Farming in northern England during the twelfth and thirteenth centuries,' *Northern History* 11 (1976 for 1975), 1—16.

4. Pugh, R.B., 'Ministers' accounts of Norhamshire and Islandshire, 1261—2,' ibid. 17—26.

5. Capra, P., 'Pour une histoire de la monnaie anglogasconne,' *Annales du Midi* 87 (1975), 405—30.

6. Martin, G.H., 'Road travel in the middle ages: some journeys of the warden and fellows of Merton College, Oxford, 1315—1470,' *J. of Transport History* new series, 3 (1976), 159—78.

7. Taylor, R., 'The coastal salt industry of Amounderness,' *T. of the Lancashire and Cheshire Antiquarian Soc.* 78 (1975), 14–21.
8. Davis, R., 'The rise of Antwerp and its English connection, 1406–1510,' Bc9, 2–20.
9. Fryde, E.B., 'The English cloth industry and the trade with the Mediterranean, c. 1370–c. 1480.' *Atti della Seconda Settimana di Studio*; Istituto Internazionale di Storia Economica Francesco Datini, Prato (Florence; L. Olschki; 1976), 343–67.
10. Ruiz, T.F., 'Castilian merchants in England, 1248–1350,' *Order and Innovation in the Middle Ages: essays in honor of Joseph R. Strayer* (ed. W.C. Jordan, B. McNab, T.F. Ruiz; Princeton UP; 1976), 173–85.
11. Haslop, G.S., 'A Selby kitchener's roll of the early fifteenth century,' *Yorkshire Arch. J.* 48 (1976), 119–33.
12. Postles, D., 'The estate stewards of Oseney Abbey, c. 1245–1340,' *Oxoniensia* 40 (1976 for 1975), 326–8.
13. Reed, C.G., 'The profits of cultivation in England during the later middle ages,' *Agricultural History* 50 (1976), 645–8.
14. Archibald, M.M., 'The Coventry hoard of coins of Edward I to Edward III,' *British Numismatic J.* 43 (1976 for 1973), 60–6.
15. Beresford-Jones, R.D., 'The salutes of Henry VI,' ibid. 67–79.
16. Bridbury, A.R., 'The Hundred Years' War: costs and profits,' Bc9, 80–95.
17. Coleman, O., 'What figures? Some thoughts on the use of information by medieval governments,' Bc9, 96–112.

(g) *Social Structure and Population*

1. Platt, C. *The English medieval town.* London; Secker & Warburg; 1976. Pp 219.
2. White, S.D., 'English feudalism and its origins [review article],' *American J. of Legal History* 19 (1975), 138–55.
3. Rosenthal, J.T. *Nobles and the noble life, 1295–1500.* London; Allen & Unwin; 1976. Pp 207.
4. Jones, A., 'A dispute between the abbey of Ramsey and its tenants,' *English Historical R.* 91 (1976), 341–3.
5. McKinley, R.A. *Norfolk and Suffolk surnames in the middle ages* (foreword by A. Everitt). London; Phillimore; 1975. Pp xiii, 175.
6. Gwynne, T.A., 'Domesday society in Shropshire,' *T. of the Shropshire Arch. Soc.* 59/2 (1976 for 1971/2), 91–103.
7. Mason, E., 'The resources of the earldom of Warwick in the thirteenth century,' *Midland History* 3 (1975), 67–76.
8. Naughton, K.S. *The gentry of Bedfordshire in the thirteenth and fourteenth centuries.* Leicester UP; 1976. Pp 90.
9. Dainton, C., 'Medieval hospitals of England,' *History Today* 26 (1976), 532–8.

10. Harte, N.B., 'State control of dress and social change in pre-industrial England,' Bc9, 132—65.
11. David, N. (ed.). *Paston letters and papers of the fifteenth century; part 2.* Oxford; Clarendon; 1976. Pp 664.
12. Vale, M.G.A., 'Piety, charity and literacy among the Yorkshire gentry, 1370—1480,' *Borthwick Papers* 50 (1976); pp. iv, 32.
13. DeWindt, A., 'Peasant power structures in fourteenth-century King's Ripton,' *Mediaeval Studies* 38 (1976), 236—67.
14. Kennedy, M.J.O., 'Resourceful villeins: the Cellarer family of Wawne in Holderness,' *Yorkshire Arch. J.* 48 (1976), 107—17.
15. Searle, E., 'Freedom and marriage in medieval England; an alternative hypothesis,' *Economic History R.* 2nd ser. 29 (1976), 482—6.
16. Scammell, J., 'Wife-rents and merchet,' ibid. 487—90.
17. Raftis, J.A., 'Geographical mobility in lay subsidy rolls,' *Mediaeval Studies* 38 (1976), 385—403.
18. Kaye, J.M. (ed.). *The cartulary of God's House, Southampton* (2 vols). Southampton UP (Southampton Records Series, 19 and 20); 1976. Pp 481.
19. Davis, R.H.C. *The early history of Coventry.* Stratford-upon-Avon; Dugdale Soc.; 1976. Pp 30.
20. Contamine, P. *La vie quotidienne pendant la guerre de Cent ans: France et Angleterre (xive siècle).* Paris; Hachette; 1976. Pp 287.
21. Harvey, S.P.J., 'Evidence for settlement study: Domesday Book,' Bc15, 195—9.
22. McIntosh, M.K., 'The privileged villeins of the English ancient demesne,' *Viator* 7 (1976), 295—328.
23. Owen, D., 'Chapelries and rural settlement: an examination of some of the Kesteven evidence,' Bc15, 66—71.

(h) *Naval and Military*

1. Cole, H. *The Black Prince.* London; Hart-Davis MacGibbon; 1976. Pp 223.
2. Allmand, C.T., 'The Black Prince,' *History Today* 26 (1976), 100—8 and 137.
3. Brooke, R. *Visits to fields of battle in England of the fifteenth century* [repr. of 1857 ed.]. Dursley; Alan Sutton; 1975. Pp viii, 342.
4. Vale, M.G.A., 'New techniques and old ideals: the impact of artillery on war and chivalry at the end of the Hundred Years' War,' Ea3, 57—72.
5. Armstrong, C.A.J., 'Sir John Fastolf and the law of arms,' Ea3, 46—56.
6. Keen, M.H., 'Chivalry, nobility and the men-at-arms,' Ea3, 32—45.
7. Lander, J.R., 'The Hundred Years' War and Edward IV's 1475 campaign in France,' Eb9, 220—41.

8. Brown, R.A. *English castles*. London; Batsford; 1976. Pp 240.
9. Emery, A., 'The development of Raglan Castle and keeps in late medieval England,' *Archaeological J.* 132 (1976 for 1975), 151–86.
10. Taylor, A.; Woodward, P., 'Cainhoe Castle excavations 1973,' *Bedfordshire Arch. J.* 10 (1976 for 1975), 41–52.
11. Ellison, M., 'Excavation at Aydon Castle, Northumberland, 1975,' *Archaeologie Aeliana* 5th ser. 4 (1976), 133–8.
12. Reynolds, N., 'Investigations in the Observatory Tower, Lincoln Castle,' *Medieval Archaeology* 19 (1975), 201–5.
13. Williams, D., 'Fortified manor houses,' *T. of the Leicestershire Arch. and Historical Soc.* 50 (1976 for 1974–5), 1–16.
14. Smith, T.P., 'The date of the King's Lynn south gate,' *Norfolk Archaeology* 36 (1976), 224–32.
15. Alebon, P.H.; Davey, P.J.; Robinson, D.J., 'The Eastgate Chester, 1972,' *J. of the Chester Arch. Soc.* 59 (1976), 37–49.
16. Gardiner, D. (ed.). *A calendar of early chancery proceedings relating to West Country shipping 1388–1493*. Devon & Cornwall Record Soc. new ser. 21 (1976). Pp 131.

(i) *Intellectual and Cultural*

1. Alexander, J.J.G.; Gibson, M.T. (ed.). *Medieval learning and literature: essays presented to Richard William Hunt*. Oxford; Clarendon; 1976. Pp xiii, 455.
2. Ker, N.R., 'The beginnings of Salisbury Cathedral library,' Ei1, 23–49.
3. Pollard, G., 'Describing medieval bookbindings,' Ei1, 50–65.
4. Parkes, M.B., 'The influence of the concepts "ordinatio" and "compilatio" on the development of the book,' Ei1, 115–41.
5. Scott, A.B., 'Some poems attributed to Richard of Cluny,' Ei1, 181–99.
6. Anon., 'La tradition manuscrite des "Quaestiones Nicolai peripatetici",' Ei1, 200–19.
7. Southern, R.W., 'Master Vacarius and the beginning of an English academic tradition,' Ei1, 257–86.
8. Rathbone, E., 'Peter of Corbeil in an English setting,' Ei1, 287–306.
9. Smalley, B., 'Oxford University sermons, 1290–1293,' Ei1, 307–27.
10. Dean, R.J., 'Nicholas Trevet, historian,' Ei1, 328–52.
11. Emden, A.B., 'Oxford academical halls in the later middle ages,' Ei1, 353–65.
12. Boyle, L.E., ' "E cathena et carcere": the imprisonment of Amaury de Montfort, 1276,' Ei1, 379–97.
13. Brehm, E., 'Roger Bacon's place in the history of alchemy,' *Ambix* 23 (1976), 53–8.

14. Rothwell, W., 'The role of French in thirteenth-century England,' *B. of the John Rylands Library* 58 (1976), 445—66.

15. Clark, C., 'People and languages in post-Conquest Canterbury,' *J. of Medieval History* 2 (1976), 1—33.

16. Levy, B.J., 'Waltheof "earl" de Huntingdon et de Northampton: la naissance d'un heros anglo-normand,' *Cahiers de Civilisation Médiévale* 18 (1975), 183—96.

17. Legge, M.D., 'Anglo-Norman hagiography and the romances,' *Medievalia et Humanistica new series*, 6 (1975), 41—9.

18. Shirley, J. (trs.). *Garnier's Becket: translated from the 12th-century 'Vie Saint Thomas le Martyr de Cantorbire' of Garbier of Pont-Sainte-Maxence.* London; Phillimore; 1975. Pp xxi, 191.

19. Keeler, L. *Geoffrey of Monmouth and the late Latin chroniclers, 1300—1500.* Norwood, Pa.; Norwood Editions; 1975. Pp viii, 151.

20. Thomson, R.M., 'The reading of William of Malmesbury,' *Revue bénédictine* 85 (1975), 362—402.

21. Dobson, E.J. *The origins of 'Ancrene Wisse'.* Oxford; Clarendon; 1976. Pp xi, 441.

22. Seymour M.C. (ed.). *On the properties of things: John Trevisa's translation of Bartholomaeus Anglicus 'De proprietatibus rerum'.* Oxford; Clarendon; 1975. 2 vols; pp. 1397.

23. Jolliffe, P.S., 'Two middle English tracts on the contemplative life,' *Mediaeval Studies* 37 (1975), 85—121.

24. Colledge, E., 'Fifteenth- and sixteenth-century English versions of "The Golden Epistle of St Bernard",' ibid. 122—9.

25. Coleman, J., 'Jean de Ripa O.F.M. and the Oxford Calculators,' ibid. 130—89.

26. Kennedy, E.D., 'Malory's King Mark and King Arthur,' ibid. 190—234.

27. Bornstein, D., 'Military manuals in fifteenth-century England,' ibid. 469—77.

28. Gervers, M., 'The medieval cartulary tradition and the survival of archival material as reflected in the English Hospitaller Cartulary of 1442,' ibid. 504—14.

29. Taylor, J., 'The Plumpton letters, 1416—1552,' *Northern History* 10 (1975), 72—87.

30. Deacon, R. *A biography of William Caxton: the first English editor, printer, merchant and translator.* London; Muller; 1976. Pp viii, 198.

31. Hay, D., 'England and the humanities in the fifteenth century,' *Itinerarium Italicum: the profile of the Italian Renaissance in the mirror of its European transformation* (dedicated to P.O. Kristeller; ed. H.A. Oberman with T.A. Brady; Studies in Medieval and Renaissance Thought, vol. 14; Leiden; Brill; 1975), 302—67.

32. Royal Commission on Historical Monuments (England). *Sherborne Abbey: the early church*. London; HMSO; 1975.
33. Swanton, M.J. (ed.). *Studies in medieval domestic architecture*. London; Royal Archaeological Institute Monographs; 1975. Pp 154.
34. Smith, J.T., 'Timber-framed building in England,' Ei33, 1—26.
35. Smith, J.T., 'Medieval aisled halls and their derivations,' Ei33, 27—44.
36. Smith, J.T., 'Medieval roofs: a classification,' Ei33, 45—83.
37. Faulkner, P.A., 'Domestic planning from the twelfth to the fourteenth centuries,' Ei33, 84—117.
38. Faulkner, P.A., 'Medieval undercrofts and town houses,' Ei33, 118—33.
39. Emery, A., 'Dartington Hall, Devonshire,' Ei33, 134—52.
40. Lazar, M., 'Cupid, the Lady and the Poet: modes of love at Eleanor of Aquitaine's court,' Ea2, 35—59.
41. Baltzer, R.A., 'Music in the life and times of Eleanor of Aquitaine,' Ea2, 61—80.
42. Ayres, L.M., 'English painting and the continent during the reign of Henry II and Eleanor,' Ea2, 115—46.
43. Robbins, R.H., 'The vintner's son: French music in English bottles,' Ea2, 147—72.
44. Vantuono, W., 'A name in the Cotton Ms Nero A.X, article 3 [John de Mascy],' *Mediaeval Studies* 37 (1975) 537—42.
45. Nau, L.T., 'A note regarding four early fellows of Oriel College, Oxford,' ibid. 543—5.
46. Baker, D., 'The genesis of Cistercian chronicles in England: the foundation history of Fountains Abbey (III),' *Analecta Cisterciensia* 31 (1976 for 1975), 179—212.
47. Flint, V.I.J., 'The date of the chronicle of "Florence" of Worcester,' *Revue Bénédictine* 86 (1976), 115—19.
48. Sargent, M.G., 'The transmission by the English Carthusians of some late medieval spiritual writings,' *J. of Ecclesiastical History* 27 (1976), 225—40.
49. Backhouse, J. *The Madresfield Hours: a fourteenth-century manuscript in the library of Earl Beauchamp*. Oxford; Roxburgh Club no. 237; 1975. Pp 33 (46 plates).
50. Tudor-Craig, P. *One half of our noblest art: a study of the sculptures of Wells west front*. Friends of Wells Cathedral; 1976.
51. McCarthy, M.R., 'The medieval kilns on Nash Hill, Lacock, Wiltshire,' *Wiltshire Arch. and Natural History Magazine* 69 (1976 for 1974), 97—160.
52. Drury, P.J.; Pratt, G.D., 'A late 13th and early 14th-century tile factory at Danbury, Essex,' *Medieval Archaeology* 19 (1975), 92—164.
53. McGlashan, N.D.; Sandell, R.E., 'The bishop of Salisbury's House

at his manor of Potterne,' *Wiltshire Arch. and Natural History Magazine* 69 (1976 for 1974), 85–96.

54. Miles, T.J.; Saunders, A.D., 'The "chantry priest's" house at Farleigh Hungerford Castle,' *Medieval Archaeology* 19 (1975), 165–94.

55. Ketteringham, L.L. *Alsted: excavation of a thirteenth-fourteenth century sub-manor house with its ironworks in Netherne Wood, Merstham, Surrey*. Guildford; Surrey Arch. Soc.; 1976. Pp v, 73.

56. Coldstream, N., 'English decorated shrine bases,' *J. of the British Arch. Association* 129 (1976), 15–34.

57. Fernie, E., 'The ground plan of Norwich cathedral and the square root of two,' ibid. 77–86.

58. Keen, L.; Thackray, D., 'Helpston parish church, Northants: the remains of a medieval tile pavement,' ibid. 87–92.

59. Bailey, J.M., 'Decorated fourteenth-century tiles at Northill church, Bedfordshire,' *Medieval Archaeology* 19 (1975), 209–13.

60. Greene, J.P.; Keen, L.; Noake, B., 'The decorated mosaic tile floor from Warrington friary: a re-assessment,' *J. of the Chester Arch. Soc.* 59 (1976), 52–9.

61. Norton, E.C., 'The medieval paving tiles of Winchester College,' *P. of the Hampshire Field Club and Arch. Soc.* 31 (1976 for 1974), 23–41.

62. Barton, K.J.; Brears, P.C.D., 'A medieval pottery kiln at Bentley, Hants,' ibid. 71–5.

63. Drury, P.J.; Petchey, M.R., 'Medieval potteries at Mile End and Great Horhesley, near Colchester,' *Essex Archaeology and History* 7 (1976 for 1975), 33–60.

64. Smith, J.R.; Wadhams, M.S., 'Robert D'Arcy's chantry priest's house, Maldon, Essex,' *Medieval Archaeology* 19 (1975), 213–19.

65. Parkin, E.W., 'The Old Chantry House, Bredgar,' *Archaeologia Cantiana* 91 (1976 for 1975), 87–97.

66. Wilson, C., 'The original design of the City of London Guildhall,' *J. of the British Arch. Association* 129 (1976), 1–14.

67. Smith, T.P., 'The early brickwork of Someries Castle, Bedfordshire, and its place in the history of English brick building,' ibid. 42–58.

68. Smith, T.P., 'Rye House, Hertfordshire, and aspects of early brickwork in England,' *Arch. J.* 132 (1976 for 1975), 111–50.

69. Barley, M.W., 'Florc's house, Oakham, Rutland,' *T. of the Leicestershire Arch. and Historical Soc.* 50 (1976 for 1974/5), 37–40.

70. Keen, L., 'Baguley Hall, Manchester,' *J. of the Chester Arch. Soc.* 59 (1976), 60–5.

71. Fletcher, J., 'The medieval hall at Lewknor,' *Oxoniensia* 40 (1976 for 1975), 247–53.

72. Rigold, S.E., 'Structural aspects of medieval timber bridges,' *Medieval Archaeology* 19 (1975), 48–91.
73. Holden, E.W., 'New evidence relating to Bramber Bridge,' *Sussex Arch. Collections* 113 (1976 for 1975), 104–17.
74. King, A., 'A medieval town house in German Street, Winchelsea,' ibid. 124–45.
75. Finlaison, M., 'A medieval house at 13 and 13a Old Street, St Helier,' *Société Jersiaise Annual B.* 21 (1976), 477–93.
76. Dawson, G.J. *The Black Prince's palace at Kennington, Surrey.* Oxford; British Arch. Reports 26 (1976). Pp 213.
77. Harvey, J., 'The Black Prince and his artists,' *Canterbury Cathedral Chronicle* 70 (1976), 29–34.
78. Humphery-Smith, C., 'The tomb of Henry IV,' ibid. 35–41.
79. Bond, M.F. (ed.). *The Saint George's Chapel quincentenary handbook.* Windsor; Oxley & Son; 1975. Pp 76.
80. Kidson, P., 'The architecture of St George's Chapel,' Ei79, 29–39.
81. Lander, J.R., 'The historical background to St George's Chapel,' Ei79, 9–18.
82. Evans, A.K.B., 'The College of Saint George, 1348 to 1975,' Ei79, 19–28.
83. Not used.
84. Judy, A.G. (ed.). *Robert Kilwardby: De Ortu Scientiarum.* Leiden; Brill for British Academy; 1976. Pp lxii, 255.
85. North, J.D. (ed.). *Richard of Wallingford: an edition of his writings with introduction, English translation and commentary,* 3 vols. London; Oxford UP; 1976. Pp 1236.
86. Orme, N. *Education in the west of England, 1066–1548.* Exeter; The University; 1976. Pp 239.
87. Evans, G.R., 'St Anselm and teaching,' *History of Education* 5 (1976), 89–102.
88. Cobban, A., 'Decentralized teaching in medieval English universities,' ibid. 193 ff.
89. Gransden, A., 'The growth of the Glastonbury traditions and legends in the twelfth century,' *J. of Ecclesiastical History* 27 (1976), 337–58.
90. Thomson, R.M., 'The reading of William of Malmesbury: addenda et corrigenda,' *Revue bénédictine* 86 (1976), 327–35.
91. McGurk, J.J.N., 'William of Malmesbury, twelfth-century historian,' *History Today* 26 (1976), 707–14.
92. Thomson, R.M., 'William of Malmesbury and some other western writers on Islam,' Bc1, 179–87.
93. Stein, P., 'Vacarius and the civil law,' Bc14, 119–37.
94. Cheney, M., 'William FitzStephen and his life of Archbishop Thomas,' Bc14, 139–56.
95. Harris, M.A., 'Alan of Tewkesbury and his letters; I,' *Studia Monastica* 18 (1976), 77–108.

96. Dronke, P., 'Peter of Blois and poetry at the court of Henry II,' *Medieval Studies* 38 (1976), 185–235.

97. Hill, K.D., 'Robert Grosseteste and his work on Greek translation,' Bc4, 213–22.

98. Green, R.F., 'King Richard II's books revisited,' *The Library* 5th ser. 31 (1976), 235–9.

99. Lagario, V.M., 'The *Joseph of Arimathie*: English hagiography in transition,' Bc1, 91–101.

100. Pearsall, D., 'John Capgrave's *Life of St Katherine* and popular romance style,' Bc1, 121–37.

101. Hirsh, J.C., 'Author and scribe in *The Book of Margery Kempe*,' *Medium Aevum* 44 (1975), 145–50.

102. Hunt, R.W., 'A Manuscript containing extracts from the *Distinctiones Monasticae*,' ibid. 238–41.

103. Cox, D.C., 'The French Chronicle of London,' ibid. 201–8.

104. Owen, A.E.B., 'The collation and descent of the Thornton manuscript,' *T. of the Cambridge Bibliographical Soc.* 6 (1976 for 1975), 218–25.

105. Stern, K., 'The London "Thornton" Miscellany: a new description of B.M. Add. MS. 31042,' *Scriptorium* 30 (1976), 26–37.

106. Watson, A.G., 'A St Augustine's Abbey, Canterbury, manuscript reconstructed: Trinity College, Cambridge, MS R.14.30 and British Library MSS Egerton 823 and 840A,' *T. of the Cambridge Bibliographical Soc.* 6 (1975), 211–17.

107. Watson, A.G., 'A Merton College manuscript reconstructed: Harley 625; Digby 178, fols. 1–14, 88–115; Cotton Tiberius B.IX, fols 1–4, 225–35,' *Bodleian Library Record* 9 (1976), 207–17.

108. Hull, P.L., 'Thomas Chiverton's Book of Obits, part IV,' *Devon and Cornwall Notes and Queries* 33 (1976), 236–9.

109. Sandler, L.F., 'An early fourteenth-century breviary at Longleat,' *J. of the Warburg and Courtauld Institutes* 39 (1976), 1–20.

110. Turner, D.H., 'The Wyndham Payne Crucifixion (Add. MS. 58078),' *British Library J.* 2 (1976), 8–26.

111. Alexander, J.J.G.; Crossley, P. *Medieval and early Renaissance treasures in the north west* (catalogue of an exhibition at Whitworth Art Gallery, Manchester). Manchester; 1976. Pp 129.

112. Childs, E.L. *William Caxton: a portrait in a background.* London; Northwood Publications; 1976. Pp 190.

113. Blake, N.F. *Caxton: England's first publisher.* London; Osprey Publishing; 1976. Pp xi, 220.

114. Painter, G.D. *William Caxton: a quincentenary biography of England's first printer.* London; Chatto & Windus; 1976. Pp xi, 227.

115. Backhouse, J.; Foot, M.; Barr, J. *William Caxton: an exhibition to commemorate the quincentenary of the introduction of printing*

into England; British Library, 1976—77 (a catalogue). London; British Museum Publications; 1976. Pp 94.

116. Nixon, H.M., 'Caxton in the British Library,' *British Library J.* 2 (1976), 91—101.

117. Barker, N., 'Quiring and the binder: quire-marks in some manuscripts in fifteenth-century blind-stamped bindings,' Bc7, 11—31.

118. *Journal of the Printing Historical Society* 11 (1976—7). [Special number: papers presented to the Caxton International Congress, 1976].

119. Corsten, S., 'Caxton in Cologne,' Ei118, 1—18.

120. Hellings, L. and W., 'Caxton in the Low Countries,' Ei118, 19—32.

121. Veyrin-Forrer, J., 'Caxton and France,' Ei118, 33—47.

122. Balsamo, L., 'The origins of printing in Italy and England,' Ei118, 48—63.

123. Blake, N.F., 'Caxton: the man and his work,' Ei118, 64—80.

124. Moran, J., 'Caxton and the city of London,' Ei118, 81—91.

125. Nixon, H.M., 'Caxton and bookbinding,' Ei118, 92—113.

126. Barker, N., 'Caxton's typography,' Ei118, 114—33.

(j) *Topography*

1. *Medieval deeds of Bath and district*: I. Deeds of St John's Hospital, Bath (ed. B.R. Kemp); II. Walker-Heneage deeds (ed. D.M.M. Shorrocks). Somerset Record Soc. vol. 73; 1974. Pp 240.

2. Beresford, G. *The medieval clay-land village: excavations at Goltho and Barton Blount.* London; Soc. for Medieval Archaeology; 1975. Pp xi, 106.

3. Hooper, M.D., 'Which Winwick?,' *Northamptonshire Past and Present* 5 (1976), 305—8.

4. Reece, R.; Catling, C. *Cirencester: the development and buildings of a Cotswold town.* Oxford; British Arch. Reports; 1975. Pp 78.

5. Jones, A.D. *The priory of Hatfield Regis, AD 1135—1536.* Hatfield Broad Oak; the author; 1975. Pp 16.

6. Forrest, D. *The making of a manor: the story of Tickenham Court.* [Bradford-on-Avon]; Moonraker Press; 1975. Pp x, 123.

7. Urwin, A.C.B. *Twickenham, Whitton, Isleworth, Hounslow and Heston in 1086: an analysis of the entry in Domesday Book.* Twickenham Local History Soc.; n.d. Pp 21.

8. Drury, J.L., 'Early settlement in Stanhope Park, Weardale, c. 1406—79,' *Archaeologia Aeliana* 5th ser. 4 (1976), 139—49.

9. Bond, C.J., 'The medieval topography of the Evesham Abbey estates: a supplement,' *Vale of Evesham Historical Soc. Research Papers* 5 (1975), 51—9.

10. Sheppard, J., 'Medieval village planning in northern England: some evidence from Yorkshire,' *J. of Historical Geography* 2 (1976), 3—20.

11. Hindle, B.P., 'The road network of medieval England and Wales,' ibid. 207—21.

12. Wilson, P.A., 'Brougham Castle and early communications in the Eden valley,' *T. of the Cumberland and Westmorland Antiquarian and Arch. Soc.* new ser. 76 (1976), 67—76.

13. Jones, B.C., 'The topography of medieval Carlisle,' ibid. 77—96.

14. May, P., 'Newmarket 500 years ago,' *P. of the Suffolk Institute of Archaeology* 33 (1976 for 1975), 253—74.

15. Biddle, M. (ed.). *Winchester Studies, vol. 1. Winchester in the early middle ages: an edition and discussion of the Winton Domesday*, by F. Barlow, M. Biddle, O. von Feilitzen and D.J. Keene, with contributions by T.J. Brown, H.M. Nixon and F. Wormald. Oxford; Clarendon; 1976. Pp 612.

16. Burgess, L.A. (ed.). *The Southampton Terrier of 1454* (with introduction by L.A. Burgess, P.D.A. Harvey and A.D. Saunders). London; HMSO; 1976. Pp 172.

17. Hassall, J., 'Excavations at Willington, 1973,' *Bedfordshire Arch. J.* 10 (1976 for 1975), 25—40.

18. Thornhill, L.; Rigold, S.E.; Tookey, G.W., 'A double-moated site at Beckenham,' *Archaeologia Cantiana* 91 (1976 for 1975), 145—63.

19. 'Excavations at the Moat Site, Walsall, Staffs., 1972—4,' *T. of the South Staffordshire Arch. and Historical Soc.* 16 (1976 for 1974/5), 19—53.

20. Tebbutt, C.E., 'An abandoned medieval industrial site at Parrock, Hartfield,' *Sussex Arch. Collections* 113 (1976 for 1975), 146—51.

21. Green, H.J.M., 'Excavations of the palace defences and abbey precinct wall at Abingdon Street, Westminster, 1963,' *J. of the British Arch. Association* 129 (1976), 59—76.

22. Drewett, P.; Stuart, I., 'Excavations in the Norman gate tower, Bury St Edmunds Abbey,' *P. of the Suffolk Institute of Archaeology* 33 (1976 for 1975), 241—52.

23. Sherlock, D., 'Discoveries at Horsham St Faith Priory, 1970—1973,' *Norfolk Archaeology* 36 (1976), 202—23.

24. Woodhouse, J., *Barrow Mead, Bath, 1964: excavation of a medieval peasant house*. Oxford; British Arch. Reports 28; 1976. Pp 73.

25. Butler, L.A.S., 'The evolution of towns: planned towns after 1066,' Bc16, 32—47.

26. Platt, C., 'The evolution of towns: natural growth,' Bc16, 48—56.

27. Barley, M.W., 'Town defences in England and Wales after 1066,' Bc16, 57—70.

28. Keene, D.J., 'Suburban growth,' Bc16, 71—82.

F. ENGLAND AND WALES 1500—1714

See also: Aa8, 17, 32, 35, 42, 48, 55, b16, 29, c17; Ei86; Gh11, i36, 54.

(a) *General*

1. Scott, A.F. (compiler). *Every one a witness: commentaries of an era: the Tudor Age.* London; White Lion Publishers; 1975. Pp xv, 291.
2. Flegel, K.M., 'Was a sick man beheaded?,' [Thomas More] *Moreana* 49 (1976), 15—27.
3. Morris, G.C. *The Tudors* (revd. ed.). London; Severn House; 1976. Pp 202.
4. De Beer, E.S. (ed.). *The correspondence of John Locke*, vols. 1 & 2. Oxford; Clarendon; 1976. Pp xcxi, 707; vii, 805.
5. Northcote-Parkinson, C. *Gunpowder, treason and plot.* London; Weidenfeld & Nicolson; 1976. Pp 139.
6. Hurstfield, J., 'Queen and state: the emergence of an Elizabethan myth,' Bc3, 58—77.
7. Hoskins, W.G. *The age of plunder: King Henry's England, 1500—1547.* London; Longman; 1976. Pp xviii, 262.
8. Burton, E. *The early Tudors at home, 1485—1558.* London; Allen Lane; 1976. Pp xi, 305.

(b) *Political*

1. Downie, J.A., 'The commission of public accounts and the formation of the Country Party,' *English Historical R.* 91 (1976), 33—51.
2. Hamshere, C., 'The Ridolfi Plot, 1571,' *History Today* 26 (1976), 32—9.
3. Morrill, J.S. *The revolt of the provinces: conservatives and radicals in the English Civil War.* London; Allen & Unwin; 1976. Pp 234.
4. Fletcher, A.J. *A county community in peace and war: Sussex 1600—1660.* London; Longman; 1975. Pp xi, 445.
5. Fletcher, A.J., 'Petitioning and the outbreak of the Civil War in Derbyshire,' *Derbyshire Arch. J.* 93 (1975 for 1973), 33—44.
6. Speck, W.A., 'Brackley: a study in the growth of oligarchy,' *Midland History* 3 (1975), 30—41.
7. Lloyd, H.A., 'Corruption and Sir John Trevor,' *T. of the Honourable Soc. of Cymmrodorion* 1975, 77—102.
8. Edwards, A.C. *John Petre: essays on the life and background of John, 1st Lord Petre, 1549—1613.* London; Regency Press; 1975. Pp 156.
9. Smith, L.B. *Elizabeth Tudor: portrait of a queen.* Boston; Little, Brown; 1975. Pp xi, 234.

10. Edwards, F. *Mary and Ridolfi: design for destruction*. Ilford; Royal Stuart Soc.; 1975. Pp 18.

11. Jordan, W.K.; Gleason, M.R. *The Saying of John late duke of Northumberland upon the scaffold, 1553*. Cambridge, Mass.; Harvard College; 1975. Pp 72.

12. Walton, M. *The prisons of Mary Queen of Scots in Yorkshire and Derbyshire* (2nd ed.). [Sheffield City Libraries]; 1975.

13. Hurd, D.G.E. *Sir John Mason, 1503–1566*. [Abingdon; Abbey Press]; 1975. Pp vi, 48.

14. Slavin, A.J., 'The fall of Lord Chancellor Wriothesley: a study in the politics of conspiracy,' *Albion* 7 (1975), 265–86.

15. Fronville, M. *Jane Grey, reine de 9 jours (1537–1554)*. Geneva; Perret-Gentil; 1975. Pp 111.

16. Hansford-Miller, F.H. *John Hampden: an illustrated life of John Hampden, 1594–1643*. Princes Risborough; Shire Publications; 1976. Pp 48.

17. Harvey, N.L. *The rose and the thorn: the lives of Mary and Margaret Tudor*. New York; Macmillan; 1975. Pp xiv, 270.

18. Kelly, H.A. *The matrimonial trials of Henry VIII*. Stanford UP; 1976. Pp xiv, 333.

19. Sjögren, G. *Walter Ralegh: den siste elisabetanen*. Stockholm; Askild & Kärnekull; 1975. Pp 244.

20. Otto, O.J. *James I*. New York; Mason/Charter; 1976. Pp 472.

21. Snyder, H.L. (ed.). *The Marlborough-Godolphin correspondence* (3 vols.). Oxford; Clarendon; 1975. Pp xxxix, 1794.

22. Wyndham, V. *The Protestant duke: a life of Monmouth*. London; Weidenfeld & Nicolson; 1976. Pp xi, 193.

23. Hosford, D.H. *Nottingham, nobles and the north: aspects of the revolution of 1688*. Hamden, Conn.; Archon Books; 1976. Pp xvi, 182.

24. Bennett, G.V. *The tory crisis in Church and State, 1688–1730: the career of Francis Atterbury, bishop of Rochester*. Oxford; Clarendon; 1976. Pp xvii, 335.

25. Hamilton, E. *Henrietta Maria*. London; Hamilton; 1976. Pp xiv, 290.

26. Latham, R.; Matthews, W. (ed.). *The diary of Samuel Pepys: a new and complete transcription*; vol. 9: 1668–1669. London; Bell; 1976. Pp xiii, 590.

27. Rowse, A.L., 'The Godolphin-Marlborough duumvirate,' *History Today* 26 (1976), 402–7.

28. Willen, D., 'Lord Russell and the western counties, 1539–1555,' *J. of British Studies* 15 (1975), 26–45.

29. Russell, C., 'Parliamentary history in perspective, 1604–1629,' *History* 61 (1976), 1–27.

30. Thirsk, J. *The Restoration*. London; Longman; 1976. Pp xxiv, 205.

31. Manning, B. *The English people and the English revolution, 1640–1649*. London; Heinemann Educational; 1976. Pp x, 390.

32. Beer, B.L., ' "The commoyson in Norfolk, 1549,": narrative of popular rebellion in sixteenth-century England,' *J. of Medieval Renaissance Studies* 6 (1976), 73–99.

33. Flemion, J.S., 'The nature of opposition in the House of Lords in the early seventeenth century: a reevaluation,' *Albion* 8 (1976), 17–34.

34. Allen, D., 'The political function of Charles II's Chiffinch,' *Huntington Library Q.* 39 (1976), 277–90.

35. Harris, B., 'The trial of the third duke of Buckingham — a revisionist view,' *American J. of Legal History* 20 (1976), 15–26.

36. Davies, E.T., 'The "popish plot" in Monmouthshire,' *J. of the Historical Soc. of the Church in Wales* 25 (1976), 32–45.

37. Cornwall, J., 'The Ecclesden outrage: a fresh interpretation,' *Sussex Arch. Collections* 113 (1975), 7–15.

38. Du Maurier, D. *The winding stair: Francis Bacon, his rise and fall.* London; Gollancz; 1976. Pp 254.

39. Gruenfelder, J.M., 'Electoral influence of the earls of Huntingdon, 1603–1640,' *T. of the Leicestershire Arch. and Historical Soc.* 50 (1976 for 1974–5), 7–29.

40. Schwoerer, L.G., 'A Jornal of the Convention at Westminster begun the 22 of January 1688/9,' *B. of the Institute of Historical Research* 49 (1976), 242–63.

41, Donagan, B., 'A courtier's progress: greed and consistency in the life of the earl of Holland,' *Historical J.* 19 (1976), 317–53.

42. Elton, G.R., 'Tudor government: the points of contact. III: the court,' *T. of the Royal Historical Soc.* 5th ser. 26 (1976), 211–28.

43. Edwards, P.S., 'The mysterious parliamentary election at Cardigan borough in 1547,' *Welsh History R.* 8 (1976), 172–87.

44. Allen, D., 'Political clubs in Restoration London,' *Historical J.* 19 (1976), 561–80.

45. Edie, C.A., 'The popular idea of monarchy on the eve of the Stuart Restoration,' *Huntington Library Q.* 39 (1976), 343–73.

46. Weinstein, M.F., 'Queen's power: the case of Katherine Parr,' *History Today* 26 (1976), 788–93.

47. Styles, P., 'The royalist government of Worcestershire during the civil war 1642–6,' *T. of the Worcestershire Arch. Soc.* 3rd ser. 5 (1976), 23–39.

48. Tittler, R. *Nicholas Bacon: the making of a Tudor statesman.* London; Cape; 1976. Pp 253.

49. Haley, K.H.D., ' "No Popery" in the reign of Charles II,' Bc3, 102–19.

50. Jacob, M.C. *The Newtonians and the English Revolution, 1688–1720.* Hassocks; Harvester Press; 1976. Pp 288.

(c) *Constitution, Administration and Law*

1. Marcotte, E., 'Shrieval administration of Ship Money in Cheshire, 1637: limitations of early Stuart governance,' *B. of the John Rylands Library* 58 (1975), 137–72.
2. Bond, S.; Evans, N., 'The process of granting charters to English boroughs, 1547–1649,' *English Historical R.* 91 (1976), 102–20.
3. Forster, G.C.F., 'The North Riding justices and their sessions, 1603–1625,' *Northern History* 10 (1975), 102–25.
4. Marwil, J.L. *The trials of counsel: Francis Bacon in 1621.* Detriot; Wayne State UP; 1976. Pp 236.
5. Goring, J.; Wake, J. (ed.). *Northamptonshire lieutenancy papers and other documents, 1580–1614.* Northamptonshire Record Soc.; 1975. Pp xxxiv, 113.
6. Forster, G.C.F., 'Faction and county government in early Stuart Yorkshire,' *Northern History* 11 (1976 for 1975), 70–86.
7. Carter, D.P., 'The "Exact Militia" in Lancashire, 1625–1640,' ibid. 87–106.
8. Stoate, T.L. (ed.). *The Somerset Protestation returns and lay subsidy rolls, 1641–2.* Bristol; T.L. Stoate; 1975. Pp xxii, 344.
9. Kitching, C.J., 'Probate during the Civil War and Interregnum; part I: the survival of the prerogative court in the 1640s,' *J. of the Soc. of Archivists* 5 (1976), 283–93.
10. Christianson, P., 'The causes of the English Revolution: a reappraisal,' *J. of British Studies* 15 (1976), 40–75.
11. Thomas, G.W., 'James I, equity, and Lord Keeper John Williams,' *English Historical R.* 91 (1976), 506–28.
12. Guy, J.A., 'Wolsey, the council and the council courts,' ibid. 481–505.
13. Morrill, J.S. *The Cheshire grand jury, 1625–1659: a social and administrative study.* Leicester UP; 1976. Pp 60.
14. Cockburn, J.S. *Calendar of assize records: Sussex indictments, James I.* London; HMSO; 1975. Pp vii, 215.
15. Cockburn, J.S. *Calendar of assize records: Hertfordshire indictments, James I.* London; HMSO; 1975. Pp vii, 385.
16. Shapiro, B., 'Law reform in seventeenth century England,' *American J. of Legal History* 19 (1975), 280–312.
17. Hoak, D.E. *The king's council in the reign of Edward VI.* Cambridge UP; 1976. Pp x, 374.
18. Brooks, C.; Sharpe, K., 'History, English law and the Renaissance' (with rejoinder by D.R. Keeley), *Past & Present* 72 (1976), 133–46.
19. Higgins, G.P., 'The government of early Stuart Cheshire,' *Northern History* 12 (1976), 32–52.
20. Forster, G.C.F., 'County government in Yorkshire during the Interregnum,' ibid. 84–104.

21. Beckett, J.V., 'Local custom and the "new taxation" in the seventeenth and eighteenth centuries: the example of Cumberland,' ibid. 105—26.
22. Guy, J.A., 'A conciliar court of audit at work in the last months of the reign of Henry VII,' *B. of the Institute of Historical Research* 49 (1976), 289—95.
23. Heinze, R.W. *The proclamations of the Tudor kings.* Cambridge UP; 1976. Pp xii, 317.
24. Youngs, F.A. *The proclamations of the Tudor queens.* Cambridge UP; 1976. Pp xiv, 277.
25. Bond, M.F. (ed.). *The diaries and papers of Sir Edward Dering, second baronet, 1644 to 1684* (House of Lords Record Office Occasional Publications, no. 1). London; HMSO; 1976. Pp viii, 237.
26. Kitching, C.J., 'Probate during the civil war and interregnum; part II: the court of probate, 1653—1660,' *J. of the Soc. of Archivists* 5 (1976), 346—56.
27. Hollis, D.W., 'The model survey of 1649,' *B. of the Institute of Historical Research* 49 (1976), 299—301.
28. Harris, M., 'Newspaper distribution during Queen Anne's reign: Charles Delafaye and the Secretary of State's office,' Bc7, 139—51.
29. Peck, L.L., 'Problems in Jacobean administration: was Henry Howard, earl of Northampton, a reformer?,' *Historical J.* 19 (1976), 831—58.
30. Holmes, G.S. *The electorate and the national will in the first age of party* (inaugural lecture). Kendal; for the author; 1976. Pp 33.

(d) *External Affairs*

1. Belcher, G.L., 'Spain and the Anglo-Portuguese alliance of 1661: a reassessment of Charles II's foreign policy at the Restoration,' *J. of British Studies* 15 (1975), 67—88.
2. Huttenbach, H.R., 'Anthony Jenkinson's 1566 and 1567 missions to Muscovy reconstructed from unpublished sources,' *Canadian-American Slavic Studies* 9 (1975), 179—203.
3. Sellin, P.R., 'John Donne: the poet as diplomat and divine,' *Huntington Library Q.* 39 (1976), 267—75.
4. Karsten, P., 'Plotters and proprietaries, 1682—83: the "Council of Six" and the colonies: plans for colonization or front for revolution?,' *The Historian* 38 (1976), 474—84.
5. Bell, G.M., 'John Man: the last Elizabethan resident ambassador in Spain,' *Sixteenth Century J.* 7 (1976), 75—93.
6. Quinn, D.B., 'Renaissance influences in English colonization,' *T. of the Royal Historical Soc.* 5th ser. 26 (1976), 73—93.
7. Korr, C.P. *Cromwell and the new model foreign policy: England's*

policy towards France, 1649–1658. Berkeley; University of
California Press; 1976. Pp x, 268.

8. Quinn, D.B. (intr.) *The last voyage of Thomas Cavendish, 1591–
1592: the autograph manuscript of his own account of the
voyage, written shortly before his death.* Chicago; University of
Chicago Press; 1975 [i.e. 1976]. Pp ix, 165.

9. Simmons, R.C., 'The Massachusetts charter of 1691,' Bc5, 66–87.

(e) *Religion*

1. Betteridge, A., 'Early baptists in Leicestershire and Rutland (4),'
Baptist Q. 26 (1976), 209–23.

2. Pineas, R., 'George Joye's *Exposicion of Daniel*,' *Renaissance Q.*
28 (1975), 332–42.

3. Davies, G.J., 'Evidence against John Wesly (c. 1636–70),' *P. of
the Welsh Historical Soc.* 40 (1975), 80–4.

4. Clark, S.; Morgan, P.T.J., 'Religion and magic in Elizabethan
Wales: Robert Holland's dialogue on witchcraft,' *J. of Ecclesiastical History* 27 (1976), 31–46.

5. Haigh, C.A., 'Slander and the Church courts in the sixteenth century,' *T. of the Lancashire and Cheshire Antiquarian Soc.* 78
(1975), 1–13.

6. Kitching, C.H. (ed.). *The Royal Visitation of 1559: act book for
the northern province.* Durham; Surtees Soc.; 1975. Pp xxxvi,
146.

7. Tobriner, A., 'Vives' prayers in English Reformation worship,'
Catholic Historical R. 61 (1975), 505–15.

8. Sheils, W.J., 'The Restoration and the temporalities: Archbishop
Frewen's commissioners 1661–1662,' *Borthwick Institute B.* 1
(1975), 17–30.

9. O'Day, R.; Heal, F. (ed.). *Continuity and Change: personnel and
administration of the Church of England 1500–1642.* Leicester
UP; 1976. Pp 303.

10. O'Day, R.; Heal, F., 'Introduction,' Fe9, 13–29.

11. Foster, A., 'The function of a bishop: the career of Richard Neile,
1562–1540,' Fe9, 33–54.

12. O'Day, R., 'The reformation of the ministry, 1558–1642,' Fe9,
55–76.

13. O'Day, R., 'The role of the registrar in diocesan administration,'
Fe9, 77–94.

14. Heal, F., 'Clerical tax collection under the Tudors: the influence
of the Reformation,' Fe9, 97–122.

15. Marcombe, D., 'The Durham Dean and Chapter: old abbey writ
large,' Fe9, 125–44.

16. Haigh, C.A., 'Finance and administration in a new diocese:
Chester 1541–1641,' Fe9, 145–66.

17. Sheils, W.J., 'Some problems of government in a new diocese: the

bishop and the puritans in the diocese of Peterborough,' Fe9, 167–87.

18. Kitching, C.H., 'The Prerogative Court of Canterbury from War-ham to Whitgift,' Fe9, 191–214.

19. Lander, S., 'Church courts and the Reformation in the diocese of Chichester,' Fe9, 215–38.

20. Houlbrooke, R., 'The decline of ecclesiastical jurisdiction under the Tudors,' Fe9, 239–58.

21. Redwood, J. *Reason, ridicule and religion: the age of enlighten-ment in England, 1660–1750.* London; Thames & Hudson; 1976. Pp 287.

22. Anstruther, G., 'The last days of the London Blackfriars,' *Archivum Fratrum Praedicatorum* 45 (1975), 213–36.

23. Parmiter, G. de C., 'Plowden, Englefield and Sandford: 1, 1558–85,' *Recusant History* 13 (1976), 159–77.

24. Somerville, C.J., 'Religious typologies and popular religion in Restoration England,' *Church History* 45 (1976), 32–41.

25. O'Day, R., 'Immanuel Bourne: a defence of the ministerial order,' *J. of Ecclesiastical History* 27 (1976), 101–14.

26. Smart, I.M., 'Edward Gee and the matter of authority,' ibid. 115–27.

27. Duffy, E., ' "Whiston's affair": the trials of a primitive Christian 1709–1714,' ibid. 129–50.

28. Bluhm, H., ' "Fyve sundry interpreters": the sources of the first printed English Bible,' *Huntington Library Q.* 39 (1976), 107–16.

29. Simpson, M.A. (ed.). *John Knox and the Troubles begun at Frankfurt.* West Linton; the author; 1975. Pp 155.

30. Williams, J.A. (ed.). *Post-Reformation Catholicism at Bath*, vol. 1. London; Catholic Record Soc.; 1975. Pp viii, 258.

31. Houlbrooke, R.A. (ed.). *The Letter Book of John Parkhurst, bishop of Norwich, compiled during the years 1571–5.* Norwich; Norfolk Record Soc.; 1975. Pp 288.

32. Knowles, D. *Bare Ruined Choirs: the dissolution of the English monasteries.* Cambridge UP; 1976. Pp 329. [Abridged ed. of *Religious Orders in England*, vol. 3].

33. Greaves, R.L., 'The organizational response of nonconformity to repression and indulgence: the case of Bedfordshire,' *Church History* 44 (1975), 472–84.

34. Flynn, D., 'Donne's catholicism: II,' *Recusant History* 13 (176); 178–95.

35. MacDonald Wigfield, W., '*Ecclesiastica, the Book of Remembrance* of the Independent congregations of Axminster and Chard,' *Somerset Archaeology and Natural History* 119 (1974/5), 51–5.

36. O'Day, R., 'Cumulative debt: the bishops of Coventry and Lich-field and their economic problems,' *Midland History* 3 (1975), 77–93.

37. McGee, J.S., 'Conversion and the imitation of Christ in anglican and puritan writing,' *J. of British Studies* 15 (1976), 21–39.

38. Cargill Thompson, W.D.J., 'Thomas Brett's puritan papers: a lost collection of Elizabethan manuscripts,' *J. of Ecclesiastical History* 27 (1976), 285–302.

39. Zell, M.I., 'The prebendaries' plot of 1543: a reconsideration,' ibid. 241.

40. Nuttall, G.F., 'Church life in Bunyan's Bedfordshire,' *Baptist Q.* 26 (1976), 305–13.

41. Jarrott, C.A., 'John Colet on justification,' *Sixteenth Century J.* 7 (1976), 59–72.

42. Schwarz, M.L., ' "Twenty-Four Arguments": Sir Robert Cotton confronts the Catholics and the Church of England,' *Albion* 8 (1976), 35–49.

43. Greaves, R.L., 'The social awareness of John Knox,' *Renaissance and Reformation* 12 (1976), 36–48.

44. Bond, R.B., 'Cranmer and the controversy surrounding publication of *Certain Sermons or Homilies* (1547),' ibid. 28–35.

45. McCann, T.J., 'Some notes on the family of George Gervase of Bosham, martyr,' *Sussex Arch. Collections* 113 (1975), 152–6.

46. Marshall, W.M. *George Hooper, 1640–1727, bishop of Bath and Wells.* Sherborne; Dorset Publishing Co.; 1976. Pp 221.

47. Howard, K.W.H. (ed.). *The Axminster Ecclesiastica.* Sheffield; Gospel Tidings Publications; 1976. Pp xv, 280.

48. Jones, F., 'A rent roll of the temporalities of the see of St David's, 1685,' *J. of the Historical Soc. of the Church in Wales* 25 (1976), 46–65.

49. Griffiths, G.M., 'A visitation of the archdeaconry of Carmarthen, 1710 (part 2),' *National Library of Wales J.* 19 (1976), 311–26.

50. Williams, G., 'The diocese of St David's from the end of the middle ages to the Methodist revival,' *J. of the Historical Soc. of the Church in Wales* 25 (1976), 11–31.

51. Painter, G.D.; Rhodes, D.E.; Nixon, H.M., 'Two missals printed for Wynkyn de Worde,' *British Library J.* 2 (1976), 159–71.

52. Sherr, M.F., 'Religion and the legal profession: a study of the religious sensibilities of 16th century London lawyers,' *Historical Magazine of the Protestant Episcopal Church* 45 (1976), 211–24.

53. Shipps, K., 'The "political puritan",' *Church History* 45 (1976), 196–205.

54. Horle, C.W., 'Quakers and Baptists 1647–1660,' *Baptist Q.* 26 (1976), 344–62.

55. Martin, J.W., 'English protestant separatism at its beginnings: Henry Hart and the Free-Will Men,' *Sixteenth Century J.* 7/2 (1976), 55–74.

56. Greaves, R.L., 'Traditionalism and the seeds of revolution in the social principles of the Geneva bible,' ibid. 94–109.

57. Donagan, B., 'The clerical patronage of Robert Rich, second earl of Warwick, 1619–1642,' *P. of the American Philosophical Soc.* 120 (1976), 388–419.

58. Sprunger, K.L., 'John Yates of Norfolk: the radical puritan preacher as Ramist philosopher,' *J. of the History of Ideas* 37 (1976), 697–706.

59. Buckroyd, J., 'Lord Broghill and the Scottish Church, 1655–1656,' *J. of Ecclesiastical History* 27 (1976), 359–68.

60. Norman, M., 'Dame Gertrude More and the English mystical tradition,' *Recusant History* 13 (1976), 196–211.

61. Clancy, T.H., 'Papist-protestant-puritan: English religious taxonomy 1565–1665,' ibid. 227–53.

62. Hidgetts, M., 'Elizabethan priest-holes; V: the north,' ibid. 254–79.

63. Cooter, R.J., 'Lady Londonderry and the Irish catholics of Seaham Harbour: "No Popery" out of context,' ibid. 288–98.

64. Briggs, E.R., 'An apostle of the incomplete reformation: Jacops Aconcio (1500–1567),' *P. of the Huguenot Soc. of London* 22 (1976), 481–95.

65. Griffiths, D.N., 'The Huguenot links with St George's Chapel, Windsor,' ibid. 496–508.

66. Gwynn, R., 'The distribution of Huguenot refugees in England; II: London and its environs,' ibid. 509–68.

67. Thorp, M.R., 'The anti-Huguenot undercurrent in late-seventeenth century England,' ibid. 569–80.

68. Guy, J.R., 'William Beaw: bishop and secret agent,' *History Today* 26 (1976), 796–803.

69. Parmiter, G. de C. *Elizabethan popish recusants in the Inns of Court.* B. of the Institute of Historical Research, special supplement no. 11 (1976). Pp vii, 60.

70. Cuming, G.J., 'Eastern liturgies and Anglican divines, 1510–1622,' Bc4, 231–8.

71. McGee, J.S. *The godly man in Stuart England: Anglicans, puritans and the two tables, 1620–1670.* New Haven/London; Yale UP; 1976. Pp xix, 299.

(f) *Economic affairs*

1. Challis, C.E., 'Spanish bullion and monetary inflation in England in the later sixteenth century,' *J. of European Economic History* 4 (1975), 381–92.

2. Shammas, C., 'The "invisible merchant" and property rights: the misadventures of an Elizabethan joint stock company,' *Business History* 17 (1975), 95–108.

3. Beresford, M.W., 'Leeds in 1628: a "Ridings Observation" from the city of London,' *Northern History* 10 (1975), 126–40.

4. Challis, C.E., 'The ecclesiastical mints of the early Tudor period: their organization and possible date of closure,' ibid. 88–100.

5. Doe, V.S., 'The common fields of Beeley in the seventeenth century,' *Derbyshire Arch. J.* 93 (1975 for 1973), 45–54.

6. Nathanson, A.J. *Thomas Simon: his life and work, 1618–1665.* London; Seaby; 1976. Pp 60.

7. Davis, R. *English merchant shipping and Anglo-Dutch rivalry in the seventeenth century.* London; HMSO; 1975. Pp 37.

8. Clemens, P.G.E., 'The rise of Liverpool, 1665–1750,' *Economic History R.* 2nd series 29 (1976), 211–25.

9. Rapley, J., 'Handframe knitting: the development of patterning and shaping,' *Textile History* 6 (1975), 18–51.

10. Drury, P.J., 'Post-medieval brick and tile kilns at Russell Green, Danbury, Essex,' *Post-Medieval Archaeology* 9 (1975), 203–11.

11. Henstock, A., 'The monopoly in Rhenish stoneware imports in late Elizabethan England,' ibid. 219–24.

12. Godfrey, E.S. *The development of English glassmaking, 1560–1640.* Oxford; Clarendon; 1975 [i.e. 1976]. Pp xii, 288.

13. Galgano, M.J., 'Iron-mining in Restoration Furness: the case of Sir Thomas Preston,' *Recusant History* 13 (1976), 212–8.

14. Yates, E.M., 'Aspects of Staffordshire farming in the seventeenth and eighteenth centuries,' *North Staffordshire J. of Field Studies* 15 (1975), 26–40.

15. Holderness, B.A., 'Credit in a rural community, 1660–1800,' *Midland History* 3 (1975), 94–116.

16. O'Connell, L.S., 'Anti-entrepreneurial attitudes in Elizabethan sermons and popular literature,' *J. of British Studies* 15 (1976), 1–20.

17. Holderness, B.A., 'Credit in English rural society before the nineteenth century, with special reference to the period 1650–1720,' *Agricultural History R.* 24 (1976), 97–109.

18. Appleby, J.O., 'Ideology and theory: the tension between political and economic liberalism in seventeenth-century England,' *American Historical R.* 81 (1976), 499–515.

19. Appleby, J.O., 'Locke, liberalism and the natural law of money,' *Past and Present* 71 (1976), 43–69.

20. Dyer, A.D., 'Wood and coal: a change of fuel,' *History Today* 26 (1976), 598–607.

21. Summers, D. *The great level: a history of drainage and land reclamation in the Fens.* Newton Abbot; David & Charles; 1976. Pp 295.

22. Willan, T.S. *The inland trade: studies in English internal trade in the sixteenth and seventeenth centuries.* Manchester UP; 1976. Pp vi, 154.

23. Kempson, E.G.H., 'Indictments for the coining of tokens in seventeenth-century Wiltshire,' *British Numismatic J.* 43 (1976 for 1973), 126–31.

24. Adams, S.L., 'The Composition of 1564 and the earl of Leicester's tenurial reformation in the lordship of Denbigh,' *B. of the Board of Celtic Studies* 26 (1976), 479–511.
25. Kepler, J.S. *The exchange of Christendom: the international entrepot at Dover, 1622–1651.* Leicester UP; 1976. Pp 191.
26. Sherman, A.A., 'Pressure from Leadenhall: the East India Company lobby, 1660–1678,' *Businss History R.* 50 (1976), 329–55.
27. Patten, J., 'Patterns of migration and movement of labour in three pre-industrial East Anglian towns,' *J. of Historical Geography* 2 (1976), 111–29.
28. Stoker, D., 'The early history of paper-making in Norfolk,' *Norfolk Archaeology* 36 (1976), 241–52.
29. John, A.H., 'English agricultural improvement and grain exports, 1660–1765,' Bc9, 45–67.
30. Ashton, R., 'Conflicts of concessionary interests in early Stuart England,' Bc9, 113–31.
31. Hammersley, G., 'The state and the English iron industry in the sixteenth and seventeenth centuries,' Bc9, 166–86.
32. Coleman, D.C., 'Politics and economics in the age of Anne: the case of the Anglo-French trade treaty of 1713,' Bc9, 187–211.
33. Blanchard, I., 'English lead and the international bullion crisis of the 1550s,' Bc9, 21–44.
34. Berry, G.; Morley, P., 'A revised survey of the seventeenth-century tokens of Buckinghamshire,' *British Numismatic J.* 43 (1976 for 1973), 96–125.

(g) *Social History (General)*

1. Roberts, B.F., 'Edward Lhuyd's debts,' *B. of the Board of Celtic Studies* 26 (1975), 353–9.
2. Kishlansky, M., 'The sales of crown lands and the spirit of the Revolution,' *Economic History R.* 2nd ser. 29 (1976), 125–30.
3. Gentles, I., 'The sales of crown lands: a rejoinder,' ibid. 131–5.
4. De Mare, E. *Wren's London.* London; Folio Soc.; 1975. Pp 128.
5. Batho, G.R., 'Gilbert Talbot, seventh earl of Shrewsbury (1553–1616): the "Great and Glorious Earl"?,' *Derbyshire Arch. J.* 93 (1975 for 1973), 23–32.
6. Gibson, J., 'A disputed inheritance,' *Cake and Cockhorse* 6 (1976), 83–6.
7. Ferguson, C., 'The Stationers' Company Poor Book, 1608–1700,' *Library* 5th series, 31 (1976), 37–51.
8. Wrightson, K., 'Infanticide in earlier seventeenth-century England,' *Local Population Studies* 15 (1975), 10–22.
9. Holman, J.R., 'Orphans in pre-industrial towns: the case of Bristol in the late seventeenth century,' ibid. 40–4.

10. Campion, L. *The family of Edmund Campion.* London; Research Publishing Company; 1975. Pp 58.

11. Deacon, R. *Matthew Hopkins, witch finder general.* London; Muller; 1976. Pp 223.

12. Cressy, D. (ed.). *Education in Tudor and Stuart England.* London; Arnold; 1975. Pp ix, 141.

13. Bittle, W.G.; Land, R.T., 'Inflation and philanthropy in England: a reassessment of W.K. Jordan's data,' *Economic History R.* 2nd series, 29 (1976), 203—10.

14. Pasold, E.W., 'In search of William Lee,' *Textile History* 6 (1975), 7—17.

15. Dixon, P., 'Excavations at Richmond Palace, Surrey,' *Post-Medieval Archaeology* 9 (1975), 103—16.

16. Haslam, J., 'The excavation of a 17th century pottery site at Cove, E. Hampshire,' ibid. 164—87.

17. Alcock, N.W., 'Warwickshire timber-framed houses: a draft and a contract,' ibid. 212—8.

18. Holmes, M. *Proud northern lady: Lady Anne Clifford 1590—1676.* London; Phillimore; 1975. Pp 181.

19. Rawcliffe, C., 'A Tudor nobleman as archivist: the papers of Edward, third duke of Buckingham,' *J. of the Soc. of Archivists* 5 (1976), 294—300.

20. Coats, A.W., 'The relief of poverty, attitudes to labour, and economic change in England, 1660—1782,' *International R. of Social History* 21 (1976), 98—115.

21. Bush, R.J.E., 'The Tudor Tavern, Fore Street, Taunton,' *Somerset Archaeology and Natural History* 119 (1974/5), 15—21.

22. Robinson, W.R.B., 'The officers and household of Henry, earl of Worcester, 1526—49,' *Welsh History R.* 8 (1976), 26—41.

23. Jaggar, G., 'Colonel Edward Whalley, his regimental officers and crown land, with particular relation to the manors of Terrington and West Walton, Norfolk, 1650 to the Restoration,' *Norfolk Archaeology* 36 (1975), 149—66.

24. Ambler, R.W.; Watkinson, M., 'The agrarian problem in sixteenth century Lincolnshire: two cases from the court of star chamber,' *Lincolnshire History and Archaeology* 11 (1976), 13—19.

25. Beckwith, I., 'Captain John Smith: the yeoman background,' *History Today* 26 (1976), 444—51.

26. Hunter, M., 'The social basis and changing fortunes of an early scientific institution: an analysis of the membership of the Royal Society, 1660—1685,' *Notes and Records of the Royal Soc. of London* 31 (1976), 9—114.

27. Brent, C.E., 'Urban employment and population in Sussex between 1550 and 1660,' *Sussex Arch. Collections* 113 (1975), 35—50.

28. Allen, D.G., 'A tale of two towns: persistent English localism in seventeenth-century Massachusetts,' Bc5, 1—35.

29. Emmison, F.E. *Elizabethan life; vol. 3: Home, work and land, from Essex wills and sessions and manorial records.* Chelmsford; Essex County Council; 1976. Pp x, 364.

30. Dickinson, R. and F. (ed.) *The register of Prescot parish church,* part 2: 1632—1666. [Manchester] ; Lancashire Parish Register Soc.; 1975. Pp vii, 155.

31. Sunderland, N. *Tudor Darlington*, part 2. Durham County Council; 1976. Pp iv, 85.

32. Murray, I.G. (ed.). *Court rolls of the manor of Tottenham, 23 Henry VIII to 1 Edward VI (1531—1546).* London; Borough of Harringey 1975. Pp vii, 225.

33. Slater, M., 'The weightiest business: marriage in an upper-gentry family in seventeenth-century England,' *Past & Present* 72 (1976), 25—54.

34. Blackwood, B.G., 'The economic state of the Lancashire gentry on the eve of the civil war,' *Northern History* 12 (1976), 53—83.

35. Slack, P. (ed.). *Poverty in early-Stuart Salisbury.* Devizes; Wiltshire Record Soc.; 1975. Pp viii, 181.

36. Macfarlane, A. (ed.). *The diary of Ralph Josselin, 1616—1683.* London; Oxford UP for British Academy; 1976. Pp xxvi, 727.

37. Machin, R. (ed.). *Probate inventories and manorial excepts of Chetnole, Leigh and Yetminster.* Bristol; Dept of Extra-Mural Studies; 1976. Pp 37.

38. DeMolen, R.L., 'Ages of admission to educational institutions in Tudor and Stuart England (with comment by K. Charlton),' *History of Education* 5 (1976), 207—26.

39. Feyerharm, W.R., 'The status of the schoolmaster and the continuity of education in Elizabethan East Anglia,' ibid. 103—16.

40. Smith, A., 'Private schools and schoolmasters in the diocese of Lichfield and Coventry in the seventeenth century,' ibid. 117—26.

41. Tittler, R., 'Education and the gentleman in Tudor England: the case of Sir Richard Bacon,' ibid. 3—10.

42. Cameron, A., 'Some social consequences of the dissolution of the monasteries in Nottinghamshire,' *T. of the Thoroton Soc.* 79 (1976 for 1975), 50—9.

43. Falkus, M., 'Lighting in the dark ages of English economic history: towns streets before the Industrial Revolution.' Bc9, 248—73.

(h) *Social Structure and Population*

1. Hanley, H., 'Population mobility in Buckinghamshire 1578—1583,' *Local Population Studies* 15 (1975), 33—9.

2. Spencer, W.M. (ed.). *Parochial chapelry of Colne: marriages from 1654 to 1754.* Burnley; Colne Register Transcriptions; 1975. Pp ix, 146.

3. Hirst, D.M., 'The seventeenth-century freeholder and the statistician: a case of terminological confusion,' *Economic History R.* 2nd series, 29 (1976), 306—16.
4. Thompson, F.M.L., 'A terminological confusion confounded,' ibid. 311—3 [answer to Fh3].
5. Pound, J.F., 'Vagrants and the social order in Elizabethan England (with rejoinder by A.L. Beier),' *Past and Present* 71 (1976), 126—34.
6. Walter, J.; Wrightson, K., 'Dearth and the social order in early modern England,' ibid. 22—42.
7. Clark, P., 'Popular protest and disturbance in Kent, 1558—1640,' *Economic History R.* 2nd ser. 29 (1976), 365—82.
8. Sayer, M.J., 'Norfolk visitation families: a short social structure,' *Norfolk Archaeology* 36 (1975), 176—82.
9. Faraday, M.A., 'The Ludlow poll-tax return of 1667,' *T. of the Shropshire Arch. Soc.* 59 (1976 for 1971—2), 104—23.
10. Crafts, N.F.R.; Ireland, N.J., 'Family limitation and the English demographic revolution: a simulation approach,' *J. of Economic History* 36 (1976), 598—623.
11. Cressy, D.A., 'Describing the social order in Elizabethan and Stuart England,' *Literature and History* 3 (1976), 29—44.
12. Brown, R., 'Clandestine marriages in Wales,' *J. of the Historical Soc. of the Church in Wales* 25 (1976), 66—71.
13. Roy, I., 'The English civil war and English society,' Bc11, 24—43.
14. Corfield, P., 'Urban development in England and Wales in the sixteenth and seventeenth centuries,' Bc9, 214—47.
15. Smith, S.R., 'Growing old in seventeenth century England,' *Albion* 8 (1976), 125—41.

(i) *Naval and Military*

1. Rodger, N.A.M., 'The Ordnance Board in 1666,' *Mariner's Mirror* 62 (1976), 91—4.
2. Young, P. *Oliver Cromwell and his times* (revd. ed.). London; Severn House; 1975. Pp 152.
3. Roy, I. (ed.). *The Royalist Ordnance Papers, 1642—1646*, part 2. Oxfordshire Record Soc,; 1976. Pp [231—536].
4. Kightly, C. *Flodden: the Anglo-Scottish war of 1513.* London; Almark Publishing Co.; 1975. Pp 48.
5. Holmes, R. *Cromwell's Ely.* Ely Local History Publications Board; 1975. Pp viii, 55.
6. Ashley, M., 'George Goring, royalist commander and debauchee,' *History Today* 26 (1976), 188—93.
7. Boxer, C.R., 'Admiral de Ruyter through English eyes,' ibid. 232—40.
8. Powell, J.R., 'John Bourne, sometime vice-admiral,' *Mariner's Mirror* 62 (1976), 109—17.

9. Martin, C. *Full fathom five: wrecks of the Spanish Armada.* New York; Viking Press; 1975. Pp 288.

10. Childs, J. *The army of Charles II.* London; Routledge; 1976. Pp xii, 304.

11. Courtney, T.W., 'Excavations at the Royal Dockyard, Woolwich, 1972–1973, Part 2,' *Post-Medieval Archaeology* 9 (1975), 45–102.

12. Ames, H.S., 'Recent excavations at Camber Castle,' ibid. 233–6.

13. Ritchie, N., 'Sir Robert Dudley: expatriate in Tuscan service,' *History Today* 26 (1976), 385–92.

14. Lyndon, B., 'Military dress and uniformity 1680–1720,' *J. of the Soc. for Army Historical Research* 54 (1976), 108–20.

15. Roddie, A., 'Jacob, the diver,' *Mariner's Mirror* 62 (1976), 253–70.

16. Ellis, P.B. *The Boyne Water: the battle of the Boyne, 1690.* London; Hamilton; 1976. Pp xii, 163.

17. Verney, P. *The battle of Blenheim.* London; Batsford; 1976. Pp 192.

18. Thomson, G.M. *Warrior prince: Prince Rupert of the Rhine.* London; Secker & Warburg; 1976. Pp ix, 238.

19. Le Fevre, P., 'The earl of Torrington's speech to the Commons, November 1690,' *Mariner's Mirror* 62 (1976), 386.

20. Taylor, C., 'The Phillipps manuscript. A chapter in early Welsh migration to the West Indies and to the United States,' *National Library of Wales J.* 19 (1976), 243.

21. Parker, G., 'If the Armada had landed,' *History* 61 (1976), 358–68.

22. Ashley, M. *Rupert of the Rhine.* London; Hart-Davis, MacGibbon; 1976. Pp viii, 199.

23. Ollard, R. *This war without an enemy: a history of the English civil wars.* London; Hodder & Stoughton; 1976. Pp 224.

24. Gillingham, J.B. *Cromwell: portrait of a soldier.* London; Weidenfeld & Nicolson; 1976. Pp vii, 149.

25. Morrah, P. *Prince Rupert of the Rhine.* London; Constable; 1976. Pp xiii, 480.

26. Allen, H.R. *Buccaneer: Admiral Sir Henry Morgan.* London; Barker; 1976. Pp xi, 193.

27. Adair, J. *A life of John Hampden, the patriot (1594–1643).* London; Macdonald and Jane's; 1976. Pp viii, 261.

28. Gentles, I., 'Arrears of pay and ideology in the army revolt of 1647,' *Bc11, 44–66.

(j) *Political Thought and the History of Ideas*

1. Barnard, T.C., 'Provost Huntington: injunctions to schoolmasters in 1684,' *Hermathena* 119 (1975), 71–3.

2. Smith, G.R., 'Shakespeare's Henry V: another part of the critical forest,' *J. of the History of Ideas* 37 (1976), 3—26.

3. Eccleshall, R., 'Richard Hooker's synthesis and the problem of allegiance,' ibid. 111—24.

4. Davies, S., 'John Milton on liberty,' *Manchester Literary and Philosophical Soc. Memoirs and P.* 117 (1974—5), 37—51.

5. Orgel, S. *The illusion of power: political theater in the English Renaissance.* Berkeley/London; University of California Press; 1975. Pp xi, 95.

6. Davis, J.C., 'Gerrard Winstanley and the restoration of true magistracy,' *Past & Present* 70 (1976), 76—93.

7. Weigall, D., 'Sir Robert Filmer of East Sutton,' *Archaeologia Cantiana* 91 (1975), 99—105.

8. Morton, A.L. (ed.). *Freedom in arms: a selection of Leveller writings.* London; Lawrence & Wishart; 1975 [i.e. 1976]. Pp 356.

9. Pocock, J.G.A., 'The classical theory of deference,' *American Historical R.* 81 (1976), 516—23.

10. Mackie, J.L. *Problems for Locke.* Oxford; Clarendon; 1976. Pp ix, 237.

11. Hoppen, T., 'The nature of the early Royal Society, Part II,' *British J. for the History of Science* 9 (1976), 243—73.

12. Moore, J.T., 'Locke's analysis of language and the assent to scripture,' *J. of the History of Ideas* 37 (1976), 707—14.

13. Gough, J.W., 'James Tyrrell, whig historian and friend of John Locke,' *Historical J.* 19 (1976), 581—610.

14. Weinberger, J., 'Science and rule in Bacon's Utopia: an introduction to the reading of the *New Atlantis*,' *American Political Science R.* 70 (1976), 865—85.

15. Holeczek, H., 'Die humanistische Bildung des Thomas More und ihre Beurteilung durch Erasmus von Rotterdam,' *Zeitschrift für historische Forschung* 3 (1976), 165—204.

16. Hampsher-Monk, I., 'The political theory of the Levellers: Putney, property and Professor Macpherson,' *Political Studies* 24 (1976), 397—422.

17. Pocock, J.G.A., 'Modes of political and historical time in early eighteenth-century England,' Bc13, 87—102.

18. Earle, P., 'The economics of stability: the views of Daniel Defoe,' Bc9, 274—92.

(k) *Cultural (including History of Science)*

1. Doughty, D.W., 'Renaissance books, bindings and owners in St Andrews and elsewhere: the humanists,' *Bibliotheck* 7 (1975), 117—33.

2. Weiner, A.D., 'Raphael's Eutopia and More's *Utopia*: Christian humanism and the limits of reason,' *Huntington Library Q.* 39 (1975), 1—27.

3. Edmond, M., 'New light on Jacobean painters,' *Burlington Magazine* 118 (1976), 74—83.
4. Cowie, L.W., 'More's house in Chelsea,' *History Today* 26 (1976), 118—24.
5. Westfall, R.S., 'The changing world of the Newtonian industry,' *J. of the History of Ideas* 37 (1976), 175—84.
6. Fisher, R.M., 'William Crashawe's library at the Temple,' *Library* (1975), 116—24.
7. Bergeron, D.M., 'Civic pageants and historical drama,' *J. of Medieval and Renaissance Studies* 5 (1975), 89—105.
8. Hunter, M. *John Aubrey and the realm of learning.* London; Duckworth; 1975. Pp 256.
9. Stephens, J. *Francis Bacon and the style of science.* Chicago/ London; University of Chicago Press; 1975. Pp xi, 188.
10. Aubrey, J. *Brief lives: a selection based upon existing contemporary portraits* (ed. R. Barber). London; Folio Soc.; 1975.
11. Betts, B.J.T. *The foundations of Newton's alchemy, or The hunting of the green lyon.* Cambridge UP; 1975. Pp xv, 300.
12. Hutchison, H.F. *Sir Christopher Wren: a biography.* London; Gollancz; 1976. Pp 191.
13. Webster, C. *The great instauration: science, medicine and reform, 1626—1660.* London; Duckworth; 1975. Pp xvi, 630.
14. Pepper, J.V., 'Harriot's manuscript on the theory of impacts,' *Annals of Science* 33 (1976), 131—51.
15. Blair, W.J., 'Nicholas Stone's design for the Bodley monument,' *Burlington Magazine* 118 (1976), 23—4.
16. Höltgen, K.J., 'Anne Bradstreet, the first American poetess, and her father, Governer Thomas Dudley,' *Northamptonshire Past and Present* 5 (1976), 325—32.
17. Wernham, R.B., 'Christopher Marlowe at Flushing in 1592,' *English Historical R.* 91 (1976), 344—5.
18. Ross, R.P., 'The social and economic causes of the revolution in the mathematical sciences in mid-seventeenth century England,' *J. of British Studies* 15 (1975), 46—66.
19. Devereux, E.J., 'John Rastell's press in the English Reformation,' *Moreana* 49 (1976), 29—47.
20. Wilkinson, R.S. *The younger John Winthrop and seventeenth-century science.* Faringdon; E.W. Classey; 1975. Pp vi, 29.
21. Dearing, V.A.; Brunet, S.E.; Hall, J.H.; Tamarelli, R.G., 'Dryden's *Heroique Stanzas* on Cromwell: a new critical text,' *Papers of the Bibliographical Soc. of America* 69 (1975), 502—26.
22. Streitberger, W.R., 'The Tyllney Manuscript at the Folger Library,' ibid. 449—64.
23. Forbes, E.G. (ed.). *The Gresham lectures of John Flamsteed.* London; Mansell Information Publishing; 1976. Pp xvii, 479.
24. Anderson, A.H., 'The books of Thomas, Lord Paget (c. 1544—1590),' *T. of the Cambridge Bibliographical Soc.* 6 (1975), 226—42.

25. Leedy, W.C., 'The design of the vaulting of Henry VII's Chapel, Westminster: a reappraisal,' *Architectural History* 18 (1975), 5–11.

26. Nelson, N.H., 'Astrology, *Hudibras* and the puritans,' *J. of the History of Ideas* 37 (1976), 521–36.

27. Killeen, J., 'Restoration and early eighteenth century drama: a study of cultural change,' *Sociological R.* new ser. 24 (1976), 213–43.

28. Whittingham, S., 'Some portraits of Bishop Burnet around 1690,' *Burlington Magazine* 118 (1976), 649–50.

29. Wilson, K.J., 'More and Holbein: the imagination of death,' *Sixteenth Century J.* 7 (1976), 51–8.

30. Hepworth, P.L., 'Humfrey Wanley and "friends" of the Bodleian, 1695–98,' *Bodleian Library Record* 9 (1976), 219–30.

31. Underwood, T.L., 'Quakers and the Royal Society of London in the seventeenth century,' *Notes and Records of the Royal Soc. of London* 31 (1976), 133–50.

32. Hoppen, T.K., 'The early Royal Society; part I,' *British J. for the History of Science* 9 (1976), 1–24.

33. Russell, J.L., 'Action and reaction before Newton,' ibid. 25–38.

34. Downie, J.A., 'Robert Harley, Charles Davenant and the authorship of the *Worcester Queries*,' *Literature and History* 3 (1976), 83–99.

35. Speck, W.A.; Downie, J.A. (ed.), ' "Plain English to all who are honest or would be so if they knew how": a tract by Robert Harley,' ibid. 100–10.

36. Hall, A.R.; Tilling, L. (ed.). *The correspondence of Isaac Newton*; vol. 6: 1713–1718. Cambridge UP; 1976. Pp xxxix, 499.

37. Hobbes, T. *Thomas White's 'De mundo' examined* [the Latin translated by H.W. Jones]. Bradford UP; 1976. Pp xl, 518.

38. Airs, M. *The making of the English country house, 1500–1640*. London; Architectural Press; 1975. Pp viii, 208.

39. Hock, J. *The baroque age in England*. London; Thames & Hudson; 1976. Pp 207.

40. Percival, R. and A. *The court of Elizabeth the First*. London; Stainer & Bell; 1976. Pp 110.

41. Ifans, D., 'William Bodwrda (1593–1660) [in Welsh],' *National Library of Wales J.* 19 (1976), 300–10.

42. Landon, M., ' "The learned Glynne and Maynard" — two characters "dashed out" of Samuel Butler's *Hudibras*,' *P. of the American Philosophical Soc.* 120 (1976), 205–10.

43. Renaldo, J.J., 'Bacon's empiricism, Boyle's science, and the Jesuit response in Italy,' *J. of the History of Ideas* 37 (1976), 689–95.

44. Meyer, B.H., 'The first tomb of Henry VII of England,' *Art B.* 58 (1976), 358–67.

45. Guinness, D.; Sadler, J.T. *The Palladian style in England, Ireland and America*. London; Thames & Hudson; 1976. Pp 184.

46. DeMolen, R.L., 'Richard Mulcaster: an Elizabethan savant,' *Shakespeare Studies* 8 (1976), 29–82.
47. Hollister-Short, G., 'Leads and lags in late seventeenth century English technology,' *History of Technology*, vol. 1 (ed. A.R. Hall and N. Smith). London; Mansell; 1976. Pp 159–83.
48. Bennett, J.A., 'A note on theories of respiration and muscular action in England c. 1660,' *Medical History* 20 (1976), 59–69.
49. Birrell, T.A. *The library of John Morris: the reconstruction of a seventeenth-century collection.* London; British Museum Publications Ltd; 1976. Pp xxiv, 83.
50. Sylvester, R.S. (ed.). *St Thomas More: the history of King Richard III and Latin poems.* New Haven; Yale UP; 1976. Pp xxviii, 168.
51. Miner, E., 'Time, sequence and plot in Restoration literature,' Bc13, 67–85.
52. Rogal, S.J., 'The selling of sex: Mandeville's *Modest defence of Publick Stews*,' Bc13, 141–50.
53. Cohen, M., 'Sensible words: linguistic theory in late seventeenth-century England,' Bc13, 229–52.
54. Hookyas, R., 'The reception of Copernicanism in England and the Netherlands,' Bc12, 33–44.
55. Hall, A.R., 'Huygens and Newton,' Bc12, 45–59.
56. Wazink, J.H., 'Erasmus and his influence on Anglo-Dutch philology,' Bc12, 60–72.
57. Morgan, P., 'The Oxford book trade: letters relating to the Oxford book trade found in bindings in Oxford College libraries,' Bc7, 71–89.
58. Vaisey, D.G., 'Anthony Stephens: the rice and fall of an Oxford bookseller,' Bc7, 91–117.
59. Carter, H., 'Early accounts of the University Press, Oxford,' Bc7, 119–38.
60. Thompson, R., 'The puritans and prurience: aspects of the Restoration book trade,' Bc5, 36–65.
61. Cressy, D.A., 'Educational opportunity in Tudor and Stuart England,' *History of Education Q.* (1976), 301–20.

G. ENGLAND 1715–1815

See also: Aa17, 18, 35, b11, 18, 23, 36, c10; Ba5; Ff8, 14, 15, 17, 29, g20, i11; Hb6, f103, j4.

(a) *General*

1. K.G. Davies (ed.). *Documents of the American Revolution, 1770–*

1783 (Colonial Office series); vol. 9: Transcripts, 1775 January to June. Dublin; Irish UP; 1875. Pp vi, 237.

2. K.G. Davies (ed.). *The Same*; vol. 8: Transcripts, 1774. Dublin; Irish UP; 1975. Pp vi, 290.

3. K.G. Davies (ed.). *The Same*; vol. 7: Calendar, 1774—30 June 1775. Dublin; Irish UP; 1974. Pp vi, 432.

4. Cartwright, J.L., 'Oundle in the eighteenth century through the eyes of John Clifton,' *Northamptonshire Past and Present* 5 (1976), 339—46.

5. Weitzman, A.J., 'Eighteenth-century London: urban paradise or fallen city,' *J. of the History of Ideas* 36 (1975), 469—80.

6. Holme, T. *Prinny's daughter: a life of Princess Charlotte of Wales.* London; Hamilton; 1976. Pp 261.

7. Jessup, R. *Man of many talents: an informal biography of James Douglas, 1753—1819.* London; Phillimore; 1975. Pp xiv, 310.

8. Livesley, B. *Galen, George III and geriatrics.* [London; Soc. of Apothecaries] ; 1976. Pp 31.

9. Moore, D. (ed.). *Wales in the eighteenth century.* Swansea; C. Davies; 1976. Pp 181.

10. Public Record Office (Northern Ireland). *An Anglo-Irish dialogue: a calendar of the correspondence between John Foster and Lord Sheffield, 1774—1821.* [Belfast; Record Office; 1976]. Pp xx, 102.

11. Williams, G.A., 'Welsh Indians: the Madoc legend and the first Welsh radicalism,' *History Workshop* 1 (1976), 137—54.

12. Tims, M. *Mary Wollstonecraft, a social pioneer.* London; Millington; 1976. Pp xii, 374.

13. Edwardes, M. *Warren Hastins: king of the nabobs.* London; Hart-Davis, MacGibbon; 1976. Pp 208.

(b) *Political*

1. Ayling, S.E. *The elder Pitt, earl of Chatham.* London; Collins; 1976. Pp 478.

2. Derry, J.W. *Castlereagh.* London; Allen Lane; 1976. Pp viii, 247.

3. Thomas, P.D.G. *Lord North.* London; Allen Lane; 1976. Pp viii, 176.

4. Dixon, P. *Canning: politician and statesman.* London; Weidenfeld & Nicolson; 1976. Pp 355.

5. Fritz, P.S. *The English ministers and Jacobitism between the rebellions of 1715 and 1745.* University of Toronto Press; 1975. Pp viii, 180.

6. Kemp, B. *Sir Robert Walpole.* London; Weidenfeld & Nicolson; 1976. Pp x, 147.

7. Penny, N.B., 'The whig cult of Fox in early nineteenth-century sculpture,' *Past and Present* 70 (1976), 94—105.

8. Wright, E. *The War of American Independence*. London; Historical Association; 1976. Pp 46.
9. Brewer, J. *Party ideology and popular politics at the accession of George III*. Cambridge UP; 1976. Pp ix, 382.
10. Derry, J.W. *English politics and the American Revolution*. London; Dent; 1976. Pp vii, 215.
11. Moore, D.C.; Davis, R.W., 'Is "The other face of reform" in Bucks an "Hallucination"?,' [with answer, 'Yes'], *J. of British Studies* 15 (1976), 150–61.
12. Bonwick, C.C., 'An English audience for American revolutionary pamphlets,' *Historical J.* 19 (1976), 355–74.
13. Christie, I.R.; Labaree, B.W. *Empire or independence, 1760–1776: a British-American dialogue on the coming of the American revolution*. Oxford; Phaidon Press; 1976. Pp xiii, 332.
14. Davies, K.G. (ed.). *Documents of the American revolution, 1770–1783*; vol. 10: Calendar, 1 July 1775–1776. Dublin; Irish UP; 1976. Pp vi, 516.
15. Davies, K.G. (ed.). *The same*; vol. 11: Transcripts 1775 July–December. Ibid; 1976. Pp vi, 239.
16. Jupp, P., 'The aims and achievements of Lord Grenville,' Bc2, 93–103.
17. Jarrett, J.D., 'The myth of "patriotism" in eighteenth-century English politics,' Bc3, 120–40.
18. Conwick, C.C., 'English dissenters and the American revolution,' Bc5, 88–112.
19. Raymond, A., ' "I fear God and honour the king": John Wesley and the American revolution,' *Church History* 45 (1976), 316–28.
20. Ritcheson, C.R. *Edmund Burke and the American revolution*. Leicester UP; 1976. Pp 15.

(c) *Constitution, Administration and Law*

1. Davies, K.G. *The end of British administration in the North American colonies*. London; Oxford UP for British Academy; 1975. Pp 24.
2. Dickinson, H.T., 'The eighteenth century debate on the "Glorious Revolution",' *History* 61 (1976), 28–45.
3. Sainty, J.C., 'The evolution of the parliamentary and financial secretaryships of the treasury,' *English Historical R.* 91 (1976), 566–84.
4. Cross, R., 'Blackstone v. Bentham,' *Law Q.R.* 92 (1976), 516–27.
5. Dickinson, H.T., 'The eighteenth century debate on the sovereignty of parliament,' *T. of the Royal Historical Soc.* 5th ser. 26 (1976), 189–210.
6. Heward, E., 'Lord Mansfield's note books,' *Law Q.R.* 92 (1976), 438–55.

7. Smith, R.W., 'Edmund Burke's negro code,' *History Today* 26 (1976), 215—23.
8. Lambert, S., 'House of Commons papers of the eighteenth century,' *Government Publications R.* 3 (1976), 195—202.

(d) *External Affairs*

1. Clark, M.E. *Peter Porcupine in America: the career of William Cobbett, 1792—1800.* Norwood, Pa; Norwood Editions; 1975 [repr. of 1939 ed.]. Pp v, 193.
2. Scott, H.M., 'Great Britain, Poland and the Russian alliance, 1763—1767,' *Historical J.* 19 (1976), 53—74.
3. Ward, J.M. *Colonial self-government: the British experience, 1759—1856.* London; Macmillan; 1976. Pp ix, 399.
4. Jones, H., 'Anglophobia and the Aroostook war,' *New England Quarterly* 48 (1975), 519—39.
5. Langford, P. *The eighteenth century, 1688—1815* [Modern British Foreign Policy series]. London; Black; 1976. Pp vii, 264.
6. Ingram, E., 'Lord Mulgrave's proposals for the reconstruction of Europe in 1804,' *Historical J.* 19 (1976), 511—20.
7. Kirby, D.G., 'The balance of the north and Baltic trade: George Mackenzie's Relation, August 1715,' *Slavonic and East European R.* 54 (1976), 429—50.
8. Martin, G.W., 'The foundation of Botany Bay, 1778—90: a reappraisal,' Hd12, 44—74.
9. Hyam, R., 'Imperial interests and the Peace of Paris (1763),' Hd12, 21—43.
10. Wright, E., 'The loyalists,' Bc5, 113—48.
11. Watson, G.E., 'The United States and the Peninsular War,' *Historical J.* 19 (1976), 859—76.

(e) *Religion*

1. Austin, M.R., 'Religion and society in Derbyshire during the industrial revolution,' *Derbyshire Arch. J.* 93 (1975 for 1973), 75—89.
2. Coleman, W., 'Providence, capitalism, and environmental degradation: English apologetics in an era of economic revolution,' *J. of the History of Ideas* 37 (1976), 27—44.
3. Duffy, E., ' "Over the Wall": converts from popery in eighteenth-century England,' *Downside R.* 93 (1976), 1—25.
4. Peeke, C., 'Dr Johnson's sermon,' *Historical Magazine of the Protestant Episcopal Church* 45 (1976), 79—87.
5. Rose, E.A., 'Methodism in Cheshire to 1800,' *T. of the Lancashire and Cheshire Antiquarian Soc.* 78 (1975), 22—37.
6. Stein, S.J., 'A note on Anne Dutton, eighteenth-century evangelical,' *Church History* 44 (1975), 485—91.

7. White, B.R., 'Baptist beginnings in Watford,' *Baptist Q.* 26 (1976), 205—8.
8. Cragg, G.R. (ed.). *The Works of John Wesley*; vol. 11: The appeals to men of reason and religion and certain related open letters. Oxford; Clarendon; 1976. Pp xiii, 593.
9. Andrews, S., 'John Wesley and America,' *History Today* 26 (1976), 353—9.
10. Hunt, G., 'A real-life "Jane Austen clergyman",' *Theology* 79 (1976), 151—7.
11. Linker, R.W., 'The English Roman Catholics and emancipation: the politics of persuasion,' *J. of Ecclesiastical History* 27 (1976), 151—80.
12. Manley, K.R., 'The making of an Evangelical Baptist leader: John Rippon's early years 1751—1773,' *Baptist Q.* 26 (1976), 254—74.
13. Owen, R.J., 'William Hawkins, 1790—1853,' ibid. 275—88.
14. Baker, D.S., 'Charles Wesley and the American War of Independence (part I),' *P. of the Wesley Historical Soc.* 40 (1976), 125—34.
15. Not used.
16. Curtis, T.C.; Speck, W.A., 'The Societies for the Reformation of Manners: a case study in the theory and practice of moral reform,' *Literature and History* 3 (1976), 45—64.
17. Durden, S., 'A study of the first Evangelical magazines, 1740—1748,' *J. of Ecclesiastical History* 27 (1976), 255—76.
18. Garrett, C. *Respectable Folly: millenarianism and the French Revolution in France and England.* Baltimore; Johns Hopkins UP; 1975. Pp xii, 237.
19. Gilbert, A.D. *Religion and society in industrial England: church, chapel and social change, 1740—1914.* London; Longman; 1976. Pp x, 251.
20. Anon., 'Correspondence of Theophilus Lindsey with the countess of Huntingdon, 1762—9,' *T. of the Unitarian Historical Soc.* 16 (1976), 82—8.
21. Payne, E.A., 'Abraham Atkins and the General Commission,' *Baptist Q.* 26 (1976), 314—9.
22. Peaston, A.E., 'The Unitarian liturgical tradition,' *T. of the Unitarian Historical Soc.* 16 (1976), 63—81.
23. Thomas, D.O., 'Proposed protest concerning Dissenters: Richard Price and the earl of Chatham,' ibid. 49—62.
24. Williams, B. *The making of Manchester Jewry, 1740—1875.* Manchester UP; 1976. Pp x, 454.
25. Amey, B., 'Baptist Missionary Society radicals,' *Baptist Q.* 26 (1976), 363—76.
26. Aspinwall, B., 'Some aspects of Scotland and the Catholic revival in the early nineteenth century,' *Innes R.* 26 (1975), 3—19.
27. Gaskin, J.C.A., 'Hume's critique of religion,' *J. of the History of Philosophy* 14 (1976), 301—11.

28. Holmes, G.S., 'The Sacheverell riots: the crowd and the Church in early eighteenth-century London,' *Past & Present* 72 (1976), 55—85.
29. Jones, C., 'Debates in the House of Lords on "the Church in danger", 1705, and on Dr Sacheverell's impeachment, 1710,' *Historical J.* 19 (1976), 759—71.
30. Nuttall, G.F., 'George Whitefield's "Curate": Gloucestershire dissent and the revival,' *J. of Ecclesiastical History* 27 (1976), 369—86.
31. Schneider, F.D., 'Scottish episcopalians and English politicians: the limits of toleration,' *Historical Magazine of the Protestant Episcopal Church* 45 (1976), 275—95.
32. Bossy, J.A., 'Catholic Lancashire in the eighteenth century,' Bc2, 54—69.
33. Ware, K., 'The fifth earl of Guildford (1766—1827) and his secret conversion to the Orthodox Church,' Bc4, 247—56.
34. Ferguson, J.P. *Dr Samuel Clarke: an eighteenth century heretic.* Kineton; Roundwood Press; 1976. Pp vii, 255.

(f) *Economic Affairs*

1. Anderson, D. *The Orrell coalfield, Lancashire, 1740—1850.* Buxton; Moorland Publishing Co.; 1975. Pp 208.
2. Chamberlin, E.R. *The awakening giant: Britain in the industrial revolution.* London; Batsford; 1976. Pp 168.
3. Chapman, J., 'Parliamentary enclosure in the uplands: the case of the North York Moors,' *Agricultural History R.* 24 (1976), 1—17.
4. Devine, T.M., 'The rise and fall of illicit whisky-making in northern Scotland, c. 1780—1840,' *Scottish Historical R.* 44 (1975), 155—77.
5. Devine, T.M., 'The colonial trades and industrial investment in Scotland, c. 1700—1815,' *Economic History R.* 2nd ser. 29 (1976), 1—13.
6. Dunlop, J., 'The British Fisheries Society: 1787 questionnaire,' *Northern Scotland* 2 (1975), 37—55.
7. Durie, A.J., 'Linen-spinning in the north of Scotland, 1746—1773,' ibid. 13—36.
8. Flinn, M.W., 'Real wage trends in Britain, 1750—1850: a reply,' *Economic History Rev.* 2nd ser. 29 (1976), 143—5 [see Gf10].
9. Fussell, G.E., 'Agricultural science and experiment in the eighteenth century: an attempt at a definition,' *Agricultural History R.* 24 (1976), 44—7.
10. Gourvish, T.R., 'Flinn and real wage trends in Britain, 1750—1850: a comment,' *Economic History R.* 2nd ser. 29 (1976), 136—42 [see Gf8].
11. Hanson, H. *The canal boatmen, 1760—1914.* Manchester UP; 1975. Pp xxii, 244.

12. Lindsay, J.M., 'Some aspects of the timber supply in the Highlands, 1700–1850,' *Scottish Studies* 19 (1975), 39–53.
13. Mountfield, D. *The coaching age.* London; Hale; 1976. Pp 191.
14. Parker, R.A.C. *Coke of Norfolk: a financial and agricultural study, 1707–1842.* Oxford; Clarendon; 1975. Pp xiii, 222.
15. Perkins, E.J. *Financing Anglo-American trade: the House of Brown, 1800–1880.* Cambridge, Mass.; Harvard UP; 1975. Pp xiii, 323.
16. Richards, E.; Hunter, J.; Sutherland, S.R., 'The Sutherland clearances: (I) New evidence from Dunrobin; (II) Sutherland in the industrial revolution; (III) Ethics and economics in the Sutherland clearances,' *Northern Scotland* 2 (1975), 57–83.
17. Smith, K.J. (ed.); Williams, N.J. (intr.). *Warwickshire apprentices and their masters, 1710–1760.* Oxford UP for Dugdale Soc.; 1975. Pp xv, 195.
18. Willies, L., 'The Barker family and the eighteenth century lead business,' *Derbyshire Arch. J.* 93 (1975 for 1973), 55–74.
19. Adams, I.H., 'Sources for Scottish local history — 5. Estate plans,' *Local Historian* 12 (1976), 26–30.
20. Adams, I.H., 'George Taylor, a surveyor o' pairts,' *Imago Mundi* 27 (1975), 55–63.
21. Boud, R.C., 'The early development of British geological maps,' ibid. 73–96.
22. Crafts, N.F.R., 'English economic growth in the eighteenth century: a re-examination of Deane and Cole's estimates,' *Economic History R.* 2nd series, 29 (1976), 226–35.
23. Eagley, R.V.; Smith, V.K., 'Domestic and international integration of the London money market, 1731–1789,' *J. of Economic History* 36 (1976), 198–216.
24. Fairclough, R.H., ' "Sketches of the roads in Scotland, 1785": the manuscript roadbook of George Taylor,' *Imago Mundi* 27 (1975), 65–72.
25. Hardman, B.M., 'The iron and steel industry of Northern Staffordshire and South Cheshire in the pre-coke smelting era,' *North Staffordshire J. of Field Studies* 15 (1975), 83–92.
26. Hornshaw, T.R. *Copper mining in Middleton Tyas.* North Yorkshire County Council; 1975. Pp 153.
27. Knight, D., 'Agriculture and chemistry in Britain around 1800,' *Annals of Science* 33 (1976), 187–96.
28. Lindsay, J. *The Scottish poor law: its operation in the north-east from 1745 to 1845.* Ilfracombe; Stockwell; 1975. Pp 265.
29. Lindsay, J.M., 'The commercial use of Highland woodland, 1750–1870: a reconsideration,' *Scottish Geographical Magazine* 92 (1976), 30–40.
30. Miers, S. *Britain and the ending of the slave trade.* London; Longman; 1975. Pp xvi, 405.
31. Pawson, E. *The turnpike trusts of the eighteenth century: a study*

of innovation and diffusion. University of Oxford (School of Geography); 1975. Pp 40.

32. Stockport Public Library. *Stockport poor rate, 1731 and 1781: indexes of people and places.* [Stockport; The Library]; 1975. Pp 22.

33. Thomas, C., 'Colonization, enclosure and the rural landscape,' *The National Library of Wales J.* 19 (1975), 132–46.

34. Turner, M., 'Sources for agricultural history – 4. Recent progress in the study of parliamentary enclosure,' *Local Historian* 12 (1976), 18–25.

35. Devine, T.M., 'A Glasgow tobacco merchant during the American War of Independence: Alexander Speirs of Elderslie, 1775–1781,' *William and Mary Q.* 3rd ser. 23 (1976), 501–13.

36. Drescher, S., 'Le "déclin" du système esclavagiste britannique et l'abolition de la traite,' *Annales* 31 (1976), 414–35.

37. England, R.W., 'The cluster potato: John Howard's achievement in scientific farming,' *Agricultural History R.* 24 (1976), 144–8.

38. Dixon, C., 'The Exeter Whale Fisher Company, 1754–1787,' *Mariner's Mirror* 62 (1976), 225–31.

39. Evans, E.J. *The contentious tithe: the tithe problem and English agriculture, 1750–1850.* London; Routledge; 1976. Pp xiv, 185.

40. Harris, J.R., 'Skills, coal and British industry in the eighteenth century,' *History* 61 (1976), 167–82.

41. Hueckel, G., 'Relative prices and supply response in English agriculture during the Napoleonic Wars,' *Economic History R.* 2nd ser. 29 (1976), 401–14.

42. Hutton. W.E., 'The burial place of Abraham Darby, I,' *T. of the Shropshire Arch. Soc.* 50 (1976 for 1971/2), 124–6.

43. MacMillan, D.S., 'Russo-British trade relations under Alexander I,' *Canadian-American Slavic Studies* 9 (1975), 437–48.

44. Ponting, K.G., 'Wiltshire woolen mills: insurance returns,' *Wiltshire Arch. and Natural History Magazine* (1976 for 1974), 161–72.

45. Robinson, J.M., 'Model farm buildings of the age of improvement,' *Architectural History* 19 (1976), 17–31.

46. Sexauer, B., 'English and French agriculture in the late eighteenth century,' *Agricultural History* 50 (1976), 491–505.

47. Turner, M.E. *Land shortage as a prelude to parliamentary enclosure: the example of Buckingham.* University of Sheffield: Dept of Economic and Social History; 1975. Pp 22.

48. Baldwin, M.W., 'The engineering history of Hull's earliest dock,' *T. of the Newcomen Soc.* 46 (1973–4), 1–12.

49. Colyer, R.J., 'The size of farms in late eighteenth and early nineteenth century Cardiganshire,' *B. of the Board of Celtic Studies* 27 (1976), 119–26.

50. Dodgshon, R.A., 'The economics of sheep farming in the southern

uplands during the age of improvement, 1750–1833,' *Economic History R.* 2nd ser. 29 (1976), 551–69.

51. Emery, F., 'The mechanics of innovation: clover cultivation in Wales before 1750,' *J. of Historical Geography* 2 (1976), 35–48.

52. Gale, W.K.V., 'The Bessemer steelmaking process,' *T. of the Newcomen Soc.* 46 (1973–4), 17–26.

53. Harris, T.R. *Sir Goldsworthy Gurney, 1793–1875.* Truro; Trevethick Soc.; 1975. Pp 100.

54. Harvey, W.S., 'Mr Symington's improved atmospheric engine,' *T. of the Newcomen Soc.* 46 (1973–4), 27–32.

55. Jenkins, D.T. *The West Riding wool textile industry 1770–1835: a study of fixed capital formation.* Edington; Pasold Research Fund Ltd.; 1975. Pp xvi, 336.

56. Johnson, C.P.C., 'Phillips Glover and the duchess of Kingston's French estates,' *Lincolnshire History and Archaeology* 11 (1976), 29–34.

57. Little, A.J. *Deceleration in the eighteenth-century British Economy.* London; Croom Helm; 1976. Pp 111.

58. Malet, H. *The duke of Bridgewater and the 18th century fuel crisis.* University of Salford; 1976. Pp 10.

59. Patrick, A. *Canals in Nottinghamshire: a survey of industrial archaeology.* Nottingham; Dept of Planning and Transportation; [1976]. Pp 36.

60. Schofield, R.B., 'Bagshawe v. The Leeds and Liverpool Canal Company: a study in engineering history, 1790–99,' *B. of the John Rylands Library* 59 (1976–7), 188–225.

61. Skempton, A.W., 'William Chapman (1749–1832), civil engineer,' *T. of the Newcomen Soc.* 46 (1973–4), 45–82.

62. Watney, J. *Mother's ruin: a history of gin.* London; Owen; 1976. Pp 152.

63. Fleeman, J.D., 'The revenue of a writer: Samuel Johnson's literary earnings,' Bc7, 211–30.

64. Stern, W.M., 'Fish marketing in London in the first half of the eighteenth century,' Bc9, 68–77.

65. Harwood Long, W., 'Facets of farm labour and wages, mainly in the 18th and 19th centuries,' *J. of the Royal Agricultural Soc.* 136 (1975), 46–55.

66. Durie, A.J., 'The fine linen industry in Scotland, 1707–1822,' *Textile History* 7 (1976), 173–85.

67. Handford, M. *The stroudwater canal; vol. 1: 1729–1763.* Bradford-on-Avon; Moonraker Press; 1976. Pp viii, 93.

(g) *Social Structure and Population*

1. Forrest, R. *Annan parish censuses, 1801–1821*; ed. G. Gilchrist. Edinburgh; Scottish Record Soc.; 1975. Pp ix, 139.

2. Dickinson, R. (ed.). *Marriage bonds for the deaneries of Lonsdale, Kendal, Furness, Copeland & Amounderness in the archdeaconry of Richmond*; part 7: 1746–1755. Chester; Record Soc. of Lancashire and Cheshire; 1975. Pp 162.

3. Fontaine, J.L. (ed.). *The parish registers of Oldswinford, Worcestershire*; vols. 4–5: 1736–58. Birmingham and Midland Soc. for Genealogy and Heraldry; 1975. Pp iv, 254.

4. Farrant, J. and S. *Brighton before Dr Russell: an interim report.* University of Sussex: Centre for Continuing Education; 1976. Pp 33.

5. Flett, J. *Lodge Kirkwall Kilwinning No. 38(2): the story from 1736.* Lerwick; Shetland Times Ltd.; 1976. Pp x, 162.

6. Reid, A.D., 'The decline of Saint Monday 1766–1876,' *Past and Present* 71 (1976), 76–101.

7. Williams, D.E., 'Were "hunger" rioters really hungry? — some demographic evidence,' ibid. 70–5.

8. Martin, J.M. *The rise in population in eighteenth-century Warwickshire.* Stratford-upon-Avon; Dugdale Soc.; 1976. Pp 52.

9. Marshall, J.D.; Dyhouse, C.A., 'Social transition in Kendal and Westmorland, c. 1760–1860,' *Northern History* 12 (1976), 127–57.

10. Pickles, M.F., 'Mid-Wharfedale 1721–1812: economic and demographic change in a Pennine dale,' *Local Population Studies* 16 (1976), 12–44.

11. Redford, A. *Labour migration in England, 1800–1850* (3rd ed. revd. by W.H. Challoner). Manchester UP; 1976. Pp xvi, 209.

12. Wilson, C.H., 'The Anglo-Dutch establishment in eighteenth century England,' Bc12, 11–32.

13. Rosen, G., 'A slaughter of innocents: aspects of child health in the eighteenth century city,' Bc13, 293–316.

14. Stephens, W.B., 'Illiteracy in Devon during the industrial revolution, 1754–1844,' *J. of Educational Administration and History* 8 (1976), 1–5.

15. Chapman, S.D., 'Workers' housing in the cotton factory colonies 1770–1850,' *Textile History* 7 (1976), 112–39.

16. Haynes, A., ' "The first great lady" — Margaret, duchess of Newcastle,' *History Today* 26 (1976), 724–33.

(h) *Naval and Military*

1. Farley, M.F., 'The battle of Sullivan's Island, 1776,' *History Today* 26 (1976), 83–91.

2. Hawkey, A. *Bligh's other mutiny.* London; Angus & Robertson; 1975. Pp 202.

3. Kennedy, L. *Nelson and his captains* [rev. ed.]. London; Collins; 1975. Pp 353.

4. Kverndal, R., 'Memoirs of the founder of seamen's missions in 1801,' *Mariner's Mirror* 62 (1976), 47–51.

5. Lawford, J.P. *Clive, proconsul of India: a biography*. London; Allen & Unwin; 1976. Pp 432.

6. Lunt, J. *John Burgoyne of Saratoga*. London; Macdonald & Jane's; 1976. Pp xiv, 369.

7. Marini, A.J., 'Parliament and the Marine regiments, 1739,' *Mariner's Mirror* 62 (1976), 55–65.

8. Padfield, P. *Nelson's war*. London; Hart-Davis MacGibbon; 1976. Pp 200.

9. Pococke, T. *A soldier of the Seventy-first: the journal of a soldier of the Highland Light Infantry, 1806–1815* [new ed. with intr. by C. Hibbert]. London; Cooper; 1975. Pp xv, 121.

10. Allen, K.S. *'That Bounty bastard': the true story of Captain William Bligh*. London; Hale; 1976. Pp 224.

11. Chandler, D. *The art of warfare in the age of Marlborough*. London; Batsford; 1976. Pp 317.

12. Clark, G., 'Naval blockmaking in the eighteenth and nineteenth centuries,' *Mariner's Mirror* 62 (1976), 137–44.

13. Crossley, D.W., 'Cannon-manufacture at Pippingford, Sussex: the excavation of two iron furnaces of c. 1717,' *Post-Medieval Archaeology* 9 (1975), 1–37.

14. Gilbert, A.N., 'Recruitment and reform in the East India Company Army, 1760–1800,' *J. of British Studies* 15 (1975), 89–111.

15. Gilbert, A.N., 'Law and honour among eighteenth-century British army officers,' *Historical J.* 19 (1976), 75–87.

16. Graham, G.S. *The Royal Navy in the War of American Independence*. London; HMSO; 1976. Pp 26.

17. Teague, J. and D. (ed.). *Where duty calls me: the experience of William Green of Lutterworth in the Napoleonic wars*. West Wickham; Synjon Books; 1975. Pp 65.

18. Guilbert, G.C., 'A Napoleonic fire beacon on Moel y Gaer, Clwyd,' *Post-Medieval Archaeology* 9 (1975), 188–202.

19. Parkinson, R. *Moore of Corunna*. London; Hart-Davis MacGibbon; 1976. Pp viii, 245.

20. Syrett, D., 'The organization of British trade convoys during the American war, 1775–83,' *Mariner's Mirror* 62 (1976), 169–81.

21. Glover, M., 'Beresford and his fighting cocks,' *History Today* 26 (1976), 262–8.

22. Barker, A.J. *Redcoats: the British soldier in America*. London; Dent; 1976. Pp 85.

23. Barker, A.J. *Redcoats*. London; Gordon & Cremonesi; 1976. Pp xii, 156.

24. Calderhead, W.L., 'Naval innovation in crisis: war in the Chesapeake, 1813,' *American Neptune* 36 (1976), 206–21.

25. Duffy, M., ' "A particular service": the British government and the Dunkirk expedition of 1793,' *English Historical R.* 91 (1976), 529—54.

26. Gilbert, A.N., 'The regimental courts martial in the eighteenth century British army,' *Albion* 8 (1976), 50—66.

27. Gilbert, A.N., 'An analysis of some eighteenth century army recruiting records,' *J. of the Soc. for Army Historical Research* 54 (1976), 38—47.

28. Hopkinson, D., 'The naval career of Jane Austen's brother,' *History Today* 26 (1976), 576—83.

29. Kemp, A. *Yorktown.* London; Altmark Publishing; 1976. Pp 48.

30. King, D.W., 'The Surrey local militia: the 1813 regiments,' *J. of the Soc. for Army Historical Research* 54 (1976), 48—53.

31. Neave, D., 'Anti-militia riots in Lincolnshire, 1757 and 1796,' *Lincolnshire History and Archaeology* 11 (1976), 21—7.

32. Rumsby, J.H. *The Durhams in the Peninsula.* Derby; English Life Publications; 1975.

33. Savory, R. (ed.), 'John Tory's journal, 1758—1762 [operations in Germany],' *J. of the Soc. for Army Historical Research* 54 (1976), 70—95.

34. Terraine, J. *Trafalgar.* London; Sedgwick & Jackson; 1976. Pp 209.

35. Tomlinson, H.C., 'Wealden gunfounding: an analysis of its demise in the eighteenth century,' *Economic History R.* 2nd Ser. 29 (1976), 383—400.

36. Gwyn, J. (ed.). *The Royal Navy and North America: the Warren papers, 1736—1752.* Navy Records Soc.; 1975. Pp xlv, 463.

37. Calderhead, W.L., 'Naval innovation in a crisis: war in the Chesapeake, 1813,' *American Neptune* 36 (1976), 206—21.

38. Garrett, R. *Robert Clive.* London; Barker; 1976. Pp 224.

39. Haarmann, A.W., 'Contemporary observations on the Hesse-Cassell troops sent to North America, 1776—1781,' *J. of the Soc. for Army Historical Research* 54 (1976), 130—4.

40. Katcher, P., 'Loyalist militia in the War of American Independence,' ibid. 136—9.

41. Katcher, P., 'The provincial corps of the British army, 1775—1783,' ibid. 164—71.

42. Katcher, P., 'Officers and other ranks in the War of American Independence,' ibid. 171—5.

43. Morriss, R.A., 'Labour relations in the Royal Dockyards, 1801—1805,' *Mariner's Mirror* 62 (1976), 337—46.

44. Neal, W.K.; Black, D.H.L. *Great British gunmakers, 1740—1790: the history of John Twigg and the Packington gun.* London; Sotheby Parke Bernet Publications Ltd; 1975. Pp 196.

45. Pemble, J., 'Resources and techniques in the second Maratha war,' *Historical J.* 19 (1976), 375—404.

46. Sullivan, F.B., 'The naval schoolmaster during the eighteenth cen-

tury and the early nineteenth century,' *Mariner's Mirror* 62 (1976), 311—26.

47. Sullivan, J.A., 'Nelson and influence,' ibid. 385—6.
48. Taylor, W. *The military roads in Scotland.* Newton Abbot; David & Charles; 1976. Pp 197.
49. Yerxa, D.A., 'Vice-admiral Samuel Graves and the North American Squadron 1774—1776,' *Mariner's Mirror* 62 (1976), 371—85.
50. Hearl, T., 'Military education and the school curriculum 1800—1870,' *History of Education* 5 (1976), 251—64.
51. Crowe, K., 'Thomas Burn Catherwood and the medical department of Wellington's army, 1809—1814,' *Medical History* 20 (1976), 22—40.
52. Humble, R. *Captain Bligh.* London; Barker; 1976. Pp xii, 212.
53. Humble, R. *Before the Dreadnought: the Royal Navy from Nelson to Fisher.* London; Macdonald & Jane's; 1976. Pp viii, 216.

(i) *Intellectual and Cultural*

1. Bader, W.C., 'Jeremy Bentham: businessman or "philanthropist"?,' *Albion* 7 (1975), 245—54.
2. Belanger, T., 'Booksellers' trade sales, 1718—1768,' *Library* 5th ser. 30 (1975), 281—302.
3. Clifford T.; Legouix, S., 'James Jefferys, historical draughtsman (1751—84),' *Burlington Magazine* 118 (1976), 148—57.
4. Constable, F. *John Constable: a biography, 1776—1837.* Lavenham; Dalton; 1975. Pp 151.
5. Cruickshank, D.; Wyld, P. *London, the art of Georgian building.* London; Architectural Press; 1975. Pp 232.
6. Daiches, D. *James Boswell and his world.* London; Thames & Hudson; 1976. Pp 128.
7. Gadney, R. *Constable and his world.* London; Thames & Hudson; 1976. Pp 128.
8. Gottzeit, M. *David Ricardo.* New York; Columbia UP; 1975. Pp xi, 90.
9. Hatley, V.A., 'Literacy at Northampton, 1761—1900: a third interim report,' *Northamptonshire Past and Present* 5 (1976), 347—8.
10. Mackintosh, I.; Ashton, G. (designers). *The Georgian playhouse: actors, artists, audiences and architecture, 1730—1830*: [catalogue of an exhibition held at the] Hayward Gallery. London; Arts Council; 1975. Pp [128].
11. Kinsley, J., 'Burns and the peasantry, 1785,' *P. of the British Academy* 60 (1975 for 1974), 135—53.
12. Macaulay, J. *The Gothic revival, 1745—1845.* Glasgow; Blackie; 1975. Pp xx, 451.

13. Melvin, P.H., 'Burke on theatricality and revolution,' *J. of the History of Ideas* 36 (1975), 447—68.
14. Napoleoni, C. *Smith, Ricardo, Marx*; translated J.M.A. Gee. Oxford; Blackwell; 1975. Pp vii, 198.
15. Noblett, W., 'From Sheffield to North Carolina,' *History Today* 26 (1976), 23—31.
16. Skinner, A.S.; Wilson, T. (ed.). *Essays on Adam Smith.* Oxford; Clarendon; 1975. Pp xvi, 647.
17. Smart, A.; Brooks, A. *Constable and his country.* London; Elek; 1976. Pp 144.
18. Smith, A. *An enquiry into the nature and causes of the wealth of nations*; ed. R.H. Campbell, A.S. Skinner, W.B. Todd. Oxford; Clarendon; 1976. Pp viii; vii; 1080.
19. Venning, C., 'Hume on property, commerce and empire in the good society: the role of historical necessity,' *J. of the History of Ideas* 37 (1976), 79—92.
20. Wertz, S.K., 'Hume, history, and human nature,' ibid. 36 (1975), 481—96.
21. White, L., 'On a passage of Hume incorrectly attributed to Jefferson,' ibid. 37 (1976), 133—5.
22. Baker, W.J., 'Beyond port and prejudice: Oxford's renaissance exemplified, 1808—1811,' *Huntington Library Q.* 39 (1976), 133—49.
23. Hill, B.W. (ed.). *Edmund Burke on government, politics and society.* London; Fontana [Hassocks; Harvester Press]; 1975. Pp 382.
24. Donohue, J. *Theatre in the age of Kean.* Oxford; Blackwell; 1975. Pp x, 201.
25. Fitzsimons, R. *Edmund Kean: fire from heaven.* London; Hamilton; 1976. Pp xiii, 255.
26. Gibson, J.S.W., 'Three lost Northamptonshire houses and their owners,' *Northamptonshire Past and Present* 5 (1976), 311—22.
27. Warwick, L. *Drama that smelled: or 'early drama in Northampton and hereabouts'.* Northampton; the author; 1975. Pp 231.
28. Haskell, F. *Rediscoveries in art: some aspects of taste, fashion and collecting in England and France.* London; Phaidon Press; 1976. Pp x, 246.
29. Kemp, M., 'Dr William Hunter on the Windsor Leonardos and his volume of drawings attributed to Pietro da Cortona,' *Burlington Magazine* 118 (1976), 144—8.
30. Knight, R.D. *Hambledon's cricket glory*; vol. 2: 1756. Weymouth; the author; 1975. Pp 69.
31. McCarthy, M., 'The building of Hagley Hall, Worcestershire,' *Burlington Magazine* 118 (1976), 214—25.
32. McMordie, M., 'Picturesque pattern books and pre-Victorian designers,' *Architectural History* 18 (1975), 44—60.

33. Matteson, R.S., 'The early library of Archbishop William King,' *Library* 5th series, 30 (1975), 303—14.
34. Norman, A.V.B., 'A note on highland dress after the '45,' *P. of the Soc. of Antiquaries of Scotland* 105 (1975 for 1972/4), 316—8.
35. Riesman, D.A. *Adam Smith's sociological economics*. London; Croom Helm; 1976. Pp 274.
36. Rothblatt, S. *Tradition and change in English liberal education: an essay in history and culture*. London; Faber; 1976. Pp 216.
37. Sisson, C.H. *David Hume*. Edinburgh; Ramsay Head Press; 1976. Pp 93.
38. Thomas, D.O. *Richard Price and America: an essay*. [Cardiff; Welsh Tourist Board] ; 1975. Pp 41.
39. Thomas, D.O. *Richard Price, 1723—1791*. University of Wales Press; 1976. Pp 102.
40. Thomas, D.O. *Richard Price and America (1723—91)*. Aberystwyth; the author; 1975. Pp 44.
41. Thomas, H.M. *Merthyr Mawr house, mid-Glamorgan: an account of the building of Sir John Nicholl's country mansion*. Cardiff; Glamorgan Archive Service; 1976. Pp 24.
42. Turner, S., 'Almack's and society,' *History Today* 26 (1976), 241—9.
43. Burke, J. *English art, 1714—1800*. Oxford; Clarendon; 1976. Pp xxxii, 425.
44. Cocke, T.H., 'James Essex, cathedral restorer,' *Architectural History* 18 (1975), 12—22.
45. Stretton, N., 'Liverpool engravers and their sources,' *The Connoisseur* 192 (1976), 264—9.
46. Parris, L.; Shields, C.; Fleming-Williams, I. (ed.). *John Constable: further documents and correspondence*. London; Boydell Press; 1975. Pp xxi, 371.
47. Fraser, J.L. *John Constable, 1776—1837: the man and his mistress*. London; Hutchinson; 1976. Pp 253.
48. Goff, M. *The Royal Pavilion, Brighton*. London; Joseph; 1976. Pp 32.
49. Gray, A., 'Adam Smith,' *Scottish J. of Political Economy* 23 (1976), 153—69;
50. Hutchison, T.W., 'The bicentenary of Adam Smith,' *Economic J.* 86 (1976), 481—92.
51. Lemahieu, D.L. *The mind of William Paley: a philosopher and his age*. Lincoln, Neb.; University of Nebraska Press; 1976. Pp xii, 215.
52. O'Brien, D.P., 'The longevity of Adam Smith's vision: paradigms, research programmes and falsifiability in the history of economic thought,' *Scottish J. of Political Economy* 23 (1976), 133—51.

53. Skinner, A.S., 'Adam Smith: the development of a system,' ibid. 111—32.

54. Burnby, J.G.L.; Robinson, A.E. *And they blew exceeding fine: Robert Uvedale, 1642—1722.* Edmonton Hundred Historical Soc.; 1976. Pp 34.

55. Burton, A. *Josiah Wedgwood: a biography.* London; Deutsch; 1976. Pp 239.

56. Hammelmann, H. *Book illustrators in eighteenth-century England* (ed. and completed by T.S.R. Boase). New Haven/London; Yale UP; 1976. Pp xiv, 121.

57. Jarrett, D. *The ingenious Mr Hogarth.* London; Joseph; 1976. Pp 224.

58. Mcnaghten, A. *Burns' Mrs Riddell; a biography.* Peterhead; Volturna Press; 1975. Pp x, 172.

59. Money, J., 'The schoolmasters of Birmingham and the West Midlands, 1750—1790: private education and cultural change in the English provinces during the early industrial revolution,' *Histoire sociale/Social History* 9/17 (1976), 129—58.

60. Watson, J.W., 'Land use and Adam Smith,' *Scottish Geographical Magazine* 92/2 (1976), 129—34.

61. White, D., 'Adam Smith's *Wealth of Nations* [review article],' *J. of the History of Ideas* 37 (1976), 715—20.

62. Dolley, M., 'A prize-medal in gold awarded to Richard Brinsley Sheridan's cousin,' Bc2, 70—9.

63. Jones, W., 'Robert Morris, the Swansea friend of John Wilkes,' Bc6, 126—36.

64. Jenkins, E., 'J.M.W. Turner in Glamorgan,' Bc6, 53—70.

65. Belanger, T., 'Tonson, Wellington and the Shakespeare copyrights,' Bc7, 195—209.

66. Nixon, H., 'Harleian bindings,' Bc7, 153—94.

67. Klinger, M.F., 'William Hogarth and London theatrical life,' Bc13, 11—27.

68. Macey, S.L., 'Hogarth and the iconography of time,' Bc13, 41—53.

69. Janes, R., 'Mary, Mary, quite contrary, Or, Mary Astell and Mary Wollstonecraft compared,' Bc13, 121—39.

70. McCarthy, M., 'The education in architecture of the man of taste,' Bc13, 337—53.

71. Harlan, R.D., 'A colonial printer as bookseller in eighteenth-century Philadelphia: the case of David Hall,' Bc13, 355—69.

72. Landon, R.G., 'Small profits do great things: James Lackington and eighteenth-century bookselling,' Bc13, 387—99.

73. Singleton, R.R., 'Defoe, Moll Flanders and the ordinary of Newgate,' *Harvard Library B.* 24 (1976), 407—13.

74. Hyde, M., 'The Thrales of Streatham Park, II: the *Family Book* — (iii) 1775—1776,' ibid. 414—74.

75. Harvey, J.H., 'Two early nurseries: Knowsley, Lancs., and Knutsford, Cheshire,' *J. of the Chester Arch. Soc.* 59 (1976), 66—83.

(k) *Science*

1. Clutton-Brock, J., 'George Garrard's livestock models,' *Agricultural History R.* 24 (1976), 18–29.
2. Donovan, A.J. *Philosophical chemistry in the Scottish Enlightenment: the doctrines and discoveries of William Cullen and Joseph Black.* Edinburgh UP; 1975. Pp x, 343.
3. Kemp, M. (ed.). *Dr William Hunter at the Royal Academy of Arts.* University of Glasgow Press; 1975. Pp 47.
4. Manley, G., 'Manchester rainfall since 1765: further comments, meteorological and social,' *Manchester Literary and Philosophical Soc. Memoirs and P.* 117 (1974–5), 93–103.
5. Paananen, V.N., 'Martin Madan and the limits of evangelical philanthropy,' *P. of the Wesley Historical Soc.* 40 (1975), 57–68.
6. Scott, E.L., 'The origins of "pneumatic medicine" and its practice in Manchester,' *Manchester Literary and Philosophical Soc. Memoirs and P.* 117 (1974–5), 75–92.
7. Williams, G.R. *The age of agony: the art of healing, c. 1700–1800.*
8. Quill, H. *John Harrison, Copley medallist and the £20,000 longitude prize.* [Ticehurst] ; Antiquarian Horological Soc.; [1976]. Pp iv, 26.
9. Stamp, T. and C. *William Scoresby, arctic scientist.* Whitby; Caedmon; [1976]. Pp xii, 253.
10. Brown, P.S., 'Medicines advertised in eighteenth-century Bath,' *Medical History* 20 (1976), 152–68.
11. Earles, M., 'The author of the *Pharmacopoeia Reformata*, 1744,' ibid. 70–5.
12. Langley, M., 'John Harrison, the hero of longitude,' *History Today* 26 (1976), 818–23.

H. BRITAIN 1815–1914

See also: Aa9, 17, 20, 33, 56, 66, b4, 11, 12, 18, 30, 32, c8, 12, 13, 14; Bb13; Gb2, e19, 24, f1, 8, 10, 11, 12, 14, 15, 29, 30, 53, 55, 65, g1, 9, 14, 15, h12, 53, i36; Ia11.

(a) *General*

1. Bell, R.C. *Unofficial farthings, 1820–1870.* London; Seaby; 1975. Pp xii, 248.
2. Smith, J.B., 'John Gwili Jenkins, 1872–1936,' *T. of the Honourable Soc. of Cymmrodorion* 1975 (for 1974–5), 191–214.
3. Parris, H., 'Sir Daniel Gooch: a biographical sketch,' *J. of Transport History* new series, 3 (1976), 203–16.

4. Mosley, N. *Julian Grenfell: his life and the times of his death, 1888—1915.* London; Weidenfeld & Nicolson; 1976. Pp x, 275.
5. Burnett, D. *A Wiltshire camera, 1835—1914.* Compton Chamberlayne; Compton Russell; 1975. Pp 108.
6. Vevers, G. *London's Zoo: an anthology to celebrate 150 years of the Zoological Society of London, with its zoos at Regent's Park and Whipsnade in Bedfordshire.* London; Bodley Head; 1976. Pp 159.
7. Blunt, W. *The ark in the park: the zoo in the nineteenth century.* London; Hamilton; 1976. Pp 256.
8. Walsh, V.J., 'The diary of a country gentleman: Sir Baldwin Leighton, Bt. (1805—71),' *T. of the Shropshire Arch. Soc.* 59 (1976 for 1971/2), 127—69.
9. Price, D., 'A Victorian parson and his people: Rector Ffoulkes at Wigginton,' *Cake and Cockhorse* 7 (1976), 23—30.
10. Douglas, R. *Land, people and politics: a history of the land question in the United Kingdom, 1878—1952.* London; Allison & Busby; 1976. Pp 239.
11. Thornes, V. *William Dronfield, 1826—1894: influences on nineteenth century Sheffield.* Sheffield City Libraries; 1976. Pp 16.
12. Castle, H.G. *Spion Kop.* London; Altmark Publishing; 1976. Pp 48.
13. Hibbert, C. *Edward VII, a portrait.* London; Allen Lane; 1976. Pp xi, 339.
14. Jones, T., 'A walk through Glamorgan, 1819,' Bc6, 109—25.
15. Hill, C.W. *Edwardian Scotland.* Edinburgh; Scottish Academic Press; 1976. Pp 182.
16. Evans, H. and M. *The party that lasted 100 days: the late Victorian season: a social study.* London; Macdonald and Jane's; 1976. Pp 162.

(b) *Politics*

1. Rich, J., 'The Bradlaugh Case: religion, respectability and politics,' *Australian J. of Politics and History* 21 (1975), 38—51.
2. Hunter, J., 'The Gaelic connection: the Highlands, Ireland, and nationalism, 1873—1922,' *Scottish Historical R.* 54 (1975), 178—204.
3. Schoenberg, M.M., 'A nineteenth-century giant, George Ward Hunt,' *Northamptonshire Past and Present* 5 (1976), 349—62.
4. Rowland, P. *Lloyd George.* London; Barrie & Jenkins; 1975. Pp xix, 872.
5. Pearce, C. *The Manningham Mills strike, Bradford, December 1890—April 1891.* University of Hull; 1975. Pp vii, 85.
6. Kirby, R.G.; Musson, A.E. *The voice of the people: John Doherty, 1789—1854: trade unionist, radical and factory reformer.* Manchester UP; 1975. Pp ix, 474.
7. Bourne, K. (ed.). *The blackmailing of the chancellor: some inti-*

mate and hitherto unpublished letters from Harriette Wilson to her friend Henry Brougham, lord chancellor of England. London; Lemon Tree Press; 1975. Pp 96.

8. Belfield, E.M.G. *The Boer War.* London; Cooper; 1975. Pp xxvi, 181.

9. Raeburn, A. *The suffragette view.* Newton Abbot; David & Charles; 1976. Pp 96.

10. Poulton, R. *Victoria, queen of a changing land.* Tadworth; World's Work; 1975. Pp 128.

11. Barltrop, R. *The monument: the story of the Socialist Party of Great Britain.* London; Pluto Press; 1975. Pp 200.

12. Mackenzie, M. *Shoulder to shoulder: a documentary.* London; Allen Lane; 1975. Pp x, 338.

13. Wheare, K.C., 'Walter Bagehot,' *P. of the British Academy* 60 (1975 for 1974), 173—97.

14. Dougan, D. *The shipwrights: the history of the Shipconstructors' and Shipwrights' Association, 1882—1963.* Newcastle/Tyne; Graham; 1975. Pp ix, 341.

15. McQuiston, J.R., 'The Lonsdale Connection and its defender, William, Viscount Lowther 1818—1830,' *Northern History* 11 (1976 for 1975), 143—79.

16. Purdue, A.W., 'Arthur Henderson and Liberal, Liberal-Labour and Labour politics in the north-east of England 1892—1903,' ibid. 195—217.

17. Snow, V.F., 'The reluctant surrender of an absurd privilege: proctorial representation in the House of Lords, 1810—1868,' *Parliamentary Affairs* 29 (1976), 60—78.

18. Epstein, J.A., 'Feargus O'Connor and the Northern Star,' *International R. of Social History* 21 (1976), 51—97.

19. Wigham, E.L. *Strikes and the government, 1893—1974.* London; Macmillan; 1976. Pp viii, 206.

20. Sack, J.J., 'The decline of the Grenvillite faction under the first duke of Buckingham and Chandos, 1817—1829,' *J. of British Studies* 15 (1975), 112—34.

21. Stewart, R., 'The Conservative Party and the "Courier" newspaper, 1840,' *English Historical R.* 91 (1976), 346—50.

22. Quinault, R.E., 'The fourth party and the Conservative opposition to Bradlaugh, 1880—1888,' ibid. 315—40.

23. Harvie, C., 'Ideology and home rule: James Bryce, A.V. Dicey and Ireland, 1880—1887,' ibid. 298—314.

24. Wright, A., 'From Fabianism to Guild Socialism: the early political thought of G.D.H. Cole,' *B. of the Soc. for the Study of Labour History* 32 (1976), 23—5.

25. Gash, N. *Peel.* London; Longman; 1976. Pp xiii, 319.

26. Trow-Smith, R. *Power on the land: a centenary of history of the Agricultural Engineers Association, 1875—1975.* London; Agripress Publicity Ltd for the Association; 1975. Pp 93.

27. Crosby, T.L. *Sir Robert Peel's administration, 1841—1846.* Newton Abbot; David & Charles; 1976. Pp

28. Reid, B.L. *The lives of Roger Casement.* New Haven, Conn.; Yale UP; 1976. Pp xx, 532.

29. Green, W.A. *British slave emancipation: the sugar colonies and the great experiment, 1830—1865.* Oxford; Clarendon; 1976. Pp xiii, 449.

30. Inglis, B. *The Opium War.* London; Hodder & Stoughton; 1976. Pp 223.

31. Fisher, G. *Bertie and Alix: anatomy of a royal marriage.* Leicester; F.A. Thorpe; 1975. Pp 350.

32. Burke, B. *Rebels with a cause: the history of Hackney Trades Council 1900—1975.* London; Hackney Trades Council; 1975. Pp 87.

33. Cunningham, H. *The Volunteer Force: a social and political history, 1859—1900.* London; Croom Helm; 1975. Pp 168.

34. Melling, E. *History of the Kent County Council, 1889—1974.* Maidstone; The Council; 1975. Pp vi, 182.

35. Russell, R.C. *Revolution in North Thoresby, Lincolnshire: the enclosure of the parish by act of Parliament, 1836—1846.* North Thoresby Workers' Educational Association; 1976. Pp 16.

36. Beresford, J., 'The Manor Street free speech controversy of 1906: how the Plymouth S.D.F. broke a pernicious circle,' Hf43, 45—57.

37. Bynyan, T. *The history and practice of the political police in Britain.* London; Friedmann; 1976. Pp xi, 320.

38. Young, K. *Local politics and the rise of party: the London Municipal Society and the Conservative intervention in local elections, 1894—1963.* Leicester UP; 1975. Pp 255.

39. Gollin, A., 'Historians and the great crisis of 1903,' *Albion* 8 (1975), 83—97.

40. Richards, E., 'The social and electoral influence of the Trentham interest, 1800—1860,' *Midland History* 3 (1975), 117—48.

41. Spring, D., 'Walter Bagehot and deference,' *American Historical R.* 81 (1976), 524—31.

42. David, R.W., 'Deference and aristocracy in the time of the Great Reform Bill,' ibid. 532—9.

43. Malchow, H.L., 'Trade unions and emigration in late Victorian England: a national lobby for state aid,' *J. of British Studies* 15 (1976), 92—116.

44. Griffiths, P.C., 'The Caucus and the Liberal party in 1886,' *History* 61 (1976), 183—97.

45. McQuiston, J.R., 'Farmers' revolt: the North Shropshire by-election of 1876,' *T. of the Shropshire Arch. Soc.* 59 (1976 for 1971/2), 170—80.

46. Foot, D. *British political crises.* London; Kimber; 1976. Pp 221.

47. Marshall, P. *Bristol and the abolition of slavery: the politics of*

emancipation. Bristol; Historical Association (Bristol Branch); 1975. Pp 28.

48. Winter, J. *Robert Lowe*. University of Toronto Press; 1976. Pp xiv, 368.

49. Wrigley, C. *David Lloyd George and the British Labour Movement: peace and war*. Hassocks; Harvester Press; 1976. Pp x, 298.

50. Kellas, J.G.; Fotheringham, P., 'The political behaviour of the working-class,' Hg43, 143—65.

51. Jones, H., 'The *Caroline* affair,' *The Historian* 38 (1976), 485—502.

52. Denholm, A., 'Lord Ripon and the Co-operative Movement,' *Historical Studies* 17 (1976), 15—26.

53. Matthew, H.C.G.; McKibbin, R.I.; Kay, J.A., 'The franchise factor in the rise of the Labour Party,' *English Historical R.* 91 (1976), 723—52.

54. Chadwick, M.E.J., 'The role of redistribution in the making of the Third Reform Act,' *Historical J.* 19 (1976), 665—83.

55. Asquith, I., 'The Whig Party and the press in the early nineteenth century,' *B. of the Institute of Historical Research* 49 (1976), 264—83.

56. Jalland, P., 'A Liberal chief secretary and the Irish Question: Augustine Birrell, 1907—1914,' *Historical J.* 19 (1976), 421—51.

57. Jowitt, J.A., 'Parliamentary politics in Halifax, 1832—1847,' *Northern History* 12 (1976), 172—201.

58. Cook, C., 'Labour and the downfall of the Liberal Party, 1906—14,' Bc8, 38—65.

59. Grigg, J., 'Liberals on trial,' Bc8, 23—37.

60. James, R.R. *The British revolution: British politics, 1880—1939; vol. 1: from Gladstone to Asquith, 1880—1914*. London; Hamilton; 1976. Pp xiv, 298.

61. Kynaston, D. *King Labour: the British working class, 1850—1914*. London; Allen & Unwin; 1976. Pp 184.

62. Mace, R. *Trafalgar Square: emblem of empire*. London; Lawrence & Wishart; 1976. Pp 338.

63. Williams, G.L. (ed.). *John Stuart Mill on politics and society*. London; Fontana; 412 pp.

64. Dinwiddy, J.R., 'Charles Hall, early English socialist,' *International R. of Social History* 21 (1976), 256—76.

65. Sachs, W.L., 'Stewart Headlam and the Fabian Society,' *Historical Magazine of the Protestant Episcopal Church* 45 (1976), 201—10.

66. Koss, S.E. *Asquith*. London; Allen Lane; 1976. Pp x, 310.

67. Graham, A.H., 'The Parliamentary Candidate Society,' Bc2, 104—116.

68. Lavin, D., 'History, morals and the politics of empire: Lionel Curtis and the Round Table,' Bc2, 117—32.

69. Feuchtwanger, E.J., 'The rise and progress of tory democracy,' Bc3, 164—83.

70. Morgan, K.O., 'The future at work: Anglo-American progressivism 1890–1917,' Bc5, 245–70.
71. Davies, E.T., 'Glamorgan and the "treachery of the Blue Books",' Bc6, 228–43.
72. Hurst, M., 'Liberal versus Liberal: 1874. A surrebuttal,' *Historical J.* 19 (1976), 1001–4.
73. Brown, K.D., 'London and the historical reputation of John Burns,' *London J.* 2 (1976), 226–38.
74. George, W.R.P. *The making of Lloyd George.* London; Faber; 1976. Pp 184.
75. Cameron, R.H., 'The Melbourne administration, the Liberals and the crisis of 1841,' *Durham University J.* 69 (1976), 83–102.
76. Woodall, R., 'Obini and the fall of Palmerston,' *History Today* 26 (1976), 636–43.

(c) *Constitution, Administration and Law*

1. Crook, M.J. *The evolution of the Victoria Cross: a study in administrative history.* Tunbridge Wells; Midas Books; 1975. Pp 321.
2. Greeves, J.W.H., 'A study of prison administration in the nineteenth century,' *Presenting Monmouthshire* 40 (1975), 23–8.
3. Cosgrove, R.A., 'The judicature acts of 1873–1875: a centennial reassessment,' *Durham University J.* 68 (1976), 196–206.
4. Peacock, S.E. *Borough government in Portsmouth, 1835–1974.* Portsmouth District Council, 1975. Pp 22.
5. Young, J.A. *The Holdenhurst parish council, 1894–1931.* Dorset County Education Committee; [1975]. Pp 25.
6. Ward, R.; Sedgwick, W.A. *The postal history of Harrogate, Knaresborough and Ripon.* Sheffield; Yorkshire Postal History Soc.; 1976. Pp 125.
7. Wilson, H.S. *TPO: a history of the Travelling Post Offices of Great Britain*; part 2: England, South of the Midland TPO. [Leicester]; Railway Philatelic Group; 1975. Pp 76.
8. Phillips, R.J., 'E.C. Tufnell: inspector of poor law schools, 1847–1874,' *History of Education* 5 (1976), 227–40.
9. Gregory, D., 'Rates and representation: Lancashire County in the nineteenth century,' *Northern History* 12 (1976), 158–71.
10. Morgan, D., 'Woman suffrage in Britain and America in the early twentieth century,' Bc5, 272–95.
11. Marsten, G., 'The centenary of the Franconia case – the persecution of Ferdinand Keyn,' *Law Q.R.* 92 (1976), 93–107.
12. Ritchie, J., 'Towards ending an unclean thing: the Molesworth Committee and the abolition of transportation to N.S.W., 1837–40,' *Historical Studies* 17 (1976), 144–64.
13. Smith, F.B., 'Labouchere's amendment to the Criminal Law Amendment Bill,' ibid. 165–75.

14. Davis, R.W., 'The mid-nineteenth century electoral structure,' *Albion* 8 (1976), 142–53.
15. Thompson, D.F. *John Stuart Mill and representative government.* Princeton UP; 1976. Pp vii, 241.

(d) *External Affairs*

1. Spring, D.W., 'The Trans-Persian Railway project and Anglo-Russian relations, 1909–14,' *Slavonic and East European R.* 54 (1976), 60–82.
2. Reinders, R.C., 'The John Anderson case, 1860–1: a study in Anglo-Canadian Imperial relations,' *Canadian Historical R.* 56 (1975), 393–415.
3. Lo, H.-M. (ed.). *The correspondence of G.E. Morrison*; 1: 1895–1912. Cambridge UP; 1976. Pp xiv, 848.
4. Wong, J.Y., 'Sir John Bowring and the question of Treaty revision in China,' *B. of the John Rylands Library* 58 (1975), 216–37.
5. Hildebrand, K., ' "British Interests" und "Pax Britannica": Grundfragen englischer Aussenpolitik im 19. und 20. Jahrhundert,' *Historische Zeitschrift* 221 (1975), 623–39.
6. Porter, B. *The lion's share: a short history of British imperialism, 1850–1970.* London; Longman; 1975. Pp xiii, 408.
7. Douglas, R., 'Britain and the Armenian question, 1894–7,' *Historical J.* 19 (1976), 113–33.
8. Randall, A., 'Lord Odo Russell and his Roman friends,' *History Today* 26 (1976), 368–76.
9. Howarth, D. *The Greek adventure: Lord Byron and other eccentrics in the war of independence.* London; Collins; 1976. Pp 253.
10. Hyam, R. *Britain's imperial century, 1815–1914: a study of empire and expansion.* London; Batsford; 1976. Pp 462.
11. Teed, P. *The move to Europe: Britain, 1880–1972.* London; Hutchinson; 1976. Pp xx, 458.
12. Hyam, R.; Martin, G.W. *Reappraisals in British imperial history.* London; Macmillan; 1975. Pp ix, 234.
13. Eames, A.; Lloyd, L.; Parry, B. (ed.). *David Evans: letters from America.* [Caernarvon]; Gwynned Archives Services; 1975. Pp 100.
14. Kent, M. *Oil and empire: British policy and Mesopotamian oil, 1900–1920.* London; Macmillan; 1976. Pp xiii, 273.
15. Marlowe, J. *Milner, apostle of empire: a life of Alfred George, the Right Honourable Viscount Milner of St James's and Cape Town, KG, GCB, GCMG, 1854–1925.* London; Hamilton; 1976. Pp xi, 394.
16. Barr, P. *The memsahibs: the women of Victorian India.* London; Secker & Warburg; 1976. Pp 210.

17. Winn, P., 'British informal empire in Uruguay in the nineteenth century,' *Past & Present* 73 (1976), 100—26.
18. Knox, B.A., 'The British government and the Governor Eyre controversy,' *Historical J.* 19 (1976), 877—900.
19. Schölch, A., 'The "men on the spot" and the English occupation of Egypt in 1882,' ibid. 773—85.
20. McLean, D., 'British finance and foreign policy in Turkey: the Smyrna-Aldin Railway Settlement 1913—1914,' ibid. 521—30.
21. Lorimer, D.A., 'The role of anti-slavery sentiment in English reactions to the American civil war,' ibid. 405—20.
22. Alonso, M.R., 'La intervención británica en España durante el gobierno progresista de Mendizábal,' *Hispania* 35 (1975), 343—90.
23. Hyam, R., 'The myth of the "magnaminous gesture": the Liberal government, Smuts and conciliation, 1606,' Hd12, 167—86.
24. Hyam, R., 'The partition of Africa: a critique of Robinson and Gallagher,' Hd12, 139—66.
25. Martin, G.W., 'The issue of "Imperial Federation",' Hd12, 121—38.
26. Martin, G.W., ' "Anti-imperialism" in the mid-nineteenth century and the nature of the British empire, 1820—70,' Hd12, 88 120.
27. Martin, G.W., 'The influence of the Durham Report,' Hd12, 75—87.
28. Colthart, J.M., 'Edward Ellice and the decision for self-government,' *Historical Papers/Communications Historiques* (of the Canadian Historical Association), 1975, 113—33.
29. Jones, M.A., 'Immigrants, steamships and governments: the steerage problem in transatlantic diplomacy,' Bc5, 178—209.
30. Campbell, C.S., 'Edward J. Phelps and Anglo-American relations,' Bc5, 210—24.
31. Temperley, H., 'Anglo-American images,' Bc5, 321—47.

(e) *Religion*

1. Richards, G., 'James Henry Cotton, dean of Bangor 1838—1868,' *National Library of Wales J.* 19 (1975), 147—80.
2. Griffin, J.R., 'The radical phase of the Oxford Movement,' *J. of Ecclesiastical History* 27 (1976), 47—56.
3. Leigh, D.J., 'Newman, Lonergan and social sin,' *The Month* 237 (1976), 41—4.
4. McPherson, A. (ed.). *History of the Free Presbyterian Church of Scotland*; vol. 2: 1893—1970. [Glasgow]; Publications Committee of the Church; [1975]. Pp 427.
5. Sayers, J.E.; Bill, E.G.W. (ed.). *Calendar of the papers of Charles Thomas Longley, archbishop of Canterbury, 1862—1868, in Lambeth Palace Library.* London; Mansell Information Publishing; 1976. Pp viii, 79.

6. Lash, N. *Newman on development: the search for an explanation in history.* London; Sheed & Ward; 1975. Pp xiii, 264.

7. Allen, L. (ed.). *John Henry Newman and the Abbé Jager: a controversy on scripture and tradition, 1834–1836.* London; Oxford UP; 1975. Pp xii, 202.

8. Holmes, J.D.; Achaval, H.M. de (ed.). *The theological papers of John Henry Newman on faith and certainty.* Oxford; Clarendon; 1976. Pp xv, 170.

9. Steer, R. *George Müller, delighted in God.* London; Hodder & Stoughton; 1975. Pp 351.

10. Jennings, D.A. *The revival of the Convocation of York, 1837–1861.* York; St Anthony's Press; 1975. Pp 27.

11. Bebbington, D.W., 'Gladstone and the Baptists,' *Baptist Q.* 26 (1976), 224–39.

12. Milburn, G.E., 'Tension in primitive methodism in the eighteen-seventies,' *P. of the Wesley Historical Soc.* 40 (1976), 93–101.

13. Dessain, C.S., 'Cardinal Newman and the eastern tradition,' *Downside R.* 94 (1976), 83–98.

14. Dessain, C.S.; Gornall, T. (ed.). *The letters and diaries of John Henry Newman;* vol. 29: the cardinalate, January 1879 to September 1881. Oxford; Clarendon; 1976. Pp xviii, 468.

15. Dessain, C.S.; Gornall, T. *The letters and diaries of John Henry Newman;* vol. 30: a cardinal's apostolate, October 1881 to December 1884. Oxford; Clarendon; 1976. Pp xviii, 488.

16. Lough, A.G. *John Mason Neale – priest extraordinary.* Newton Abbot; the author; [1975]. Pp 152.

17. Yonge, S. *Carmarthen Road United Reformed Church, Swansea, 1876–1976.* Swansea; The Church; 1976. Pp 33.

18. Bronner, E.B. *The other branch: London Yearly Meeting and the Hicksites.* London; Friends House; 1975. Pp ix, 67.

19. Donovan, R.K., 'The denominational character of English Catholic charitable effort, 1800–1865,' *Catholic Historical R.* 62 (1976), 200–23.

20. Pinnington, J.E., 'The consular chaplaincies and the Foreign Office under Palmerston, Aberdeen and Malmesbury. Two case histories: Rome and Funchal,' *J. of Ecclesiastical History* 27 (1976), 277–84.

21. Milburn, G.E., 'Tensions in Primitive Methodism in the eighteen-seventies (continued),' *P. of the Wesley Historical Soc.* 40 (1976), 135–44.

22. Bradley, I. *The call to seriousness: the evangelical impact on the Victorians.* London; Cape; 1976. Pp 224.

23. Ward, W.R. (ed.). *Early Victorian Methodism: the correspondence of Jabez Bunting, 1830–1858.* Oxford UP; 1976. Pp xxiii, 440.

24. Levesley, G. *Third jubilee: the history of the church and parish of St George, Sheffield, 1825–1975.* Sheffield; the parochial church council; [1975]. Pp vi, 115.

25. Piggin, S., 'Sectarianism versus ecumenism: the impact on British churches of the missionary movement to India, ca. 1800—1960,' *J. of Ecclesiastical History* 27 (1976), 387—402.

26. Sellers, I. *Adam Clarke, controversialist: Wesleyanism and the historic faith in the age of Bunting.* Wesley Historical Soc.; 1976. Pp 21.

27. Lambert, W.R., 'Thomas Williams, J.P., Gwaelod-y-Garth (1823—1903): a study in nonconformist attitudes and actions,' Bc6, 199—211.

28. Gurden, H., 'Primitive Methodism and agricultural trade unions in Warwickshire 1872—75,' *Soc. for the Study of Labour History* 33 (1976), 4—6.

29. Martyn, M., 'John Evans — East India chaplain,' *History Today* 26 (1976), 670—7.

30. Brown, H.M. *A century for Cornwall: the diocese of Truro, 1877—1977.* Truro; Oscar Blackford Ltd.; 1976. Pp x, 141.

(f) *Economic Affairs*

1. Thomas, H., 'The industrialization of a Glamorgan parish,' *National Library of Wales J.* 19 (1975), 194—208.

2. Smyth, A.L., 'The first Pic-Vic.,' *Manchester Literary and Philosophical Soc. Memoirs and P.* 117 (1974—5), 112—14.

3. Bouquet, M., 'The first commercial cargo of frozen meat,' *Mariner's Mirror* 62 (1976), 79—80.

4. Collins, E.J.T., 'Migrant labour in British agriculture in the nineteenth century,' *Economic History R.* 2nd ser. 29 (1976), 38—59.

5. Thompson, F.M.L., 'Nineteenth-century horse sense,' ibid. 60—81.

6. Harley, C.K., 'Goschen's conversion of the National Debt and the yield on Consols,' ibid. 101—6.

7. Musson, A.E., 'Joseph Whitworth and the growth of mass-production engineering,' *Business History* 17 (1975), 104—49.

8. Irving, R.J., 'New industries for old? Some investment decisions of Sir W.G. Armstrong, Whitworth & Co. Ltd. 1900—14,' ibid. 150—75.

9. Blackett, R., 'In search of international support for African colonization: Martin R. Delany's visit to England,' *Canadian J. of History* 10 (1975), 307—24.

10. Bone, Q., 'Legislation to revive small farming in England, 1887—1914,' *Agricultural History* 49 (1975), 653—61.

11. Hutton, K., 'The distribution of wheelhouses in the British Isles,' *Agricultural History R.* 24 (1976), 30—5.

12. Grove, R., 'Coprolite mining in Cambridgeshire,' ibid. 36—43.

13. Henthorn, F. (ed.). *Letters and Papers concerning the establishment of the Trent, Ancholme and Grimsby Railway, 1860—1862.* Lincoln Record Society; 1975. Pp lv, 130.

14. Harvie, K.G. *The tramways of South London and Croydon, 1899–1949.* (5th ed.). London; Borough of Lewisham; 1975. Pp 160.
15. Irving, R.J. *The North Eastern Railway Company, 1870–1914: an economic history.* Leicester UP; 1976. Pp 320.
16. Maggs, C. *The Bristol Port Railway & Pier and the Clifton Extension Railway.* [Blandford]; Oakwood Press; 1975. Pp 59.
17. Vaughan, C.M. *Pioneers of Welsh steel: Dowlais to Llanwern.* Risca; Starling Press; 1975. Pp 38.
18. Brewster, D.E. *Motor buses in Wales, 1898–1932.* Blandford; Oakwood Press; 1976. Pp 52.
19. Kidner, R.W. *The London motor bus, 1896–1975* (5th revd. ed.). Blandford; Oakwood Press; 1975. Pp 45.
20. Warren, K. *The geography of British heavy industry since 1800.* London; Oxford UP; 1976. Pp 60.
21. Ehrlich, C. *Social emulation and industrial progress – the Victorian piano.* Belfast; Queen's University; 1975 [inaugural lecture].
22. Braund, H.E.W. *Calling to mind: being some account of the first hundred years (1870–1970) of Steel Brothers & Co. Ltd.* Oxford; Pergamon; 1975. Pp 151.
23. Setright, L.J.K. *Rolls-Royce.* Yeovil; Foulis; 1975. Pp 160.
24. Gant, R.L., 'Perspectives on the townscape and economy of early 19th century Monmouth,' *Presenting Monmouthshire* 40 (1975), 11–23.
25. Olcott, T., 'Dead centre: the women's trade union movement in London, 1874–1914,' *London J.* 2 (1976), 33–50.
26. Hugh, R.K., 'The earl of Radnor and free trade,' *Huntington Library Q.* 39 (1976), 151–70.
27. McLean, D., 'Finance and "informal empire" before the first world war,' *Economic History R.* 2nd series, 29 (1976), 291–305.
28. Everitt, A., 'Country carriers in the nineteenth century,' *J. of Transport History* new series, 3 (1976), 179–202.
29. Parry, M.L., 'The abandonment of upland settlement in southern Scotland,' *Scottish Geographical Magazine* 92 (1976), 50–60.
30. Craig, D.; Carter, I., 'Dorset, Kincardine and peasant crisis [comment by Craig, reply by Carter],' *J. of Peasant Studies* 2 (1975), 483–9.
31. Benson, J., 'Non-fatal coalmining accidents,' *B. of the Soc. for the Study of Labour History* 32 (1976), 20–2.
32. Goode, C.T. *Railways in south Yorkshire: Clapham via Doncaster.* Dalesman; 1975. Pp 96.
33. Macdonnell, K. *Looking back at transport, 1901–1939.* Wakefield; EP Publishing; 1976. Pp 95.
34. Horne, J.B.; Maund, T.B. *Liverpool transport*; vol. 1: 1830–1900. London; Light Railway Transport League; 1975. Pp 153.

35. Gray, A. *The railways of mid-Sussex.* Blandford; Oakwood Press; [1975]. Pp 86.
36. Boyd, J.I.C. *The Festiniog railway*; vol. 2: Locomotives, rolling stock and quarry feeders. The Same; 1975. Pp 300—626.
37. Shuttleworth, S. *The Lancaster and Morecambe tramways.* The Same; 1976. Pp 42.
38. Abley, R.S. *The Byers Green branch of the Clarence railway.* Durham County Local History Soc.; 1975. Pp 47.
39. Haining, P. *The great English earthquake.* London; Hale; 1976. Pp 219.
40. Nock, O.S. *The railway race to the north* (new ed.). London; Allan; 1976. Pp 168.
41. Baddeley, G.E. (ed.). *The tramways of Kent*; vol. 2: East Kent. London; Light Railway Transport League; 1975. Pp 117—360.
42. Emrys, H.; Eames, A. *Porthmadog ships.* Caernarvon: Gwynned Archives Service; 1975. Pp 426.
43. Porter, J. (ed.). *Education and labour in the south-west.* University of Exeter, Dept. of Economic History; 1975. Pp 77.
44. Rowe, J., 'The declining years of Cornish tin-mining,' Hf43, 59—77.
45. Pigott, S. *OBM: a celebration; one hundred and twenty-five years in advertising.* London; Ogilvy Benson and Mather Ltd.; 1975. Pp 84.
46. Thomas, H., 'The industrialization of a Glamorgan parish, II,' *National Library of Wales J.* 19 (1976), 227—42.
47. Musson, A.E., 'Industrial motive power in the United Kingdom, 1800—70,' *Economic History R.* sec. ser. 29 (1976), 415—39.
48. Maloney, J., 'Marshall, Cunningham, and the emerging economics profession,' ibid. 440—51.
49. McLean, I.W., 'Anglo-American engineering competition, 1870—1914: some third-market evidence,' ibid. 452—64.
50. Perkins, J.A., 'The prosperity of farming on the Lindsey uplands, 1813—37,' *Agricultural History R.* 24 (1976), 126—43.
51. Kain, R.J.P., 'Tithe surveys and the study of land occupation,' *Local Historian* 12 (1976), 88—92.
52. Williams, L.J., 'The coalowners of South Wales, 1873—80: problems of unity,' *Welsh History R.* 8 (1976), 75—93.
53. Aspinall, P.J., 'Speculative builders and the development of Cleethorpes, 1850—1900,' *Lincolnshire History and Archaeology* 11 (1976), 43—52.
54. Boyd, J.I.C. *The Festiniog railway: a history of the narrow gauge railway linking the slate quarries of Blaenau Ffestiniog with Portmadoc, North Wales*; vol. 1: History and route, 1800—1953. [Blandford] ; Oakwood Press; 1975. Pp 297.
55. *Swindon works and its place in British railway history.* Swindon; British Rail Engineering; [1975]. Pp 42.

56. Cottrell, P.L. *British overseas investment in the nineteenth century.* London; Macmillan; 1975. Pp 79.

57. Course, E. *The railways of southern England*; vol. 3: Independent and light railways. London; Batsford; 1976. Pp ix, 189.

58. Fisher, J.R. *Clare Sewell Read, 1826–1905: a farmers' spokesman of the late nineteenth century.* University of Hull; 1975. Pp vi, 39.

59. Forwood, M.J. *The Elham Valley railway.* London; Phillimore; 1975. Pp 88.

60. Franks, D.L. *The Ashby and Nuneaton Railway, together with the Charnwood Forest Railway.* Sheffield; Turntable Publications; 1975. Pp 63.

61. Hodrien, R.C. *Cambridge's industrial relics* (2nd ed.). Cambridge Soc. for Industrial Archaeology; 1976. Pp 20.

62. Mitchell, W.R.; Mussett, N.J. *Seven years hard: building the Settle-Carlisle railway.* Clapham (N. Yorks.); Dalesman; 1976. Pp 65.

63. Phillips, D. *How the Great Western came to Berkshire: a railway history, 1833–1882.* Reading Libraries; 1975. Pp 35.

64. Reed, M.C. *Investment in railways in Britain, 1820–1844: a study in the development of the capital market.* London; Oxford UP; 1975. Pp xiv, 315.

65. Sturgess, R.W. *Aristocrat in business: the third marquis of Londonderry as coalowner and portbuilder.* [Sunderland] ; Durham County Local History Soc.; 1975. Pp 108.

66. Taylor, E. *The better temper: a commemorative history of the Midland Iron and Steel Wages Board, 1876–1976.* London; Iron and Steel Trade Confederation; 1976. Pp 38.

67. Thomas, J. *Scotland.* Newton Abbot; David & Charles; 1976. Pp 224.

68. Moorby, R.L.; Myall, D.G.A.; Ward Dyer, F.J. *A century of trade marks: a commentary on the work and history of the Trade Marks Registry.* London; HMSO; 1976. Pp iv, 56.

69. Unwin, P. *The printing Unwins: a short history of Unwin Brothers, the Gresham Press, 1826–1976.* London; Allen & Unwin; 1976. Pp 159.

70. James, F. *Walter Hancock and his common road steam carriages.* Alresford; Laurence Oxley; 1975. Pp vi, 131.

71. *The Kingston upon Hull street tramways: a history of private enterprise in Hull tramway operation, 1870–1899.* Hull; M. Charlesworth and S.F. Robinson; 1976. Pp 22.

72. Gauldie, E., 'The middle class and working class housing in the nineteenth century,' Hg43, 12–35.

73. Gray, M., 'North-east agriculture and the labour force,' Hg43, 86–104.

74. Grove, R. *The Cambridgeshire coprolite mining rush.* Cambridge; Oleander Press; 1976. Pp 51.

75. Pollard, S.; Turner, R., 'Profit-sharing and autocracy: the case of J.T. and J. Taylor of Batley, woollen manufacturers, 1892–1966,' *Business History* 18 (1976), 4–34.

76. Jones, S.R.H., 'Hall, English & Co., 1813–41: a study of entrepreneurial response in the Gloucester pin industry,' ibid. 35–65.

77. Drake, B.K., 'Continuity and flexibility in Liverpool's trade with Africa and the Caribbean,' ibid. 85–97.

78. Grampp, W.D., 'Scots, Jews and subversives among the dismal scientists,' *J. of Economic History* 36 (1976), 543–71.

79. Lant, J.L., 'The Jubilee coinage of 1887,' *British Numismatic J.* 42 (1976 for 1975), 132–41.

80. Taylor, D., 'The English dairy industry, 1860–1930,' *Economic History R.* 2nd ser. 29 (1976), 585–601.

81. Sharpless, J.B., 'The economic structure of port cities in the mid-nineteenth century: Boston and Liverpool 1840–1860,' *J. of Historical Geography* 2 (1976), 131–43.

82. Faiers, C., 'Persistence and change in farming methods in a Suffolk village,' *Oral History* 4/2 (1976), 52–62.

83. Floud, R. *The British machine tool industry, 1850–1914.* Cambridge UP; 1976. Pp xiv, 217.

84. Goodey, C. *The first hundred years: the story of Richards Shipbuilders.* Ipswich; Boydell Press; 1976. Pp 111.

85. Klapper, C.F. *London's lost railways.* London; Routledge; 1976. Pp xiv, 139.

86. Sayers, R.S. *The Bank of England, 1891–1944* (3 vols.). Cambridge UP. Pp 680; viii, 403.

87. Thomas, D.G.; Vickers, R.P. *M. Bolson & Co. Ltd., embossing press makers, Columbia Road, London E2: a short record of the firm's history, work and equipment.* London; Greater London Industrial Archaeology Soc.; 1976. Pp 22.

88. Warn, C.R. *Rails across Northumberland; part 4: Railways of the Northumberland coalfield.* Newcastle upon Tyne; Graham; 1976. Pp 60.

89. Hogle, K. *The railways of York.* Clapham (Yorks.); Dalesman; 1976. Pp 95.

90. Bellwood, J.; Jenkinson, D. *Gresley and Stanier: a centenary tribute.* London; HMSO; 1976. Pp vii, 100.

91. Parry, M.L., 'The mapping of abandoned farmland in upland Britain: an exploratory survey in S.E. Scotland,' *Geographical J.* 142 (1976), 101–10.

92. Rymer, E.A., 'The martyrdom of the mine,' *History Workshop* 1 (1976), 220–45.

93. Vale, V., 'Trusts and tycoons: British myth and American reality,' Bc5, 225–44.

94. Lewis, E.D., 'Pioneers of the Cardiff coal trade,' Bc6, 22–52.

95. Flint, A.J., ' "Neither a borrower . . . ", Sir Robert Price, Bart., M.P., Bc6, 82–97.

96. Trebilcock, C., 'The British armaments industry 1890–1914: false legend and true utility,' Bc10, 89–107.
97. Mason, J.W., 'The duke of Argyll and the land question in late-nineteenth-century Britain,' *Society for the Study of Labour History* 33 (1976), 12–14.
98. Bean, R., 'Employers' associations in the port of Liverpool, 1890–1914,' *International R. of Social History* 21 (1976), 358–82.
99. Rule, J., 'The smacksmen of the North Sea: labour recruitment and exploitation in British deep-sea fishing, 1850–90,' ibid. 383–411.
100. Dodd, J.P., 'Norfolk agriculture in 1853–54,' Norfolk Archaeology 36 (1976), 253–64.
101. Rath, T., 'The Tewkesbury hosiery industry,' *Textile History* 7 (1976), 140–53.
102. Hynes, W.G., 'British mercantile attitudes towards imperial expansion,' *Historical J.* 19 (1976), 969–79.
103. Colyer, R.J. *The Welsh cattle drovers: agriculture and the Welsh cattle trade before and during the nineteenth century.* Cardiff; University of Wales Press; 1976. Pp 155.
104. Taylor, J. *Ellermans: a wealth of shipping.* London; Wilton House Gentry Ltd.; 1976. Pp 320.

(g) *Social Structure and Population*

1. Olney, R.J. (ed.). *Labouring life in the Lincolnshire Wolds: a study of Binbrook in the mid-nineteenth century.* Sleaford; Soc. for Lincolnshire History and Archaeology; 1975. Pp 39.
2. Lowerson, J. (ed.). *Victorian and Edwardian Seaford: an embryonic Brighton?* Brighton; Centre for Continuing Education; 1975. Pp 64.
3. Parker, O. *For the family's sake: a history of the Mothers' Union, 1876–1976.* London; Mowbrays; 1975. Pp viii, 133.
4. Michell, R. *The Parish of Beddington in the year 1837.* Beddington, Carshalton and Wallington Arch. Soc.; 1975. Pp 28.
5. Cooke, A. *The American in England: Emerson to S.J. Perelman.* Cambridge UP; 1975 [Rede lecture]. Pp 30.
6. Davey, N. *Dundee by gaslight: a glimpse of 'old Dundee' through the eyes of the Victorian and Edwardian photographer.* Dundee Museum and Art Galleries; 1975. Pp 44.
7. Cowell, F.R. *The Athenaeum: club and social life in London 1824–1974.* London; Heinemann; 1975. Pp xi, 177.
8. Ashmore, O.; Bolton, T., 'Hugh Mason and the Oxford Mills and Community, Ashton-under-Lyne,' *T. of the Lancashire and Cheshire Antiquarian Soc.* 78 (1975), 38–50.
9. Perkin, H.J., 'The "social tone" of Victorian seaside resorts in the north-west,' *Northern History* 11 (1976 for 1975), 180–94.
10. Franklin, J., 'Troops of servants: labour and planning in the

country house 1840—1914,' *Victorian Studies* 19 (1975), 211—39.

11. Levine, D.C., 'The reliability of parochial registration and the representativeness of family reconstruction,' *Population Studies* 30 (1976), 107—22.

12. Fitton, A.M.H.; Day, G., 'Religion and social status in rural Wales: "Buchedd" and its lessons for concepts of stratification in community studies,' *Sociological R.* 23 (1975), 867—91.

13. Brazier, A. *West Twickenham in the 1890s: a railwayman's memories.* Twickenham Local History Soc.; 1976. Pp 24.

14. Girouard, M. *Victorian pubs.* London; Studio Vista; 1975. Pp 223.

15. Neale, K. (ed.). *Victorian Horsham: the diary of Henry Michell, 1809—1874.* Chichester; Phillimore; 1975. Pp iv, 109.

16. Porter, E. *Victorian Cambridge: Josiah Chater's diaries, 1844—1884.* London; Phillimore; 1975. Pp xvii, 227.

17. Cross, R.L. *The living past — a Victorian heritage: the origins, building, use and renewal of the Town Hall and Corn Exchange, Cornhill, Ipswich.* Borough of Ipswich; 1975. Pp 141.

18. Clives, S.W. *The centenary book of the Birmingham County Football Association, 1875—1975.* Birmingham: The Association; 1975. Pp 164.

19. Reyburn, W. *Twickenham: the story of a rugby ground.* London; Allen & Unwin; 1976. Pp 176.

20. Waterworth, W.E. *The story of the Huddersfield Y.M.C.A., 1875—1975.* [Huddersfield YMCA; 1975]. Pp 49.

21. Pride, E. *Rhondda my valley brave.* Risca; Starling Press Ltd; 1975. Pp 191.

22. Mills, D.R., 'A social and demographic study of Melbourn, Cambridgeshire, c. 1840,' *Archives* 12 (1976), 115—20.

23. Prynn, D., 'The Clarion Clubs, rambling and the holiday associations in Britain since the 1890s,' *J. of Contemporary History* 11 (1976), 65—77.

24. Lindgren, C., 'Nathaniel Hawthorne, consul at Liverpool,' *History Today* 26 (1976), 516—24.

25. Gwynne, T.; Sill, M., 'Census enumeration books: a study of mid-nineteenth century immigration,' *Local Historian* 12 (1976), 74—9.

26. Steel, D., 'One hundred years on: the use of a private census to compare with the mid-nineteenth century enumerators' returns,' ibid. 93—101.

27. Crossick, G., 'The labour aristocracy and its values: a study of mid-Victorian Kentish London,' *Victorian Studies* 19 (1976), 301—28.

28. Williams, G., 'The structure and process of Welsh emigration to Patagonia,' *Welsh History R.* 8 (1976), 42—74.

29. Short, B., 'The turnover of tenants on the Ashburnham estate, 1830—1850,' *Shropshire Arch. Collections* 113 (1975), 157—74.

30. Caffrey, K. *The 1900s lady.* London; Cremonesi; 1976. Pp 176.
31. Swift, A. *The story of George Cooper, Stockport's last town crier, 1824—1895.* [Stockport; the author; 1975]. Pp 38.
32. Chalkin, C.W. (ed.). *Early Victorian Tonbridge.* Kent County Council; 1975. Pp 25.
33. Gray, R.Q. *The labour aristocracy in Victorian Edinburgh.* Oxford; Clarendon; 1976. Pp x, 220.
34. Macnaghten, A.D.I.J. *Windsor in Victorian times.* Ascot; the author; 1975. Pp 142.
35. Peroni, R. *Industrial Lancashire.* Nelson; Hendon Publishing Co.; 1975. Pp 75.
36. Russell, R.C. *Friendly societies in the Caistor, Binbrook and Brigg areas in the nineteenth century.* Nettleton Branch of the Workers' Education Association; 1975. Pp 17.
37. Vansittart, J. (ed.). *Lifelines: the Stacey letters, 1836—1858.* London; P. Davies; 1976. Pp x, 180.
38. Vamplew, W. *The turf: a social and economic history of horse racing.* London; Allen Lane; 1976. Pp 288.
39. Williams, G. *The desert and the dream: a study of Welsh colonization in Chubut, 1865—1915.* Cardiff; University of Wales Press; 1975. Pp xiii, 230.
40. Aspin, C. *Gone cricket mad: the Haslingdon Club in the Victorian era.* Helmshore Local History Soc.; 1976. Pp 70.
41. Keating, P. (ed.). *Into unknown England, 1866—1913: selections from the social explorers.* Manchester UP; 1976. Pp 320.
42. Bragg, M. (ed.). *Speak for England: an essay on England, 1900—1975* (based on interviews with inhabitants of Wigton, Cumberland). London; Secker & Warburg; 1976. Pp 504.
43. MacLaren, A.A. (ed.). *Social class in Scotland: past and present.* Edinburgh; Donald; [1976]. Pp ix, 195.
44. MacLaren, A.A., 'An open society?,' Hg43, 1—11.
45. Smout, T.C., 'Aspects of sexual behaviour in nineteenth century Scotland,' Hg43, 55—85.
46. Gray, M., 'Class and culture among farm servants in the northeast, 1840—1914,' Hg43, 105—27.
47. Gray, R.Q., 'Thrift and working-class mobility in Victorian Edinburgh,' Hg43, 128—42.
48. Scott, J.; Hughes, M., 'The Scottish ruling class: problems of analysis and data,' Hg43, 166—92.
49. Petrie, C.A. *Scenes of Edwardian life.* London; Severn House; 1975. Pp 244.
50. Carter, I., 'The peasantry of northeast Scotland,' *J. of Peasant Studies* 3 (1976), 151—91.
51. Silverstone, R., 'Office work for women: a historical review,' *Business History* 18 (1976), 98—110.
52. Selby, D.E., 'Cardinal Manning, campaigner for children's rights,' *J. of Ecclesiastical History* 27 (1976), 403—12.

53. Anderson, G.L., 'Victorian clerks and voluntary associations in Liverpool and Manchester,' *Northern History* 12 (1976), 202–19.

54. Winstanley, M., 'The rural publican and his business in East Kent, before 1914,' *Oral History* 4/2 (1976), 63–78.

55. Hall, B. *Lowerhouse and the Dugdales: the story of a Lancashire mill community.* Burnley and District Historical Soc.; 1976. Pp 33.

56. Horn, P. *Labouring life in the Victorian countryside.* Dublin; Gill & Macmillan; 1976. Pp 292.

57. Hunter, J. *The making of the crofting community.* Edinburgh; Donald; 1976. Pp xiii, 309.

58. McBride, T.M. *The domestic revolution: the modernisation of household service in England and France, 1820–1920.* London; Croom Helm; 1976. Pp 160.

59. Pearsall, R. *Public purity, private shame: Victorian sexual hypocrisy exposed.* London; Weidenfeld & Nicolson; 1976. Pp 222.

60. McKenna, F., 'Victorian railway workers,' *History Workshop* 1 (1976), 26–73.

61. Weeks, J., ' "Sins and diseases": some notes on homosexuality in the nineteenth century,' ibid. 211–19.

62. Barke, M., 'The population of Brighouse, West Yorkshire, in 1851,' *Yorkshire Arch. J.* 48 (1976), 135–46.

63. Neville, R.G., 'The Yorkshire miners and the 1893 lockout: the Featherstone "massacre",' *International R. of Social History* 21 (1976), 337–57.

64. Kaijage, F.J., 'Manifesto of the Barnsley chartists,' *Society for the Study of Labour History* 33 (1976), 20–6.

65. Howkins, A., 'The Norfolk farm labourer 1900–1923,' ibid. 7–9.

66. Hostettler, E., 'Women's work in the nineteenth-century countryside,' ibid. 9–12.

67. Macdonald, S., 'The diary of an agricultural apprentice in Northumberland, 1842,' *Local Historian* 12 (1976), 139–45.

68. Meller, H.E. *Leisure and the changing city, 1870–1914.* London; Routledge; 1976. Pp x, 308.

69. Anderson, G. *Victorian clerks.* Manchester UP; 1976. Pp viii, 145.

(h) *Social Policy*

1. Brundage, A., 'Reform of the Poor Law electoral system, 1834–94,' *Albion* 7 (1975), 201–15.

2. Fraser, D. (ed.). *The new poor law in the nineteenth century.* London; Macmillan; 1976. Pp v, 218.

3. Bryan, A. *The evolution of health and safety in mines.* [London; Ashire Publishing Ltd.] ; 1975. Pp 192.

4. *The Aberlour Trust centenary year, 1875–1975.* [Stirling] ; The Trust; 1975. Pp 43.

5. Bruce, G. *Some practical good: the Cockburn Association, 1875– 1975; a hundred years' participation in planning in Edinburgh.* Edinburgh; The Association; 1975. Pp 108.

6. Manton, J. *Mary Carpenter and the children of the streets.* London; Heinemann Educational; 1976. Pp xii, 268.

7. Hazlehurst, C., 'Churchill as social reformer: the Liberal phase,' *Historical Studies* 17 (1976), 84–92.

8. Thane, P.; Musson, A.E.; Hanson, C.G., 'Craft unions, welfare benefits, and the case for trade union law reform, 1867–75,' *Economic History R.* 2nd ser. 29 (1976), 617–35.

9. Rowley, J.J., 'Drink and the public houses in Nottingham 1830– 1860,' *T. of the Thoroton Soc.* 79 (1976 for 1975), 72–83.

10. Oldfield, G., 'The fight for public health: the work of the Basford Rural Sanitary Authority, 1874–1894,' ibid. 84–95.

11. Alderman, G., 'The national free labour association: a case-study of organised strike-breaking in the late nineteenth and early twentieth centuries,' *International R. of Social History* 21 (1976), 309–36.

12. Spenceley, G.F.R., 'The health and disciplining of children in the pillow lace industry in the nineteenth century,' *Textile History* 7 (1976), 154–72.

(i) *Education*

1. Taylor, A.J., 'History at Leeds, 1877–1974: the evolution of a discipline,' *Northern History* 10 (1975), 141–64.

2. Mathieson, M. *The preachers of culture: a study of English and its teachers.* London; Allen & Unwin; 1975. Pp 231.

3. Parkin, R. *The Central Society of Education, 1836–1840.* Leeds; The University — Museum of the History of Education; 1975. Pp 37.

4. Miller, E. *Century of change, 1875–1975: one hundred years of training home economics' students in Glasgow.* [Glasgow; Queen's College; 1975]. Pp 64.

5. Bland, J., 'The impact of government on English Catholic education, 1870–1902,' *Catholic Historical R.* 62 (1976), 36–55.

6. Coulson, J., 'Newman's ideas of an open university, and its consequences today,' *Downside R.* 94 (1976), 133–45.

7. Pedersen, J., 'Schoolmistresses and headmistresses: elites and education in nineteenth-century England,' *J. of British Studies* 15 (1975), 135–62.

8. Thomas, D.W. *The history of technical education in London, 1904–1940.* Lancaster; History of Education Soc.; 1976. Pp 72.

9. Scrowston, R.M. *A hundred years of education in Walkington, 1876–1976.* Governors of Walkington County Primary School; 1976. Pp 42.

10. Whitcut, J. *Edgbaston High School, 1876–1976.* Governors of the School; 1976. Pp xi, 181.

11. Stephens, W.B., 'An anatomy of illiteracy in mid-Victorian Devon,' Hf43, 7–20.

12. Duncan, G.S., 'Adult education in early Victorian Torquay, with particular reference to the contribution of the Church,' Hf43, 21–44.

13. Jones, E.W., 'Addysg feddygol i ferched — Cyfraniadau of Gymru: agor y cyndyn ddorau [19th century female education],' *National Library of Wales J.* 19 (1976), 249–92.

14. Davies, W., 'The intermediate school in rural Wales 1897–1907: the problem of school organisation,' ibid. 293–9.

15. Horn, P., 'Oxfordshire village school teachers: 1800–1880,' *Cake and Cockhorse* 7 (1976), 3–18.

16. Boyden, B. (compiler). *Call back yesterday: a collection of reminiscences to mark the centenary of the Nottingham High School for Girls, GPDST, 1875–1975.* [Nottingham; The School; 1976]. Pp 205.

17. Munson, J.E.B., 'The education of Baptist ministers, 1870–1900,' *Baptist Q.* 26 (1976), 320–7.

18. Dyhouse, C., 'Social Darwinistic ideas and the development of women's education in England, 1880–1920,' *History of Education* 5 (1975), 41–58.

19. Roach, J.P., 'History teaching and examining in secondary schools, 1850–1900,' ibid. 127–40.

20. McClelland, V.A., 'The "free schools" issue and the general election of 1885: a denominational response,' ibid. 141–54.

21. Leinster-Mackay, D., 'The evolution of t'other schools: an examination of the nineteenth century development of the private preparatory school,' ibid. 241–9.

22. Carter, I.R., 'The mutual improvement movement in north-east Scotland in the nineteenth century,' *Aberdeen University R.* 156 (1976), 383–92.

23. Layton, D., 'The educational work of the parliamentary committee of the British Association for the Advancement of Sicence,' *History of Education* 5 (1976), 25–40.

24. Bullock, F.W.B. *A history of training for the ministry of the Church of England in England and Wales from 1875 to 1974.* London; Home Words Printing and Publishing Co.; 1976. Pp xxvi, 177.

25. Childs, H. *W.M. Childs: an account of his life and work.* Reading; the author; 1976. Pp 204.

26. Stone, D. *The National: the story of a pioneer college: the National Training College of Domestic Subjects* (2nd ed.). London; Hale; 1976. Pp xvi, 399.

27. Sewell, B., 'Frederick William Rolfe and the Scots College,' *Innes R.* 26 (1976), 20–6.

28. Lyons, N., 'The clergy in education: career structures in the 1830s,' *J. of Educational Administration and History* 8 (1976), 6–10.
29. Cummings, R., 'The log-book of a Rhondda school, 1864–1910,' Bc6, 188–98.
30. Cruickshank, M., 'Mary Dendy, 1855–1933, pioneer of residential schools for the feeble-minded,' *J. of Educational Administration and History* 8 (1976), 26–9.
31. Marcham, A.J., 'The Birmingham Education Society and the 1870 Education Act,' ibid. 11–16.
32. Horn, P., 'Mid-Victorian elementary school teachers,' *Local Historian* 12 (1976), 161–6.
33. Colls, R., ' "Oh happy English children!": coal, class and education in the north-east,' *Past and Present* 73 (1976), 75–99.

(j) *Naval and Military*

1. Lant, J.L., 'The Spithead naval review of 1887,' *Mariner's Mirror* 62 (1976), 67–79.
2. Rodger, N.A.M., 'The dark ages of the Admiralty, part II: change and decay, 1874–80,' ibid. 33–46.
3. Sharp, G. *The siege of Ladysmith.* London; Macdonald & Jane's; 1976. Pp 164.
4. Dawnay, N.P. *The standards, guidons and colours of the Household Division, 1660–1973.* Tunbridge Wells; Midas Books; 1975. Pp xxiii, 272.
5. Hamilton, C.I., 'Sir James Graham, the Baltic campaign and war-planning at the Admiralty in 1854,' *Historical J.* 19 (1976), 89–112.
6. 'Admiral Ballard's memoirs, Part II: Midshipman,' *Mariner's Mirror* 62 (1976), 23–32. [See Hj9]
7. Rodger, N.A.M., 'The dark age of the Admiralty, 1869–85; part III: peace retrenchment and reform, 1880–85,' ibid. 121–8.
8. Minchinton, W.E., 'British ports of call in the nineteenth century,' ibid. 145–57.
9. 'Admiral Ballard's memoirs; Part III: around the world, 1880–82,' ibid. 129–33. [See Hj6 and 13]
10. Marshall-Cornwall, J., 'British aid in the Carlist war, 1835–1840,' *History Today* 26 (1976), 179–87.
11. McBride, A. *The Zulu War.* London; Osprey Publishing; 1976. Pp 40.
12. Tyler, W.B., 'The British German Legion 1854–62,' *J. of the Soc. for Army Historical Research* 54 (1976), 14–29.
13. 'Admiral Ballard's memoirs, Parts IV and V: Greenwich, *Excellent*, *Vernon* and *Hecla*, 1882–84,' *Mariner's Mirror* 62 (1976), 249–52, 347–52. [See Hj9]

14. Satre, L.J., 'St John Brodrick and army reform, 1901–1903,' *J. of British Studies* 15 (1976), 117–39.
15. Abbott, P.E. *Recipients of the Distinguished Conduct Medal, 1855–1909.* London; J.B. Hayward & Son; 1975. Pp xxiv, 88.
16. Barclay, G. St J. *The Empire is marching: a study of the military effort of the British Empire, 1800–1945.* London; Weidenfeld & Nicolson; 1976. Pp ix, 276.
17. Rosa, J.G. *Colonel Colt, London: the history of Colt's London firearms, 1851–1857.* London; Arms and Armour Press; 1976. Pp 216.
18. Spiers, E.M., 'The use of the dum-dum bullet in colonial warfare,' *J. of Imperial and Commonwealth History* 4 (1975), 3–14.
19. Lindsay, A.B., 'Letters from the Abor expedition 1911–12,' *J. of the Soc. for Army Historical Research* 54 (1976), 149–63.
20. Barthrop, M., 'Some South African battlefields of 1879 and 1881,' ibid. 142–8.
21. Best, G.F.A., 'How right is might? Some aspects of the international debate about how to fight wars and how to win them, 1870–1918,' Bc10, 120–35.
22. Travers, T.H.E., 'Future warfare: H.G. Wells and British military theory, 1895–1916,' Bc11, 67–87.
23. Gooch, J., 'Attitudes to war in late Victorian and Edwardian England,' Bc11, 88–102.
24. Towle, P., 'The debate on wartime censorship in Britain, 1902–14,' Bc11, 103–16.
25. Strachan, H. *History of the Cambridge University Officers Training Corps.* Tunbridge Wells; Midas Books; 1976. Pp xiii, 289.

(k) *Science and Medicine*

1. Smith, C., ' "Mechanical philosophy" and the emergence of physics in Britain, 1800–1850,' *Annals of Science* 33 (1976), 3–29.
2. Forrester, S.D., 'The history of the development of the light fastness testing of dyed fabrics up to 1902,' *Textile History* 6 (1975), 52–88.
3. McKenna, S., 'Joseph Chessborough Dyer,' *Manchester Literary and Philosophical Soc. Memoirs and P.* 117 (1974–5), 104–11.
4. Middleton, G.E.; Knell, K.A. (ed.). *Engineering centenary 1975.* Cambridge University Engineering Department; 1975. Pp 83.
5. Thomas, K.B. *The development of unaesthetic apparatus: a history based on the Charles King Collection of the Association of Anaesthetists of Great Britain and Ireland.* Oxford; Blackwell; 1975. Pp x, 268.
6. Forrest, J.S. *One hundred years of public electricity.* [Egham] ; 1975. Pp 24.

7. Bartholomew, M.J., 'The award of the Copley Medal to Charles Darwin,' *Notes and Records* 30 (1976), 209—18.

8. Jensen, V., 'Thomas Henry Huxley's baptism into oratory,' ibid. 181—207.

9. Charlton, T.M., 'Contributions to the science of bridge-building in the nineteenth century by Henry Moseley, Hon. L.D., F.R.S., and William Pole, D.Mus., F.R.S.,' ibid. 169—79.

10. Ruse, M., 'The relationship between science and religion in Britain, 1830—1870,' *Church History* 44 (1975), 505—22.

11. Farrar, W.V.; Farrar, K.R.; Scott, E.L., 'The Henrys of Manchester, part 5: William Henry: contagion and cholera; the textbook,' *Ambix* 23 (1976), 27—52.

12. Henderson, P. *The School Health Service 1908—1974: report of the chief medical officer of the Dept. of Education and Science (with an historical review).* London; HMSO; 1975. Pp iii, 66.

13. Merrington, W.R. *University College Hospital and its medical school: a history.* London; Heinemann; 1976. Pp xvii, 305.

14. Matthews, M.H., 'The development of the synthetic alkali industry in Great Britain by 1823,' *Annals of Science* 33 (1976), 371—82.

15. Brock, W.H.; Macleod, R., 'The "Scientists' Declaration": reflexions on science and belief in the wake of *Essays and Reviews*, 1864—5,' *British J. for the History of Science* 9 (1976), 39—66.

16. Bird, A. *Paxton's palace.* London; Cassell; 1976. Pp xi, 179.

17. Body, G. *Clifton suspension bridge: an illustrated history.* Bradford-on-Avon; Moonraker Press; 1976. Pp 76.

18. Hannavy, J. *Fox Talbot: an illustrated life of William Henry Fox Talbot, 'father of modern photography', 1800—1877.* Princes Risborough; Shire Publications; 1976. Pp 48.

19. Baker, E.C. *Sir William Preece, F.R.S.: Victorian engineer extraordinary.* London; Hutchinson; 1976. Pp xiv, 377.

20. Hattersley-Smith, G., 'The British arctic expedition, 1875—76,' *Polar Record* 18 (1976), 117—26.

21. Deacon, M.; Savours, A., 'Sir George Strong Nares (1831—1915),' ibid. 127—42.

22. Bowler, P.J., 'Malthus, Darwin and the concept of struggle,' *J. of the History of Ideas* 37 (1976), 631—50.

23. Mansell, A.L., 'The influence of medicine on science education in England,' *History of Education* 5 (1976), 155—68.

24. Cardwell, D.S.L.; Hills, R.L., 'Thermodynamics and practical engineering in the nineteenth century,' *History of Technology* (ed. A.R. Hall and N. Smith; London; Mansell; 1976), vol. 1, 1—20.

25. Wilson, G.B.L., 'The small country gasworks,' *T. of the Newcomen Soc.* 46 (1973—4), 33—44.

26. Thomas, P.H., 'Medical men of Glamorgan: William Salmon of Penllin, 1790—1896,' Bc6, 98—108.

27. Cooter, R.J., 'Phrenology and British alienists, c. 1825—1845,' *Medical History* 20 (1976), 1—21, 135—51.

28. Durey, M.J., 'Bodysnatchers and Benthamites: the implications of the Dead Body Bill for the London schools of anatomy, 1820—42,' *London J.* 2 (1976), 200—25.

29. Morris, R.J. *Cholera, 1832: the social response to an epidemic.* London; Croom Helm; 1976. Pp 228.

(l) *Intellectual and Cultural*

1. Lucas, P., 'Publicity and power; James Ramsden's experiment with daily journalism,' *T. of the Cumberland and Westmorland Antiquarian and Arch. Soc.* new ser. 75 (1975), 352—75.

2. Rodgers, B., 'John Stuart Mill: the Avignon years,' *Manchester Literary and Philosophical Soc. Memoirs and P.* 117 (1974—5), 52—74.

3. Kirkham, M., 'The Edwardian critical opposition,' *University of Toronto Q.* 45 (1975), 19—34.

4. Angus-Butterworth, L.M. *Walter Butterworth, M.A., J.P. (1862—1935), a patron of art.* [Ashton-on-Mersey; the author]; 1975. Pp 20.

5. Nash, A. *A.E. Cogswell, architect within a Victorian city.* Portsmouth; School of Architecture, Portsmouth Polytechnic; 1975.

6. Lambton, L. *Vanishing Victoriana.* Oxford; Elsevier-Phaidon; 1976. Pp 143.

7. Livings, H. *That the medals and the baton be put on view: the story of a village band, 1875—1975.* Newton Abbot; David & Charles; 1975. Pp 96.

8. Maas, J. *Gambart: prince of the Victorian art world.* London; Barrie & Jenkins; 1975. Pp 320.

9. Sambrook, J. (ed.). *Pre-Raphaelitism: a collection of critical essays.* Chicago UP; 1974. Pp 277.

10. Jenkins, D.C. (ed.). *The diary of Thomas Jenkins of Llandeilo, 1826—1870.* Bala; Dragon Books; 1976. Pp 206.

11. Welland, D., 'The American writer and the Victorian north west,' *B. of the John Rylands Library* 58 (1975), 193—215.

12. Struhl, P.R., 'Mill's notion of social responsibility,' *J. of the History of Ideas* 37 (1976), 155—62.

13. Liscombe, R.W., 'The commencement of real art,' [reception of the Elgin Marbles] *Apollo* 1976, 34—9.

14. Manvell, R. *The trial of Annie Besant and Charles Bradlaugh.* London; Elek; 1976. Pp ix, 182.

15. Hook, P., 'The classical revival in English painting,' *The Connoisseur* 192 (1976), 122—7.

16. Ellis, J., 'Critics of the mid-Victorian London theatre,' *London J.* 2 (1976), 101—16.
17. Fox, C., 'The engravers' battle for professional recognition in early nineteenth century London,' ibid. 3—31.
18. Tarn, J.N., 'The restoration of Great Longstone church,' *Derbyshire Arch. J.* 93 (1975 for 1973), 90—102.
19. Lester, G.A., 'Thomas Bateman, barrow opener,' ibid. 10—22.
20. Robertson, J.C., 'A Bacon-facing generation: Scottish philosophy in the early nineteenth century,' *J. of the History of Philosophy* 14 (1976), 37—49.
21. McDonnell, J., 'Success and failure: a rhetorical study of the first two chapters of Mill's *Autobiography*,' *University of Toronto Q.* 45 (1976), 109—22.
22. Tait, A.A., 'The instant landscape of Sir Henry Steuart,' *Burlington Magazine* 118 (1976), 14—23.
23. Sterrenburg, L., 'Psychoanalysis and the iconography of revolution,' *Victorian Studies* 19 (1975), 241—64.
24. Senelick, L., 'Politics as entertainment: Victorian music-hall songs,' ibid. 149—80.
25. McCord, N., 'Research and recreation [inns],' *Local Historian* 12 (1976), 31—5.
26. Elbourne, R.P., ' "Singing away to the click of the shuttle": musical life in the handloom weaving communities of Lancashire,' ibid. 13—17.
27. Richardson, J., ' "My dearest uncle . . . ", a royal correspondence,' *History Today* 26 (1976), 250—5.
28. McLaren, A., 'Contraception and the working classes: the social ideology of the English birth control movement in its early years,' *Comparative Studies in Society and History* 18 (1976), 236—51.
29. Trudgill, E. *Madonnas and Magdalens: the origins and development of Victorian sexual attitudes.* London; Heinemann; 1976. Pp xiii, 336.
30. Service, A. (ed.). *Edwardian architecture and its origins.* London; Architectural Press; 1975. Pp 504.
31. Makin, D. *Music in Belper (1824—1975).* [Milford; the author; 1976].
32. Horsman, R., 'Origins of racial Anglo-Saxonism in Great Britain before 1850,' *J. of the History of Ideas* 37 (1976), 387—410.
33. Wiener, M.J., 'The myth of William Morris,' *Albion* 8 (1976), 67—82.
34. August, E. *John Stuart Mill: a mind at large.* London; Vision Press; 1976. Pp xii, 276.
35. Bradbrook, M.C. *Barbara Bodichon, George Eliot and the limits of feminism.* [Oxford; Somerville College; 1975] . Pp 16.
36. Brett, C.E.B. *Buildings on the island of Alderney.* Belfast; Ulster Architectural Heritage Soc.; 1976. Pp 50.

37. Brophy, B. *Beardsley and his world*. London; Thames & Hudson; 1976. Pp 128.
38. Darroch, S.J. *Ottoline: the life of Lady Ottoline Morrell*. London; Chatto & Windus; 1976. Pp 317.
39. Lennie, C. *Landseer: the Victorian paragon*. London; Hamilton; 1976. Pp 259.
40. McWatters, K.G. *Stendhal and England*. Liverpool UP; 1976. Pp 23.
41. Williams, G.L. (ed.). *John Stuart Mill on politics and society*. Hassocks; Harvester Press; 1976. Pp 412.
42. Summerson, J. *The turn of the century: architecture in Britain around 1900*. University of Glasgow Press; 1976. Pp 25.
43. Sutton, D. *Walter Sickert: a biography*. London; Joseph; 1976. Pp 272.
44. Scott, D.F.S. (ed.). *Luke Howard (1772–1864): his correspondence with Goethe and his continental journey of 1816*. York; William Sessions Ltd.; 1976. Pp viii, 99.
45. Longman, G. *The Herkomer Art School, 1883–1900*. Bushey; the author; 1976. Pp 16.
46. Ormond, L. and R. *Lord Leighton*. New Haven; Yale UP; 1975. Pp xv, 200.
47. *1850–1875, art and industry in Sheffield*. [Sheffield City Art Galleries; 1976]. Pp 36.
48. Lyle, E.B., 'The printed writings of Andrew Crawfurd,' *The Bibliotheck* 7 (1975), 141–58.
49. Attenborough, J. *A living memory: Hodder & Stoughton Publishers, 1868–1975*. London; Hodder & Stoughton; 1975. Pp 287.
50. Walton, J.M., 'Residential amenity, respectable morality and the rise of the entertainment industry: the case of Blackpool 1860–1914,' *Literature and History* 1 (1975), 62–78.
51. MacLaren, A.A., 'Bourgeois ideology and Victorian philanthropy: the contradictions of cholera,' Hg43, 36–54.
52. Žekulin, N.G., 'Turgenev in Scotland,' *Slavonic and East European R.* 54 (1976), 355–70.
53. Penny, N.B., 'English church monuments to women who died in childbed between 1780 and 1835,' *J. of the Warburg and Courtauld Institutes* 38 (1975), 314–32.
54. Collini, S., 'Hobhouse, Bosanquet and the state: philosophical idealism and political argument in England 1880–1918,' *Past and Present* 72 (1976), 86–111.
55. Fulford, R. (ed.). *Darling child: private correspondence of Queen Victoria and the Crown Princess of Prussia, 1871–1878*. London; Evans Bros.; 1976. Pp xii, 307.
56. Chadwick, O. *Acton and Gladstone* [Creighton lecture]. London; Athlone; 1976. Pp 56.

57. Holroyd, M. *Augustus John: a biography* (revd. ed.). Harmondsworth; Penguin; 1976. Pp 828.

58. Sultana, D. *Benjamin Disraeli in Spain, Malta and Albania, 1830–32: a monograph* (enlarged ed.). London;Tamesis; 1976. Pp ix, 78.

59. Fredeman, W.E. *The letters of Pictor Ignotus: William Bell Scott's correspondence with Alice Boyd, 1859–1884.* Manchester; John Rylands Library; 1976. Pp 93.

60. Shipley, S., 'The libraries of the Alliance Cabinet Makers' Association in 1879,' *History Workshop* 1 (1976), 180–4.

61. Dunbabin, J.P.D., 'Oliver Cromwell's popular image in nineteenth-century England,' Bc3, 141–63.

62. Jones, I.G., 'The building of St Elvan's Church, Aberdare,' Bc6, 71–81.

63. Munby, A.N.L., 'Dibdin's Reference Library: the sale of 26–28 June 1817,' Bc7, 279–314.

64. Turner, M.L., 'Tillotson's Fiction Bureau: agreements with authors,' Bc7, 351–78.

65. Saint, A. *Richard Norman Shaw.* New Haven/London; Yale UP; 1976. Pp xx, 487.

66. Hannavy, J. *Masters of Victorian photography.* Newton Abbot; David & Charles; 1976. Pp 96.

67. Trewin, J.C. *The Edwardian theatre.* Oxford; Blackwell; 1976. Pp xiv, 193.

68. Harrison, R., 'Marx, Gladstone and Olga Novikov,' *Soc. for the Study of Labour History* 33 (1976), 26–34.

69. Webb, I., 'The Bradford Wool Exchange: industrial capitalism and the popularity of Gothic,' *Victorian Studies* 20 (1976), 45–68.

70. Port, M.H., 'Pride and parsimony: influences affecting the development of the Whitehall quarter in the 1850s,' *London J.* 2 (1976), 171–99.

71. Sewter, A.C. *The stained glass of William Morris and his circle*, vol. 2: a catalogue. New Haven/London; Yale UP; 1975. Pp xiii, 335.

72. Clay, E.; Frederiksen, M. (ed.). *Sir William Gell in Italy: letters to the Society of Dilettanti, 1831–1835.* London; Hamilton; 1976. Pp x, 182.

73. Lee, A.J. *The origins of the popular press in England, 1855–1914.* London; Croom Helm; 1976. Pp 310.

I. BRITAIN SINCE 1914

See also: Aa14, 15, 39, 47, 49, c11; Bb13; Ha2, 6, b2, 4, 11, 14, 19, 26, 34, 38, c4, 5, d17, f13, 18, 19, 20, 22, 23, 45, 54, 66, 67, 68, 75, 80,

Ia1

83, 84, 86, 90, g3, 5, 7, 18, 19, 20, 21, 38, 42, h4, 5, i1, 2, 4, 6, 8, 9, 10, j4, 16, k4, 5, 6, 12, 13, 14, 7, 49

(a) *General*

1. Taylor, R.; Cox, M.; Dickens, I. (ed.). *Britain's planning heritage.* London; Helm; 1975. Pp ix, 230.
2. Hands, N.S. *Old Cranleighan Lodge no. 4680: a history of the Lodge's first fifty years, 1925–1975.* [Northwood; Old Cranleighan Lodge; 1975]. Pp 19.
3. Sinar, J., 'John Morton Bestall, 1921–1973: a memoir,' *Derbyshire Arch. J.* 93 (1975 for 1973), 5–8.
4. McKenzie, D. *The Red Cross mail service for Channel Islands civilians, 1940–1945.* Chippenham; Picton Publishing; 1975. Pp iv, 82.
5. Thompson, A.H. *Censorship in public libraries in the United Kingdom during the twentieth century.* Epping; Bowker; 1975. Pp xiv, 236.
6. Reith, J.C.W., Lord Reith. *The Reith diaries* (ed. C. Stuart). London; Collins; 1975. Pp 541.
7. Franzero, C.M. *Cinquant'anni a Londra.* Turin; Società editrice internazionale; 1975. Pp 296.
8. Draper, A. *The Prince of Wales.* London; New English Library; 1975. Pp 159.
9. Begley, G. *Keep Mum! – advertising goes to war.* London; Lemon Tree Press; 1975. Pp 77.
10. Branson, N. *Britain in the Nineteen Twenties.* London; Weidenfeld & Nicolson; 1975. Pp 274.
11. Eden, A. (earl of Avon). *Another world: 1897–1917.* London; Allen Lane; 1976. Pp 156.
12. Holmes, C., 'East End anti-semitism, 1936,' *B. of the Soc. for the Study of Labour History* 32 (1976), 26–33.
13. Howell, G. (ed.). *In "Vogue": six decades of fashion.* London; Allen Lane; 1975. Pp viii, 344.
14. Stevenson, W.I. *Patrick Geddes and geography: a bio-bibliographical study.* London; University College (Dept. of Geography); 1975. Pp 29.
15. Cullen, T. *The prostitutes' padre: the story of the notorious rector of Stiffkey.* London; Bodley Head; 1975. Pp 199.
16. Hohmann, D. *Londoner Skizzen.* Berlin; Der Morgen; 1975. Pp 168.
17. Sheail, J. *Nature in trust: the history of nature conservation in Britain.* Glasgow; Blackie; 1976. Pp xiv, 270.
18. Flint, R.H.; Rheinberg, N. *Fair play: the story of women's cricket.* London; Angus & Robertson; 1976. Pp 192.
19. Glynn, S.; Oxborrow, J. *Interwar Britain: a social and economic history.* London; Allen & Unwin; 1976. Pp 276.

108

20. Graves, R.P. *Lawrence of Arabia and his world*. London; Thames & Hudson; 1976. Pp 127.
21. Harrisson, T. *Living through the blitz*. London; Collins; 1976. Pp 372.
22. Vasilyeva, L., 'G.B.S. in the U.S.S.R.,' *Anglo-Soviet J.* 36/2 (1975), 20–2.
23. Wolfenden, J. *Turning points: the memoirs of Lord Wolfenden*. London; The Bodley Head; 1976. Pp 186.
24. Stevenson, 'Myth and reality: Britain in the 1930s,' Bc8, 90–109.
25. Perkin, H.L. *The age of the automobile*. London; Quartet Books; 1976. Pp xiii, 250.
26. Jenkins, A. *The thirties*. London; Heinemann; 1976. Pp 240.

(b) *Politics*

1. Gardiner, G. *Margaret Thatcher: from childhood to leadership*. London; Kimber; 1975. Pp 235.
2. Wilford, R.A., 'The federation of progressive societies and individuals,' *J. of Contemporary History* 11 (1976), 49–82.
3. Carpenter, L.P., 'Corporatism in Britain 1930–45,' ibid. 3–25.
4. Widgery, D. *The Left in Britain, 1956–68*. Harmondsworth; Penguin; 1976. Pp 549.
5. Young, K. *Stanley Baldwin*. London; Weidenfeld & Nicolson; 1976. Pp xi, 161.
6. Leruez, J. *Economic planning and politics in Britain* (trs. Martin Harrison). London; Robertson; 1975. Pp xi, 324.
7. Oldfield, A., 'The Independent Labour Party and planning,' *International R. of Social History* 21 (1976), 1–29.
8. Robinson, I.; Sims, D. *The decline and fall of Mr Heath: essays in criticism of British politics*. Swansea; Brynmill Publishing Co.; 1974. Pp 78.
9. Greenleaf, W.H., 'The character of modern British politics,' *Parliamentary Affairs* 1975, 368–85.
10. Tinker, H. *Separate and unequal: India and the Indians in the British Commonwealth, 1920–1950*. London; Hurst; 1976. Pp 460.
11. Cyr, A., 'Current trends in British politics,' *Parliamentary Affairs* 29 (1976), 27–36.
12. Woodhouse, M.; Pearce, B. *Essays on the history of communism in Britain*. London; New Park Publications; 1975. Pp xv, 248.
13. *The nine days in Birmingham: the general strike, 4–12 May 1926*. Birmingham Public Libraries; 1976. Pp vi, 43.
14. Durr, A. *Who were the guilty?: General strike, Brighton, May 1926*. Brighton Labour History Press; 1976. Pp 40.
15. Calhoun, D.F. *The united front* [British Labour and Soviet Russia]. Cambridge UP; 1976. Pp xi, 450.

16. Money, E. *Margaret Thatcher, first lady of the House*. London; Frewin; 1975. Pp 159.

17. Dewar, H. *Communist politics in Britain: the CPGB from its origins to the Second World War*. London; Pluto Press; 1976. Pp 159.

18. James, R.R. *Victor Cazalet: a portrait*. London; Hamilton; 1976. Pp xiv, 306.

19. Forester, T. *The Labour Party and the working class*. London; Heinemann Educational; 1976. Pp x, 166.

20. Layton-Henry, Z., 'Labour's lost youth,' *J. of Contemporary History* 11 (1976), 275–308.

21. Lazer, H., 'British populism: the Labor Party and the Common Market parliamentary debate,' *Political Science Q.* 91 (1976), 259–77.

22. Barker, R., 'Political myth: Ramsay MacDonald and the Labour Party,' *History* 61 (1976), 46–56.

23. Sharp, A.J., 'The Foreign Office in eclipse, 1919–22,' ibid. 198–218.

24. Cook, C. *A short history of the Liberal Party, 1900–1976*. London; Macmillan; 1976. Pp viii, 179.

25. Cousins, P.F., 'Voluntary organizations and local government in three south London boroughs,' *Public Administration* 54 (1976), 63–81.

26. Panitch, L. *Social democracy and industrial militancy: the Labour Party and incomes policy, 1945–1974*. Cambridge UP; 1976. Pp x, 318.

27. Shipley, P. *Revolutionaries in modern Britain*. London; The Bodley Head; 1976. Pp 256.

28. Gyford, J. *Local Politics in Britain*. London; Croom Helm; 1976. Pp 193.

29. Crossman, R.H.S. *The diaries of a cabinet minister. Vol. 2: lord president of the Council and leader of the House of Commons, 1966–8*. London; Hamilton/Cape; 1976. Pp 851.

30. Howell, D. *British social democracy: a study in development and decay*. London; Croom Helm; 1976. Pp 320.

31. Addison, P., 'Journey to the centre: Churchill and Labour in coalition, 1940–5,' Bc8, 165–93.

32. Koss, S., 'Asquith versus Lloyd George: the last phase and beyond,' Bc8, 66–89.

33. Roberts, D.M., 'Clement Davies and the fall of Neville Chamberlain, 1939–40,' *Welsh History R.* 8 (1976), 188–215.

34. Drucker, H.M., 'Leadership selection in the Labour Party,' *Parliamentary Affairs* 29 (1976), 378–95.

35. Volkov, F.D., ['The great October socialist revolution and the British working class,'] *Voprosy Istorii* 8 (1975), 64–77.

36. Taylor, R., 'The uneasy alliance – Labour and the unions,' *Political Q.* 47 (1976), 398–407.

37. Gilbert, M. *Winston S. Churchill, vol. 5: 1922–1939.* London; Heinemann; 1976. Pp xxvii, 1167.
38. Pelling, H. *A short history of the Labour Party* (5th ed.). London; Macmillan; 1976. Pp vii, 180.
39. Meltzer, A. *The anarchists in London, 1935–1955.* Sanday: Cienfuegos Press; 1976. Pp 41.
40. Whale, J., 'The press and Jeremy Thorpe,' *Political Q.* 47 (1976), 408–24.
41. Jones, G.W.; Hart, W., 'Sir Isaac Hayward 1884–1976,' *London J.* 2 (1976), 239–49.
42. Hyde, H.M. *Neville Chamberlain.* London; Weidenfeld & Nicolson; 1976. Pp xii, 188.
43. Mahon, J. *Harry Pollit: a biography.* London; Lawrence & Wishart; 1976. Pp 567.
44. Wichert, S., 'The enigma of fascism: the British Left on National Socialism,' Bc2, 146–58.

(c) *Constitution, Administration and Law*

1. Adams, R.J.Q., 'Delivering the goods: reappraising the Ministry of Munitions, 1915–1916,' *Albion* 7 (1975), 232–44.
2. Alderman, R.K.; Cross, J.A., 'The prime ministers and the decision to dissolve,' *Parliamentary Affairs* 28 (1975), 386–404.
3. Hermens, F.A., 'Electoral systems and political systems: recent developments in Britain,' *Parliamentary Affairs* 29 (1976), 47–59.
4. Liversidge, D. *Prince Charles: monarch in the making.* London; Barker; 1975. Pp vii, 148.
5. Craig, F.W.S. (ed.). *The most gracious speeches to parliament, 1900–1974: statements of government policy and achievements.* London; Macmillan; 1975. Pp xi, 240.
6. Laver, M., 'On introducing STV and interpreting the results: the case of Northern Ireland, 1973–1975,' *Parliamentary Affairs* 29 (1976), 211–29.
7. Bromhead, P.; Shell, D., 'The British constitution in 1975,' ibid. 135–54.
8. Burton, I.; Drewry, G., 'Public legislation: a survey of season 1974,' ibid. 155–89.
9. Walkland, S.A., 'The politics of parliamentary reform,' ibid. 190–200.
10. Alderman, R.K., 'The prime minister and the appointment of ministers: an exercise in political bargaining,' ibid. 101–34.
11. Robson, W., 'What the Crossman Diaries actually said,' *Political Q.* 47 (1976), 276–85.
12. Aster, S. *Anthony Eden.* London; Weidenfeld & Nicolson; 1976. Pp x, 176.

13. Butler, D.; Kitzinger, U. *The 1975 Referendum*. London; Macmillan; 1976. Pp xi, 315.
14. Goodhart, P. *Full-hearted consent: the story of the Referendum campaign – and the campaign for the Referendum*. London; Davis-Poynter; 1976. Pp 264.
15. Norton, P., 'The forgotten whips: whips in the House of Lords,' *The Parliamentarian* 57/2 (1976), 86–92.
16. Crispin, A., 'Local government finance: assessing the central government's contribution,' *Public Administration* 54 (1976), 45–61.
17. Winterton, G., 'The British grundnorm: parliamentary supremacy re-examined,' *Law Q.R.* 92 (1976), 591–617.
18. Yardley, D.C.M. *Modern constitutional developments: some reflections*. University of Birmingham; 1976. Pp 22.

(d) *External Affairs*

1. Calder, K.J. *Britain and the origins of the new Europe, 1914–1918*. Cambridge UP; 1976. Pp ix, 268.
2. Rose, J.D., 'The British and the northern Albanian boundary dispute,' *New R. of East-European History* 15 (1975), 3–19.
3. Hopkins, A.G., 'Imperial business in Africa; part I: sources,' *J. of African History* 17 (1976), 29–48.
4. Chan, K.C., 'Britain's reaction to Chiang Kai-shek's visit to India, February 1942,' *Australian J. of Politics and History* 21 (1975), 52–61.
5. La Feber, W., 'Roosevelt, Churchill and Indochina: 1942–45,' *American Historical R.* 80 (1975), 1277–95.
6. Graham, R.A., 'Vatican Radio between London and Berlin, 1940–1,' *The Month* 237 (1976), 125–30.
7. Pratt, L.R. *East of Malta, west of Suez; Britain's Mediterranean crisis, 1936–1939*. Cambridge UP; 1975. Pp xiii, 215.
8. Boardman, R. *Britain and the People's Republic of China, 1949–74*. London; Macmillan; 1976. Pp xi, 210.
9. Weinroth, H., 'Peace by negotiation and the British anti-war movement, 1914–1918,' *Canadian J. of History* 10 (1975), 369–92.
10. Kedourie, E. *In the Anglo-Arab labyrinth: the McMahon-Husayn correspondence and its intepretations, 1914–1939*. Cambridge UP; 1976. Pp xii, 330.
11. Heywood, R.W., 'London, Bonn, the Königswinter conferences and the problem of European integration,' *J. of Contemporary History* 10 (1975), 131–55.
12. Schroeder, P.W., 'Munich and the British tradition,' *Historical J.* 19 (1976), 223–43.
13. Conte, F., 'Lloyd George et le traité de Rapallo,' *Revue d'histoire moderne et contemporaine* 23 (1976), 44–67.

14. Medlicott, W.N.; Dakin, D.; Lambert, M.E. (ed.). *Documents on British Foreign Policy, 1919–1939, 1A series*; vol. 7: German, Austrian and Middle Eastern questions, 1929–1930. London; HMSO; 1975. Pp lv, 852.
15. Barker, E. *British policy in the Second World War.* London; Macmillan; 1976. Pp viii, 320.
16. Woodward, Sir L. *British foreign policy in the Second World War*, vol. 4. London; HMSO; 1975. Pp xvii, 550.
17. Newman, S. *March 1939, the British guarantee to Poland: a study in the continuity of British foreign policy.* Oxford; Clarendon; 1976. Pp ix, 253.
18. Lyon, P. (ed.). *Britain and Canada: survey of a changing relationship.* London; Cass; 1976. Pp xxix, 191.
19. Shay, R.P., jr., 'Chamberlain's folly: the national defence contribution of 1937,' *Albion* 7 (1975), 317–27.
20. Parrott, Sir C. *The tightrope* [memoirs]. London; Faber; 1975. Pp 223.
21. Mansergh, N. (ed.). *The transfer of power, 1942–7*; vol. 6: the post-war phase: new moves by the Labour government, 1 August 1945–22 March 1946. London; HMSO; 1976. Pp lxxxvi, 1280.
22. Medlicott, W.N.; Dakin, D.; Lambert, M.E. (ed.). *Documents on British foreign policy, 1919–1939*; second series, vol. 14: the Italo-Ethiopian dispute, March 21, 1934, to October 3, 1935. London; HMSO; 1976. Pp lxix, 790.
23. Hunt, D.W.S. *On the spot: an ambassador remembers.* London; P. Davies; 1975. Pp ix, 259.
24. Troeller, G. *The birth of Saudi Arabia: Britain and the rise of the House of Sa'ud.* London; Cass; 1976.
25. Zhigalov, I.I., 'The problem of Great Britain's participation in the 1956 Suez crisis and its reflection in historical literature,' *Voprosy Istorii* 5 (1976), 66–83.
26. Waley, D. *British public opinion and the Abyssinian war, 1935–6.* London; Temple Smith; 1975. Pp 176.
27. Blouet, B.W., 'Sir Harold Mackinder as British high commissioner to South Russia 1919–1920,' *Geographical J.* 142 (1976), 228–36.
28. Zhivkova, L. *Anglo-turetskie otnoshenia, 1933–1939.* Moscow; 1975. Pp 196.
29. Cohen, M., 'The British White Paper on Palestine, May 1939: part II, The testing of a policy, 1942–1945,' *Historical J.* 19 (1976), 727–57.
30. Hall, H.H., 'The foreign policy-making process in Britain, 1934–1935, and the origins of the Anglo-German naval agreement,' ibid. 477–99.
31. Meyers, R., 'Britain, Europe and the Dominions in the 1930s: some aspects of British, European and Commonwealth policies,' *Australian J. of Politics and History* 22 (1976), 36–50.

32. Brown, J.M., 'Imperial facade: some constraints upon and contradictions in the British position in India, 1919—35,' *T. of the Royal Historical Soc.* 5th ser. 26 (1976), 32—52.

33. Megaw, M.R., 'Australia and the Anglo-American trade agreement 1938,' *J. of Imperial and Commonwealth History* 3 (1975), 191—211.

34. Garson, R., 'The Atlantic alliance, eastern Europe, and the origins of the Cold War: from Pearl Harbor to Yalta,' Bc5, 296—320.

35. Snelling, R.C., 'Peacemaking, 1919: Australia, New Zealand and the British Empire delegation at Versailles,' *J. of Imperial and Commonwealth History* 4 (1976), 15—28.

36. Parker, R.A.C., 'Britain, France and Scandinavia, 1939—40,' *History* 61 (1976), 369—87.

37. Hanak, H., 'The visit of the Czechoslovak foreign minister Dr. Edward Beneš to Moscow in 1935 as seen by the British minister in Prague, Sir Joseph Addison,' *Slavonic and East European R.* 54 (1976), 586—92.

38. Barker, E., 'Fresh sidelights on British policy in Yugoslavia, 1942—3,' ibid. 572—85.

39. Wasserstein, B., 'Herbert Samuel and the Palestine problem,' *English Historical R.* 91 (1976), 753—75.

40. Hyam, R., 'The politics of partition in southern Africa, 1908—61,' Hd12, 187—200.

(e) *Religion*

1. Newman-Norton, S. *The time of silence: a history of the Catholic Apostolic Church, 1901—71* (3rd ed.). Leicester; Albury Soc.; 1975. Pp xi, 42.

2. Vidler, A.R., 'The limitations of William Temple,' *Theology* 79 (1976), 36—41.

3. White, G.W. *A half-century of Cornish Methodism, 1925—1975: a local preacher's experience.* Redruth; Cornish Methodist Historical Association; 1975. Pp 22.

4. Greene, T.R., 'The English Catholic press and the second Spanish republic, 1931—1936,' *Church History* 45 (1976), 70—84.

5. Thomas, J.A., 'Liturgy and architecture, 1932—60: methodist influences and ideas,' *P. of the Wesley Historical Soc.* 40 (1976), 106—13.

6. Mews, S., 'The churches,' If42, 318—37.

7. Field, C., 'A sociological profile of English Methodism, 1900—1932,' *Oral History* 4/1 (1976), 73—95.

8. Mews, S., 'Anglican intervention in the election of an Orthodox patriarch, 1925—6,' Bc4, 293—306.

(f) *Economic Affairs*

1. Minsky, H.P. *John Maynard Keynes.* London; Macmillan; 1976.
2. Buxton, N.K., 'Efficiency and organization in Scotland's iron and steel industry during the interwar period,' *Economic History R.* 2nd ser. 29 (1976), 107–24.
3. Mason, E. *The Lancashire & Yorkshire Railway in the twentieth century* (2nd ed.). London; Allan; 1975. Pp 236.
4. Duncan, T.S. *'Cautious, Belfast': the story of the first fifty years of Harris, Marrian and Co., Ltd., 1925–1975.* [Belfast]; the author; 1975. Pp 43.
5. Fausten, D.K. *The consistency of British balance of payments policies.* London; Macmillan; 1975. Pp xi, 210.
6. Phillips, G.A. *The General Strike: the politics of industrial conflict.* London; Weidenfeld & Nicolson; 1976. Pp xii, 388.
7. Skelley, J. (ed.). *The General Strike 1926.* London; Lawrence & Wishart; 1976. Pp xiv, 412.
8. Foster, J., 'Imperialism and the Labour aristocracy,' If7, 3–57.
9. Klugman, J., 'Marxism, reformism, and the general strike,' If7, 58–107.
10. Carter, P., 'The west of Scotland,' If7, 111–39.
11. McDougal, I., 'Edinburgh,' If7, 140–59.
12. Frow, E.; Frow, R., 'Manchester diary,' If7, 160–72.
13. Wyncoll, P., 'The East Midlands,' If7, 173–92.
14. Barnsbuy, S., 'The Black Country,' If7, 193–207.
15. Hastings, R.P., 'Birmingham,' If7, 208–31.
16. Francis, H., 'South Wales,' If7, 232–60.
17. Attfield, J.; Lee, J., 'Deptford and Lewisham,' If7, 261–82.
18. Tucket, A., 'Swindon,' If7, 283–311.
19. Kerrigan, P., 'From Glasgow,' If7, 315–29.
20. Davies, B., 'From St Helens,' If7, 330–9.
21. Carr, B., 'From the Yorkshire coalfield,' If7, 340–51.
22. Wilson, D.A., 'From Bradford,' If7, 352–9.
23. Jacobs, J., 'From Hackney,' If7, 360–7.
24. Watson, H., 'An incident on the river Thames,' If7, 368–71.
25. Jacques, M., 'Consequences of the General Strike,' If7, 375–404.
26. Moggridge, D.E. *Keynes.* London; Macmillan/Fontana; 1976. Pp 189.
27. Jolly, W.P. *Lord Leverhulme: a biography.* London; Constable; 1976. Pp viii, 246.
28. Aldcroft, D.H., 'A new chapter in transport history: the twentieth-century revolution,' *J. of Transport History* new series, 3 (1976), 217–39.
29. Lindley, R.M., 'Inter-industry mobility of male employees in Britain, 1959–68,' *J. of the Royal Statistical Soc.* ser. A, 139 (1976), 56–79.

30. Merton Jones, A.C. *British independent airlines since 1946.* Uxbridge; LAAS International; 1976. Pp 120.
31. New, P.T. *The Solent sky: a local history of aviation from 1908 to 1946 with special reference to Southampton (Eastleigh) Airport.* [Chandlers Ford; the author; 1976]. Pp 118.
32. Whetham, E.H. *Beef cattle and sheep, 1910–1940: a description of the production and marketing of beef cattle and sheep in Great Britain in the early 20th century to the Second World War.* Univ. of Cambridge (Dept. of Land Economy); 1976. Pp 59.
33. Hinton, J.; Hyman, R. *Trade unions and revolution: the industrial politics of the early British Communist Party.* London; Pluto Press; 1975. Pp 78.
34. Reader, W.J. *Metal Box: a history.* London; Heinemann; 1976. Pp xii, 256.
35. Sheail, J., 'Land improvement and reclamation: the experiences of the First World War in England and Wales,' *Agricultural History R.* 24 (1976), 110–25.
36. Rhys, D.G., 'Concentration in the inter-war motor industry,' *J. of Transport History* new ser. 3 (1976), 241–64.
37. Humphreys, B.K., 'Nationalization and in the independent airlines in the United Kingdom, 1945–51,' ibid. 265–81.
38. Burridge, T.D. *British Labour and Hitler's war.* London; Deutsch; 1976. Pp 206.
39. Noel, G.E. *The great lock-out of 1926.* London; Constable; 1976. Pp xii, 239.
40. Millward, R., 'Price restraint, anti-inflation policy and public and private industry in the United Kingdom, 1949–1973,' *Economic J.* 86 (1976), 226–42.
41. Miller, F., 'The unemployment policy of the National Government, 1931–1936,' *Historical J.* 19 (1976), 453–76.
42. Morris, M. (ed.). *The general strike.* Harmondsworth; Penguin; 1976. Pp 479.
43. McDonald, G.W., 'The role of British industry in 1926,' If42, 289–317.
44. Mellor, A.; Pawling, C.; Sparks, C., 'Writers and the general strike,' If42, 338–57.
45. Bhaumik, S., 'The strike in the regions, (b) Glasgow,' If42, 394–410.
46. Edwards, E.W., 'The strike in the regions, (c) The Pontypridd area,' If42, 411–25.
47. Benton, S., 'The strike in the regions, (d) Sheffield,' If42, 426–39.
48. Garside, W.R., 'Juvenile unemployment statistics between the wars,' *Soc. for the Study of Labour History* 33 (1976), 38–46.
49. Mace, R., 'The strike in the regions, (a) Battersea, London,' If42, 379–93.
50. Buxton, N.K., 'Efficiency and organization in Scotland's iron and

steel industry during the interwar period,' *Economic History R.* 2nd ser. 29 (1976), 107–24.

51. Hartman, P., 'Industrial relations in the news media,' *Industrial Relations* 6 (1976), 4–18.
52. Richards, M.A., 'The Sex Discrimination Act – equality for women?,' *Industrial Law J.* 5 (1976), 35–41.
53. Creighton, W.B., 'Enforcing the Sex Discrimination Act,' ibid. 42–53.
54. Freedland, M.R., 'Employment protection: redundancy procedures and the E.E.C.,' ibid. 24–34.
55. Benedictus, R., 'Employment protection: new institutions and trade union rights,' ibid. 12–23.
56. Drake, C.D., 'The Trade Union and Labour Relations (Amendment) Bill,' ibid. 2–11.
57. Frank, P., 'Women's work in the Yorkshire inshore fishing industry,' *Oral History* 4/1 (1976), 57–72.
58. Eaton, J.; Fletcher, A., 'Workers' participation in management: a survey of post-war organised opinion,' *Political Q.* 47 (1976), 82–92.
59. Goodman, J.F.B., 'Great Britain: towards the social contract,' *Worker Militancy and its consequences, 1965–75*, ed. S. Barkin (London; Martin Robertson/Praeger; 1976), 39–81.
60. Johnson, H., 'Oil, imperial policy and the Trinidad disturbances,' *J. of Imperial and Commonwealth History* 4 (1976), 29–54.
61. Foster, J., 'The redistributive effect of inflation on building society shares and deposits 1961–74,' *B. of Economic Research* 28/2 (1976), 67–76.
62. Capie, F., 'Consumer preference: meat in England and Wales,' ibid. 85–94.
63. Hart, P.E., 'The dynamics of earnings, 1963–73,' *Economic J.* 86 (1976), 551–65.
64. Watt, D.C., 'Britain and North Sea oil: policies past and present,' *Political Q.* 47 (1976), 377–97.
65. Green, F.H.W., 'Recent changes in land use and treatment,' *Geographical J.* 142 (1976), 12–26.
66. Kolz, A.W.F., 'British economic interests in Siberia during the Russian civil war, 1918–1920,' *J. of Modern History* 48 (1976), 483–91.
67. Hawkins, K., *British industrial relations, 1945–1975.* London; Barrie & Jenkins; 1976. Pp 223.
68. Hannah, L. *The rise of the corporate economy.* London; Methuen; 1976. Pp xii, 243.
69. Klapper, C.F. *Roads and rails of London, 1900–1933.* London; Allan; 1976. Pp 191.
70. Lavington, S.H. *A history of Manchester computers.* Manchester; NCC Publications; 1975. Pp 45.

71. Shapiro, E., 'Cyclical fluctuations in prices and output in the United Kingdom, 1921–71,' *Economic J.* 86 (1976), 746–58.

(g) *Social Structure and Population*

1. Kohler, D.F. *Ethnic minorities in Britain: statistical data* (4th ed.). London; Community Relations Commission; 1975. Pp 23.
2. Waites, B.A., 'The effect of the first World War on class and status in England, 1910–20,' *J. of Contemporary History* 11 (1976), 27–48.
3. Longmate, N. *The GIs: the Americans in Britain, 1942–1945.* London; Hutchinson; 1975. Pp xv, 416.
4. Hall, D.N., 'Little Houghton 1972 – a parish field survey,' *Northamptonshire Past and Present* 5 (1976), 295–304.
5. Jones, J., 'Village life: Redbrook on Wye, 1914–1931,' *Presenting Monmouthshire* 40 (1975), 32–5.
6. Birtill, G. *'The changing years': Chorley and district between two wars.* Chorley; Guardian Press; 1976. Pp 100.
7. Cherry, G.E. *Environment planning, 1939–1969*; vol. 2: National Parks and recreation in the countryside. London; HMSO; 1975. Pp vii, 173.
8. Craig, J. *Population density and concentration in Great Britain, 1931, 1951 and 1961.* The Same; 1975. Pp 148.
9. Oddy, D.; Miller, D. (ed.). *The making of the modern British diet.* London; Croom Helm; 1976. Pp 235.
10. Meadows, D. *Living like this: around Britain in the seventies.* London; Arrow Books; 1975. Pp 128.
11. Woods, R., 'Aspects of the scale problem in the calculation of segregation indices: London and Birmingham, 1961 and 1971,' *Tijdschrift voor Economische en Sociale Geografie* 67 (1976), 169–74.
12. Marwick, A., 'People's war and top people's peace? British society and the Second World War,' Bc8, 148–64.
13. Nicolson, I.F.; Hughes, C.A., 'A provenance of proconsuls: British colonial governors 1900–1960,' *J. of Imperial and Commonwealth History* 4 (1976), 77–106.
14. Champion, A.G., 'Evolving patterns of population distribution in England and Wales, 1951–71,' *Institute of British Geographers T.* new ser. 1 (1976), 401–20.
15. Evans, G.E. *From mouths of men.* London; Faber; 1976. Pp 202.
16. Overy, R.J. *William Morris, viscount Nuffield.* London; Europa; 1976. Pp xlvi, 151.
17. Carson, J., 'A matter of policy: the lessons of recent British race relations legislation,' *Albion* 8 (1976), 154–77.

(h) *Social Policy*

1. Mishra, R., 'Convergence theory and social change: the development of welfare in Britain and the Soviet Union,' *Comparative Studies in Society and History* 18 (1976), 28—56.
2. Gray, P., 'Grangethorpe Hospital, Rusholme, 1917—1929,' *T. of the Lancashire and Cheshire Antiquarian Soc.* 78 (1975), 51—64.
3. Bourne, R., 'Going comprehensive in Greater London,' *London J.* 2 (1976), 85—95.
4. Fenwick, I.G.K. *The comprehensive school, 1944—1970 — the politics of secondary school reorganization.* London; Methuen; 1976. Pp xi, 187.
5. Davey, C.J. *Home from home: the story of Methodist Homes for the Aged.* London; Epworth Press; 1976. Pp 168.
6. Partington, G. *Women teachers in the twentieth century in England and Wales.* Windsor; NFER; 1976. Pp ix, 107.
7. Thomson, W.P.L. (ed.). *Kirkwall grammar school, from sang school to comprehensive.* Kirkwall; Education Committee; 1976. Pp 72.
8. Andrews, L. *The Education Act, 1918.* London; Routledge; 1976. Pp xii, 107.
9. Barren, C. *The history of the West Ham College of Technology.* London; Nelpress; 1976. Pp 77.
10. Thompson, A.L. *Half a century of medical research; vol. 2: the programme of the Medical Research Council (UK).* London; HMSO; 1975. Pp xii, 402.
11. Beardsley, E.H., 'Allied against sin: American and British responses to venereal disease in World War I,' *Medical History* 20 (1976), 189—202.

(i) *Naval and Military*

1. Pitcher, A. *'Promise and fulfil': fifty years of the Royal Air Force at Odiham.* [Basingstoke]; the author; [1975]. Pp 40.
2. King-Clark, R. *George Stuart Henderson: the story of a Scottish soldier, 1893—1920.* [Helensburgh; the author]; 1975. Pp 169.
3. Fussell, P. (ed.). *The ordeal of Alfred M. Hale: the memoirs of a soldier servant.* London; Cooper; 1975. Pp vi, 185.
4. Johnson, S. *Agents extraordinary.* London; Hale; 1975. Pp 195.
5. Knightley, P. *Lawrence of Arabia.* London; Sidgwick & Jackson; 1976. Pp 84.
6. Marder, A.J. *Operation 'Menace': the Dakar expedition and the Dudley North affair.* London; Oxford UP; 1976. Pp xxv, 289.
7. Ladd, J.D. *Assault from the sea, 1939—45: the craft, the landings, the men.* Newton Abbot; David & Charles; 1976. Pp 256.

8. Macintyre, D. *The battle for the Mediterranean* (revd. ed.). London; Severn House Publishers; 1975. Pp 216.

9. Jackson, W.G.F. *The North African campaign, 1940–43*. London; Batsford; 1975. Pp 402.

10. Baker, A.; Ivelaw-Chapman, R. *Wings over Kabul: the first airlift*. London; Kimber; 1975. Pp 191.

11. Townshend, C. *The British campaign in Ireland, 1919–1921: the development of political and military policies*. London; Oxford UP; 1975. Pp xiv, 242.

12. Lipscomb, F.W. *The British submarine* (2nd revd. ed.). Greenwich; Conway Maritime Press; 1975. Pp xiv, 284.

13. Mack, J.E. *A prince of our disorder: the life of T.E. Lawrence*. London; Weidenfeld & Nicolson; 1976. Pp xxviii, 561.

14. Grant, I.; Maddren, N. *The city at war*. London; Jupiter Books; 1975. Pp 128.

15. Grant, I.; Maddren. N. *The countryside at war*. The Same; 1975. Pp 128.

16. Parkinson, R. *The war in the desert*. London; Hart-Davis Mac-Gibbon; 1976. Pp 200.

17. Chalfont, A.L. (baron). *Montgomery of Alamein*. London; Weidenfeld & Nicolson; 1976. Pp xvi, 365.

18. Crookenden, N. *Dropzone Normandy: the story of the American and British airborne assault on D Day 1944*. London; Allan; 1976. Pp 304.

19. Tree, R.T. *When the moon was high: memoirs of peace and war, 1897–1942*. London; Macmillan; 1975. Pp 208.

20. Stanhope-Palmer, R. *Tank trap 1940, or, No battle in Britain*. Ilfracombe; Stockwell; 1976. Pp 205.

21. Winstone, H.V.F. *Captain Shakespear: a portrait*. London; Cape; 1976. Pp 236.

22. Robertson, B. *Beaufort special*. London; Allan; 1976. Pp 80.

23. Hoyt, E.P. *Disaster at the Dardanelles, 1915*. London; Barker; 1976. Pp viii, 166.

24. Sixsmith, E.K.G. *Douglas Haig*. London; Weidenfeld & Nicolson; 1976. Pp xi, 212.

25. Gleeson, J. *They feared no evil: the women agents of Britain's secret armies, 1939–45*. London; Hale; 1976. Pp 173.

26. Richards, D.; Saunders, H. St G. *Royal Air Force, 1939–45*; vol. 2: The fight avails (revised ed.). London; HMSO; 1975. Pp x, 415.

27. *The same*. Vol. 3: The fight is won (revised ed.). The same; 1975. Pp x, 441.

28. Smith, P.C. *Fighting flotilla: HMS Laforey and her sister ships*. London; Kimber; 1976. Pp 224.

29. Jackson, R. *Dunkirk: the British evacuation 1940*. London; Barker; 1976. Pp 206.

30. Terraine, J., 'The texture of the Somme 1916,' *History Today* 26 (1976), 559–68.
31. Watts, A.J. *The U-boat hunters.* London; Macdonald & Jane's; 1976. Pp 192.
32. Roskill, S.W. *Naval policy between the wars;* vol. 2: the period of reluctant rearmament 1930–1939. London; Collins; 1976. Pp 525.
33. Ginns, M.; Bryans, P. *The German fortifications in Jersey.* Grouville; W.M. Ginns etc. 1975. Pp v, 93.
34. Bowyer, C. *Sunderland at war.* London; Allan; 1976. Pp 160.
35. Duncan, B. *Invergordon '31: how the men of the RN struck and won.* Southampton; the author; 1976. Pp vi, 53.
36. Gobbs, N.H. *Grand strategy, vol. 1: Rearmament policy.* London; HMSO; 1976. Pp xxvi, 859.
37. Lewin, R. *Man of armour: a study of Lieut.-General Vyvyan Pope and the development of armoured warfare.* London; Cooper; 1976. Pp 152.
38. Mockler, A. *Our enemies the French: being an account of the war fought between the French and the British, Syria 1941.* London; Cooper; 1976. Pp xix, 252.
39. Sainsbury, K. *The North African landings, 1942: a strategic decision.* London; Davis-Poynter; 1976. Pp 215.
40. Wood, D. *Attack warning red: the Royal Observer Corps and the defence of Britain, 1925 to 1975.* London; Macdonald and Jane's; 1976. Pp xi, 357.
41. Middlebrook, M. *Convoy: the battle for convoys SC.122 and HX. 229.* London; Allen Lane; 1976. Pp x, 378.
42. Costello, J.; Hughes, T. *Jutland, 1916.* London; Weidenfeld & Nicolson; 1976. Pp 240.
43. Liddle, P. *Men of Gallipoli: the Dardanelles and Gallipoli experience, August 1914 to January 1916.* London; Allen Lane; 1976. Pp 320.
44. Powers, B.D. *Strategy without slide-rule: British air strategy, 1914–1939.* London; Croom Helm; 1976. Pp 295.
45. Howard, M.E., 'Total war in the twentieth century: participation and consensus in the Second World War,' Bc11, 216–26.
46. Bialer, U., 'The danger of bombardment from the air and the making of British air disarmament policy 1932–4,' Bc11, 202–15.
47. Keegan, J., 'Regimental ideology,' Bc10, 3–18.
48. Blair, P.E., 'Air power and appeasement,' Bc2, 159–78.
49. Goold, D., 'Lord Hardinge and the Mesopotamia expedition and enquiry, 1914–1917,' *Historical J.* 19 (1976), 919–45.

(j) *Intellectual and Cultural*

1. Fletcher, H.R. *A quest of flowers: the plant explorations of Frank*

Ludlow and George Sherriff, told from their diaries and other occasional writings. Edinburgh UP; 1975. Pp xxix, 387.

2. Sewell, B. *Cecil Chesterton.* Faversham; Saint Albert's Press; 1975. Pp xii, 107.

3. Niblett, W.R.; Humphreys, D.W.; Fairhurst, J.R. *The university connection* [i.e. of teachers' training colleges] . Windsor; NFER; 1975. Pp 300.

4. Green, M.B. *Children of the sun: a narrative of 'decadence' in England after 1918.* New York; Basic Books; 1976. Pp xxi, 470.

5. Beadle, G.B., 'George Orwell and the Victorian radical tradition,' *Albion* 7 (1975), 287–99.

6. Kelly, C.M. *The Brocks: a family of Cambridge artists and illustrators.* London; Skilton; 1975. Pp 184.

7. Buitenhuis, P., 'Writers at war: propaganda and fiction in the Great War,' *University of Toronto Q.* 45 (1976), 277–94.

8. Perry, G. *The great British picture show.* Frogmore; Paladin; 1975. Pp 367.

9. Perry, G. *Movies from the mansion: a history of Pinewood Studios.* London; Elm Tree Books; 1976. Pp 186.

J. MEDIEVAL WALES

(a) *General*

1. Rees, W. (ed.). *Calendar of ancient petitions relating to Wales: thirteenth to sixteenth century.* Cardiff; University of Wales Press; 1975. Pp xxxviii, 559.

2. Chadwick, N.K. *The British heroic age: the Welsh and the men of the north.* Cardiff; University of Wales Press; 1976. Pp xi, 125.

3. Kirby, D.P., 'British dynastic history in the pre-Viking period,' *B. of the Board of Celtic Studies* 27 (1976), 81–114.

(b) *Politics*

1. Robinson, W.R.B., 'The marcher lords of Wales 1525–1531,' *B. of the Board of Celtic Studies* 26 (1975), 342–52.

2. Miller, M., 'The commanders at Arthuret,' *T. of the Cumberland and Westmorland Antiquarian and Arch. Soc.* new ser. 75 (1975), 96–118.

3. Kirby, D.P., 'Hywel Idda: anglophil?,' *Welsh History R.* 8 (1976), 1–13.

4. Smith, J.B., 'Gruffyd Llwyd and the Celtic alliance, 1315–18,' *B. of the Board of Celtic Studies* 26 (1976), 463–78.

5. Smith, J.B., 'Edward II and the allegiance of Wales,' *Welsh History R.* 8 (1976), 139–71.

6. Griffiths, R.A., 'Richard, duke of York, and the royal household in Wales, 1449–50,' ibid. 14–25.
7. Kirby, D.P., 'British dynastic history in the pre-Viking period,' *B. of the Board of Celtic Studies* 27 (1976), 81–114.

(c) *Constitution, Administration and Law*

1. Reeves, A.C., 'The Great Session in the lordship of Newport in 1503,' *B. of the Board of Celtic Studies* 26 (1975), 323–41.
2. Jenkins, D., 'Kings, lords and princes: the nomenclature of authority in thirteenth-century Wales,' *B. of the Board of Celtic Studies* 26 (1976), 451–62.
3. Jenkins, D., '*Cynghellor* and chancellor,' *B. of the Board of Celtic Studies* 27 (1976), 115–8.

(d) *External Affairs*

(e) *Religion*

1. White, R. *Early Christian Gwynnedd*. [Bangor Cathedral]; 1975. Pp 16.
2. Williams, G. *The Welsh Church from conquest to Reformation* (revd. ed.). Cardiff; University of Wales Press; 1976.
3. Williams, D.H. *White monks in Gwent and the border*. Pontypool; Hughes & Son; 1976. Pp xii, 169.

(f) *Economic Affairs*

1. Smith, L.B., 'The gage and the land market in late medieval Wales,' *Economic History R.* 2nd ser. 29 (1976), 537–50.

(g) *Social Structure and Population*

1. Jones, G.R.J., 'Early territorial organization in Gwynedd and Elmet,' *Northern History* 10 (1975), 3–27.
2. Jones, F., 'Cadets of Golden Grove: Vaughan of Derwydd,' *T. of the Honourable Soc. of Cymmrodorion* 1975 (for 1974–5), 132–61.
3. Owen, D.H., 'The Englishry of Denbigh: an English colony in medieval Wales,' ibid. 57–76.
4. Davies, R., 'Race relations in post-conquest Wales: confrontation and compromise,' ibid. 32–56.
5. McDonald, R.W., 'Cofrestri plwyf Cymry,' *National Library of Wales J.* 19 (1975), 113–31.
6. Peate, I.C., 'The antiquity of leprosy in Wales,' *B. of the Board of Celtic Studies* 26 (1975), 361–2.

7. Williams-Jones, K. (ed.). *The Merioneth lay subsidy roll, 1292—3.* Cardiff; University of Wales Press; 1976. Pp cxliv, 136.

(h) *Naval and Military*

1. Taylor, A.J., 'Who was "John Pennardd, leader of the men of Gwynedd"?,' *English Historical R.* 91 (1976), 79—97.
2. Barber, W.T., 'The castles of the Monnow,' *Presenting Monmouthshire* 40 (1975), 37—43.
3. Moore, P. *Fonmon Castle, South Glamorgan: a residence occupied since the thirteenth century.* [Cardiff] ; Glamorgan Archive Service; 1976. Pp 34.
4. Walker, R.F., 'The Hagnaby Chronicle and the battle of Maes Moydog,' *Welsh History R.* 8 (1976), 125—38.

(i) *Intellectual and Cultural*

1. Bowen, D.J., 'Cywyddau Gruffudd Hiraethog i Dri O Awduron y Dadeni,' *T. of the Honourable Soc. of Cymmrodorion* 1975 (for 1974—5), 103—31.
2. Dumville, D.N., 'The origin of the C-text of the variant version of the *Historia Regum Britannie*,' *B. of the Board of Celtic Studies* 26 (1975), 315—22.
3. Bowen, D.J., 'Canu Gruffudd Hiraethog i Degeingl,' ibid., 281—304.
4. Winterbottom, M., 'The preface to Gildas' *De Excidio*,' *T. of the Honourable Soc. of Cymmrodorion* 1975 (for 1964—5), 277—87.
5. Jones, B.L. *Arhtur y Cymry* [The Welsh Arthur]. Cardiff; Gwasg Prifysgol Cymru; 1975. Pp 96.
6. Roberts, B.F., 'Geoffrey of Monmouth and Welsh historical tradition,' *Nottingham Mediaeval Studies* 20 (1976), 29—40.
7. Paul, L.D. *Music and Bangor Cathedral Church: some historical notes.* [Bangor Cathedral] ; 1975. Pp 24.

(j) *Topography*

1. Jones, H.G. *Place names in Glamorgan.* Risca; Starling Press; 1976. Pp 56.

K. SCOTLAND BEFORE THE UNION

See also Db3

(a) *General*

1. Bingham, C. *The kings and queens of Scotland.* London; Weidenfeld & Nicolson; 1976. Pp xv, 182.
2. Duncan, A.A.M. *Scotland: the making of the Kingdom* [Edinburgh History of Scotland, vol. 1]. Edinburgh; Oliver & Boyd; 1975. Pp xii, 705.
3. McNeill, P.; Nicholson, R. (ed.). *An historical atlas of Scotland, c. 400—c. 1600.* St Andrews; Conference of Scottish Medievalists; 1975. Pp x, 213.
4. MacKie, E.W. *Scotland: an archaeological guide, from earliest times to the 12th century A.D.* London; Faber; 1975. Pp 309.
5. Stone, J.C., 'A copy of Mercator's *Scotia Regnum* with manuscript annotation,' *Imago Mundi* 27 (1975), 43—6.

(b) *Politics*

1. Stevenson, D., 'The massacre at Dunaverty, 1647,' *Scottish Studies* 19 (1975), 27—37.
2. Cowan, I.B. *The Scottish Covenanters, 1660—1688.* London; Gollancz; 1976. Pp 191.
3. Drummond, H. *The queen's man: James Hepburn, earl of Bothwell and duke of Orkney, 1536—1578.* London; Frewin; 1975. Pp 193.
4. Rubinstein, H.L. *Captain Luckless: James, first duke of Hamilton, 1606—1649.* Edinburgh; Scottish Academic Press; 1975. Pp xii, 307.
5. Watson, G. *Bothwell and the witches.* London; Hale; 1975. Pp 205.
6. Williams, R. *Montrose: cavalier in mourning.* London; Barrie & Jenkins; 1975. Pp xiii, 443.
7. Duncan, A.A.M., 'The battle of Carham, 1018,' *Scottish Historical R.* 55 (1976), 20—8.
8. Meehan, B., 'The siege of Durham, the battle of Carham and the cession of Lothian,' ibid. 1—19.
9. Duncan, A.A.M. *James I, 1424—1437.* University of Glasgow; History Department; 1976. Pp 27.
10. Barrow, G.W.S., 'Lothian in the first war of independence,' *Scottish Historical R.* 55 (1976), 151—71.
11. Cadell, P. *Sudden slaughter: the murder of the regent Moray.* Edinburgh; West Lothian History and Amenity Soc.; 1975. Pp 21.
12. Grant, A., 'Earls and earldoms in late medieval Scotland (c. 1310—1460), Bc2, 24—40.

13. Kirby, D.P., ' . . . *per universas Pictorum provincias*,' Dc3, 286–324.

(c) *Constitution, Administration and Law*

1. Robertson, A.D. *Lanark: the burgh and its councils, 1469–1880.* Lanark Town Council; 1974 [i.e. 1975]. Pp viii, 383.
2. Pinkerton, J.M. (ed.). *The minute book of the Faculty of Advocates*; vol. 1: 1661–1712. Edinburgh; Stair Society; 1976. Pp xxi, 310.
3. Lee, M. Jr., 'James VI's government of Scotland after 1603,' *Scottish Historical R.* 55 (1976), 41–53.
4. Madden, C., 'Royal treatment of feudal casualties in late medieval Scotland,' ibid. 172–94.

(d) *External Affairs*

(e) *Religion*

1. Foster, W.R. *The Church before the Covenants: the Church of Scotland, 1596–1638.* Edinburgh; Scottish Academic Press; 1975. Pp viii, 216.
2. Holmes, N.M.McQ., 'Excavations within the Tron Kirk, Edinburgh, 1974,' *Post-Medieval Archaeology* 9 (1975), 137–63.
3. Cant, R.G. *The medieval churches and chapels of Shetland.* Lerwick; Shetland Arch. and Historical Soc.; 1975. Pp 50.
4. Cowan, I.B.; Easson, D.E. *Medieval religious houses, Scotland, with an appendix on the houses in the Isle of Man* (2nd ed.). London; Longman; 1976. Pp xxviii, 252.
5. Macdiarmid, H.; Maclean, C.; Ross, A. *John Knox.* Edinburgh; Ramsay Head Press; 1976. Pp 96.
6. Ash, M., 'The diocese of St Andrews under its "Norman" bishops,' *Scottish Historical R.* 55 (1976), 105–26.
7. Ash, M., 'Dairsie and Archbishop Spottiswoode,' *Records of the Scottish Church Historical Soc.* 19 (1976), 125–32.
8. Marshall, J.S., 'Scottish trade incorporations and the Church,' ibid. 93–109.
9. Scott, P.G., 'James Blair and the Scottish Church,' *William and Mary Q.* 3rd ser. 33 (1976), 300–8.
10. Shead, N.F., 'The administration of the diocese of Glasgow in the twelfth and thirteenth centuries,' *Scottish Historical R.* 55 (1976), 127–50.
11. Sefton, H.R., 'The Scottish bishops and Archbishop Arsenius,' Bc4, 239–46.

(f) *Economic Affairs*

1. Dodshon, R.A., 'Farming in Roxburghshire and Berwickshire on the eve of improvement,' *Scottish Historical R.* 44 (1975), 140–54.
2. Skinner, B.C., 'The archaeology of the lime industry in Scotland,' *Post-Medieval Archaeology* 9 (1975), 225–30.

(g) *Social Structure and Population*

1. Dodgshon, R.A., 'Scandinavian "Solskifte" and the sunwise division of land in eastern Scotland,' *Scottish Studies* 19 (1975), 1–14.
2. Parry, M.L., 'County maps as historical sources: a sequence of surveys in south-east Scotland,' ibid. 15–26.
3. Whyte, I.D., 'Rural housing in lowland Scotland in the seventeenth century: the evidence of estate papers,' ibid. 55–68.

(h) *Naval and Military*

(i) *Intellectual and Cultural*

1. Campbell, J.L. (ed.). *A collection of Highland rites and customes: copied by Edward Lhuyd from the manuscript of the Rev. James Kirkwood (1650–1709) and annotated by him with the aid of the Rev. John Beaton.* Cambridge; D.S. Brewer; 1975. Pp 117.
2. Cameron, J.K.; Smart, R.N., 'A Scottish form of the Embleme de la Religion Reformee: the post-Reformation seal of St Mary's College in the University of St Andrews,' *P. of the Soc. of Antiquaries of Scotland* 105 (1975 for 1972/4), 248–54.
3. Sutherland, J., 'The heraldic ceiling of Balbegno Castle,' *Aberdeen University Review* 46 (1976), 268–73.
4. Enright, M.J., 'King James and his island: an archaic kingship belief?,' *Scottish Historical R.* 55 (1976), 29–40.

L. IRELAND TO c. 1640

See also: Aa61; Da8, f5; Fi16.

(a) *General*

1. Moody, T.W.; Martin, F.X.; Byrne, F.J. (ed.). *A new history of Ireland. III: Early Modern Ireland, 1534–1691.* Oxford; Clarendon; 1976. Pp xliv, 736.
2. Moody, T.W., 'Early modern Ireland,' La1, pp. xxxix–lxiii.

3. Quinn, D.B.; Nicholls, K.W., 'Ireland in 1534,' La1, 1—38.
4. Simms, J.G., 'Bibliography,' La1, 634—96.

(b) *Politics*

1. Mac Niocaill, G., 'The background of the battle of Tarbga,'
   Celtica 11 (1976), 133—40.
2. Clarke, A., 'Selling royal favours, 1624—32,' La1, 233—42.
3. Clarke, A., 'The government of Wentworth, 1632—40,' La1, 243—69.
4. Clarke, A., 'The breakdown of authority, 1640—61,' La1, 270—89.
5. Clarke, A.; Edwards, R.D., 'Pacification, plantation and the
   Catholic question,' La1, 187—232.
6. Dolley, M.; Moore, C.N., 'Some reflections on the English coin-
   ages of Sihtric Caoch, king of Dublin and York,' *British Numismatic J.* 43 (1976 for 1973), 45—59.
7. Smyth, P.A., 'Húi Failgi relations with the Húi Néill, in the century after the loss of the Plain of Mide,' *Etudes celtiques* 14
   (1975), 503—23.
8. Ellis, S.G., 'The Kildare rebellion and the early Henrician Reformation,' *Historical J.* 19 (1976), 807—30.
9. Warren, W.L., 'John in Ireland, 1185,' Bc2, 11—23.

(c) *Constitution, Administration and Law*

1. Binchy, A.A., *'Fechem, fethem, aigne,'* *Celtica* 11 (1976), 18—33.
2. Canny, N. *The Elizabethan conquest of Ireland: a pattern estab-
   lished, 1565—1576.* Hassocks; Harvester Press; 1976. Pp xii, 205.

(d) *External Affairs*

(e) *Religion*

1. Bottigheimer, K.S., 'The Reformation in Ireland revisited,'
   [review article], *J. of British Studies* 15 (1976), 140—9.
2. Edwards, R.D., 'Ecclesiastical appointments in the province of
   Tuam, 1399—1477,' *Archivium Hibernicum* 33 (1975), 91—100.
3. Kilroy, P., 'Sermon and pamphlet literature in the Irish reformed
   Church, 1613—34,' ibid. 110—21.
4. Lennon, C., 'Recusancy and the Dublin Stanyhursts,' ibid. 101—9.
5. Ryan, C., 'Religion and state in seventeenth-century Ireland,' ibid.
   122—32.
6. Dolley, M., 'Roman coins from Ireland and the date of St Patrick,'
   P. of the Royal Irish Academy 76 C (1976), 181—90.
7. Giblin, C., 'Francis MacDonnell, OFM, son of the first earl of
   Antrim (d. 1636),' *Seanchas Ardmhacha* 8 (1975—6), 44—54.

8. Gwynn, A., 'The problem of the *Dicta Patricii*,' ibid. 69—80.
9. Hayes,McCoy, G.A., 'The royal supremacy and ecclesiastical revolution, 1534—47,' La1, 39—68.
10. Hayes-McCoy, G.A., 'Conciliation, coercion and the Protestant Reformation,' La1, 69—93.
11. Hayes-McCoy, G.A., 'The completion of the Tudor conquest and the advance of the Counter-Reformation, 1571—1603,' La1, 94—141.

(f) *Economic Affairs*

1. Clarke, A., 'The Irish economy, 1600—1660,' La1, 168—86.
2. Connolly, P., 'The Irish Memoranda Rolls: some unexplored aspects,' *Irish Economic and Social History* 3 (1976), 66—74.
3. Dolley, M., 'A Hiberno-Manx coinage of the eleventh century,' *Numismatic Chronicle* 7th ser. 16 (1976), 75—84.
4. Dolley, M., 'The Irish coinage, 1534—1691,' La1, 408—19.
5. Dolley, M., 'A further find of fused coins from Rahans Lough, Magheracloone,' *Clogher Record* (1976), 76—7.

(g) *Social Structure and Population*

1. Charles-Edwards, T.M., 'The social background to Irish *peregrinatio*,' *Celtica* 11 (1976), 43—59.
2. Stone, R.C., 'Ulcombe, Ireland and the St. Legers,' *Archaeologia Cantiana* 91 (1975), 111—17.
3. Thomas, A., 'Drogheda, 1574,' *J. of the County Louth Arch. and Historical Soc.* 18 (1976 for 1975), 179—86.
4. Butlin, R.A., 'Land and people c. 1600,' La1, 142—67.
5. Charles-Edwards, T.M., 'Boundaries in Irish Law,' Bc15, 83—7.
6. Barrett, G.E.; Graham, B.J., 'Some considerations concerning the dating and distribution of ring-forts in Ireland,' *Ulster J. of Archaeology* 3rd ser. 38 (1975), 33—47.

(h) *Naval and Military*

1. McNeil, T.E., 'Ulster mottes: a checklist,' *Ulster J. of Archaeology* 3rd ser. 38 (1975), 49—56.

(i) *Intellectual and Cultural*

1. Bieler, L., 'Hagiography and romance in medieval Ireland,' *Medievalia et Humanistica* new series, 6 (1975), 13—24.
2. Harbison, P. *The archaeology of Ireland.* London; Bodley Head; 1976. Pp 120.
3. Heist, W.W., 'Irish saints' lives, romance and cultural history.' *Medievalia et Humanistica* new series, 6 (1976), 25—40.

4. Mould, D.D.C.P. *The monasteries of Ireland: an introduction.* London; Batsford; 1976. Pp 188.
5. Hall, R.A., 'A Viking grave in Phoenix Park, Co. Dublin,' *J. of the Royal Soc. of Antiquaries of Ireland* 104 (1976 for 1974), 39—43.
6. Maguire, J.B., 'Seventeenth century plans of Dublin Castle,' ibid. 5—14.
7. Bateson, J.D., 'Further finds of Roman materials from Ireland,' *P. of the Royal Irish Academy* 76 C (1976), 171—80.
8. Bliss, A., 'The development of the English language in early modern Ireland,' La1, 546—60.
9. Fanning, T., 'Excavations at Clontuskert priory, Co. Galway,' *P. of the Royal Irish Academy* 76 C (1976), 97—169.
10. Millett, B., 'Irish literature in Latin, 1550—1700,' La1, 561—86.
11. Ó Cuív, B., 'The Irish language in the early modern period,' La1, 509—45.
12. Ó Gallchóir, N., 'Aodh Mac Aingil, Gael san Eoraip (1571—1626) [An Irishman in Europe],' *Seanchas Ardmhacha* 8 (1975—6), 81—96.
13. Ó Riain, P., 'The composition of the Irish section of the calendar of saints,' *Dinnseanchas* 6 (1976 for 1975), 77—92.
14. Rynne, E., 'The La Tène and Roman finds from Lambay, County Dublin: a re-assessment,' *P. of the Royal Irish Academy* 76 C (1976), 231—44.
15. Silke, J.J., 'The Irish abroad in the age of the Counter-Reformation,' La1, 587—633.
16. Thomas, C., 'Imported late-Roman Mediterranean pottery in Ireland and western Britain: chronologies and implications,' *P. of the Royal Irish Academy* 76 C (1976), 245—55.
17. Warner, R.B., 'Some observations on the context and importation of exotic material in Ireland, from the first century B.C. to the second century A.D.,' ibid. 267—92.

M. IRELAND SINCE c. 1640

See also: Aa61, 65; Ic6

(a) *General*

1. Coogan, T.P., *The Irish: a personal view.* London; Phaidon; 1975. Pp 232.
2. Feldman, D.; Kane, W. *Handbook of Irish postal history, to 1840.* Dublin; D. Feldman Ltd.; 1975. Pp xi, 131.
3. Lebow, R.N. *White Britain and Black Ireland: the influence of*

stereotypes on colonial policy. Philadelphia; Institute for the study of Human Issues; 1976. Pp 152.

4. Martin, G.W., 'The Irish Free State and the evolution of the Commonwealth,' Hd12, 201–23.

(b) *Politics*

1. Target, G.W. *Bernadette: the story of Bernadette Devlin.* London; Hodder & Stoughton; 1975. Pp 384.
2. Owens, R. *Votes for women: Irish women's struggle for the vote.* Dublin; A.D.S. Skeffington & R. Owens; [1975]. Pp 27.
3. *What happened on the Twelfth?* Belfast; The Workers' Association; [1975]. Pp 14.
4. *British strategy in Northern Ireland: from the white paper to the fall of Sunningdale.* Dublin; Revolutionary Marxist Group; [?1975]. Pp 39.
5. Van Voris, W.H. *Violence in Ulster: an oral documentary.* Amherst; University of Massachusetts Press; 1975. Pp x, 326.
6. Hull, R.H. *The Irish triangle: conflict in Northern Ireland.* Princeton UP; 1976. Pp ix, 312.
7. O'Brien, J.V. *William O'Brien and the course of Irish politics, 1881–1918.* Berkeley; University of California Press; 1976. Pp xiii, 273.
8. Utley, T.E. *Lessons of Ulster.* London; Dent; 1975. Pp 154.
9. Foster, R.F. *Charles Stewart Parnell: the man and his family.* Hassocks; Harvester Press; 1976. Pp xx, 403.
10. Murphy, M., 'Municipal reform and the repeal movement in Cork, 1833–1844,' *J. of the Cork Historical and Arch. Soc.* 81 (1976), 1–18.
11. Rose, R. *Northern Ireland: a time of choice.* London; Macmillan; 1976. Pp 175.
12. Darby, J. *Conflict in Northern Ireland: the development of a polarised community.* Dublin; Gill & Macmillan; 1976. Pp xix, 268.
13. O'Connell, M.R., 'Daniel O'Connell and the Irish eighteenth century,' Bc13, 475–95.
14. Stewart, A.T.Q., ' "A stable unseen power": Dr William Drennan and the origins of the United Irishmen,' Bc2, 80–92.

(c) *Constitution, Administration and Law*

1. Greer, D.S.; Childs, B.A. (ed.). *Index to cases decided in the courts of Northern Ireland and reported during the period 1921–1970.* Belfast; Incorporated Council of Law Reporting for Northern Ireland; 1975. Pp xi, 303.

(d) *External Affairs*

1. D'Angelo, G. *Italy and Ireland in the 19th century: contacts and misunderstandings between two national movements.* Athlone; St Paul Publications; 1975. Pp 56.
2. Hopkinson, M.H., 'Irish Americans and the Anglo-Irish treaty of 1921,' Bc2, 133—45.

(e) *Religion*

1. Larkin, E., 'Church state and nation in modern Ireland,' *American Historical R.* 80 (1975), 1244—76.
2. Mawhinney, B.; Wells, R. *Conflict and Christianity in Northern Ireland.* Berkhamsted; Lion Publishing; 1975. Pp 128.
3. Fenning, H., 'The Irish Dominican Province at the beginning of its decline (1745—1761),' *Archivum Fratrum Preadicatorum* 45 (1975), 399—502.
4. Hill, J.R., 'Nationalism and the Catholic Church in the 1840s,' *Irish Historical Studies* 19 (1975), 371—95.
5. Mac Giolla Phadraig, B., 'Dr John Carpenter, archbishop of Dublin, 1760—1786,' *Dublin Historical Record* 30 (1976), 2—17.

(f) *Economic Affairs*

1. Simpson, N. *The Belfast Bank, 1827—1970: 150 years of banking in Ireland.* Belfast; Blackstaff Press; 1975. Pp xiii, 365.
2. Longfield, A.K. (Mrs Leask), 'Irish linen for Spain and Portugal: James Archbold's letters 1771—79,' *P. of the Royal Irish Academy* 76 (1976), 13—22.
3. Lowe, W.J., 'Landlord and tenant on the estate of Trinity College, Dublin, 1851—1903,' *Hermathena* 120 (1976), 5—24.
4. Daniel, T.K., 'Griffith and his noble head: the determining of Cumann na nGaedheal economic policy 1922—32,' *Irish Economic and Social History* 3 (1976), 55—65.
5. Donnelly, J.S., 'The Irish agricultural depression of 1859—64,' ibid. 33—54.
6. Maguire, W.A., 'Lord Donegall and the sale of Belfast: a case history from the Encumbered Estates Court,' *Economic History R.* 2nd ser. 29 (1976), 570—84.
7. Maguire, W.A., 'The 1822 settlement of the Donegall estates,' *Irish Economic and Social History* 3 (1976), 17—32.
8. Greig, W. *General report on the Gosford estates in county Armagh 1821* (with an introduction by F.M.L. Thompson and D. Tierney). Belfast; HMSO; 1976. Pp xi, 244.
9. Lees, L., 'Mid-Victorian migration and the Irish family economy,' *Victorian Studies* 20 (1976), 25—43.

(g) *Social structure and population*

1. Beames, M.R., 'Peasant movements: Ireland, 1758—95,' *J. of Peasant Studies* 2 (1975), 502—6.
2. Feingold, W.L., 'The tenants' movement to capture the Irish Poor Law Boards, 1877—1886,' *Albion* 7 (1975), 216—31.
3. Clarke, R.S.J. *Gravestone inscriptions*; vol. 15: County Down, barony of Ard. Belfast; Ulster Historical Foundation; 1975. Pp viii, 201.
4. Ross, N., 'Families at Mosstown and Philipstown in 1852,' *J. of the County Louth Arch. and Historical Soc.* 18 (1976 for 1975), 232—7.
5. Pobal, A. *Cashel and Emly census of population, 1841—1971.* Durlas; [The Archdiocese of Cashel and Emly]; 1975. Pp 121.
6. Steele, E.D., 'The Irish presence in the north of England, 1850—1914,' *Northern History* 12 (1976), 220—41.
7. Griffin, W.D., 'The Irish on the continent in the eighteenth century,' Bc13, 453—73.

(h) *Naval and Military*

1. Styles, G. *Bombs have no pity; my war against terrorism* [as told to Bob Perrin]. London; Luscombe; 1975. Pp 187.
2. Bowden, T., 'The IRA and the changing tactics of terrorism,' *Political Q.* 47 (1976), 425—37.
3. Beckett, J.C., 'The Irish armed forces, 1660—1685,' Bc2, 41—53.

(i) *Intellectual and Cultural*

1. Dixon, H. *An introduction to Ulster architecture.* Belfast; Ulster Architectural Heritage Soc.; 1975. Pp vii, 93.
2. Chinnéide, Síle ní, 'A view of Kilkenny, city and county, in 1790,' *J. of the Royal Soc. of Antiquaries of Ireland* 104 (1976 for 1974), 29—38.
3. Beckett, J.C. *The Anglo-Irish tradition.* London; Faber; 1976. Pp 159.
4. Seaby, W.A.; Brady, G., 'The extant Ormonde pistoles and double pistoles of 1646,' *British Numismatic J.* 43 (1976 for 1973), 80—95.
5. Pettit, S.F., 'The Royal Cork Institution: a reflection of the cultural life of a city,' *J. of the Cork Historical and Arch. Soc.* 81 (1976), 70—90.

AUTHOR INDEX

Cheney, M., Ei94

Cherry, B., Bb75; Df17

Cherry, G.E., Ig7

Cherry, J., Aa36, b19

Chibnall, M., Ac27

Childs, B.A., Mc1

Childs, E.L., Ei112

Childs, H., Hi25

Childs, J., Fi10

Chinnéide, Síle ní, Mi2

Chitty, E., Bd9

Chivers, K., Ba58

Christianson, P., Fc10

Christie, I.R., Gb13

Clancy, T.H., Fe61

Clark, C., Ei15

Clark, C.O., Aa46

Clark, G., Gh12

Clark, M.E., Gd1

Clark, P., Fh7

Clark, S., Fe4

Clarke, A., Lb2–5, f1

Clarke, D., Bb96

Clarke, R.S.J., Mg3

Clarkson, L.A., Ba21

Clay, E., Hl72

Clayton, P., Ab38

Clemens, P.G.E., Ff8

Clemoes, P., Da6, e1

Clifford, T., Gi3

Clifton-Taylor, A., Ba40

Clinker, C.R., Ab30

Clives, S.W., Hg18

Clogan, P.M., Bc1

Close-Brooks, J., Ca61

Clough, T.H.McK., Da7

Clutton-Brock, J., Df14; Gk1

Coad, J., Aa36

Coats, A.W., Fg20

Cobban, A.B., Ei88

Cochrane, H., Bb59

Cockburn, J.S., Fc14, 15

Cocke, T.H., Gi44

Cockerell, H.A.L., Ba63

Cohen, M., Fk53

Cohen, Michael, Id29

Coldstream, N., Ei56

Cole, H., Eh1

Coleman, D.C., Bc9; Ff32

Coleman, J., Ei25

Coleman, O., Ef17

Coleman, W., Ge2

Colledge, E., Ee34, i24

Collini, S., Hl54

Collins, E.J.T., Hf4

Colls, R., Hi33

Colthart, J.M., Hd28

Colyer, C., Ca39

Colyer, R.J., Gf49; Hf103

Compton-Reeves, A., Ee6

Conlee, J.W., Ee25

Connolly, P., Lf2

Connolly, S.J., Aa72

Constable, F., Gi4

Contamine, P., Eg20

Conte, F., Id13

Conwick, C.C., Gb18

Coogan, T.P., Ma1

Cook, C., Aa1; Bc8; Hb58; Ib24

Cooke, A., Hg5

Coopland, G.W., Ed6

Cooter, R.J., Fe63; Hk27

Corder, J., Bd7

Corfield, P., Fh14

Cornwall, J., Fb37

Corsten, S., Ei119

Cosgrove, R.A., Hc3

Costello, J., Ii42

Cottrell, P.L., Hf56

Coulson, J., Hi6

Course, E., Hf57

Courtney, T., Bb64

Courtney, T.W., Fi11

Cousins, P.F., Ib25

Cowan, I.B., Kb2, e4

Cowell, F.R., Hg7

Cowie, L.W., Bb87; Fk4

Cox, D.C., Ei103

Cox, Margaret, Ia1

Cox, Marjorie, Bb37

Crafts, N.F.R., Ff10; Gf22

Cragg, G.R., Ge8

Craig, D., Hf30

Craig, F.W.S., Ic5

Frankforter, A.D., Aa78
Franklin, J., Hg10
Franks, D.L., Hf60
Franzero, C.M., Ia7
Fraser, D., Hh2
Fraser, J.L., Gi47
Fredeman, W.E., Hl59
Frederiksen, M., Hl72
Freedland, M.R., If54
Frere, S.S., Ca25
Freshwater, P.B., Ab1, 47
Fritz, P., Gb5
Fronville, M., Fb15
Frow, E., If12
Frow, R., If12
Fryde, E.B., Ef9
Fulford, M., Ca7
Fulford, R., Hl55
Fussell, G.E., Ba36; Gf9

Gadney, R., Gi7
Gale, W.K.V., Gf52
Galgano, M.J., Ff13
Gant, R.L., Ac19; Hf24
Gardiner, D., Eh16
Gardiner, G., Ib1
Garlick, T., Ca53
Garrett, C., Ge18
Garrett, R., Gh38
Garside, P.D., Ac5
Garside, W.R., If48
Garson, R., Id34
Gash, N., Hb25
Gaskin, J.C.A., Ge27
Gatch, M.McC., De3
Gauldie, E., Hf72
Geddes, R.S., Bb99
Gee, J.M.A., Gi14
Gelling, M., Ac32; Da5
Gentles, I., Fg3, h28
George, W.R.P., Hb74
Gervers, M., Ei28
Gibbs, N.H., Ii36
Giblin, C., Le7
Gibson, J., Fg6
Gibson, J.S.W., Gi26
Gibson, M.T., Ei1

Gilbert, A.D., Ge19
Gilbert, A.N., Gh14, 15, 26, 27
Gilbert, M., Ib37
Gilbert, V.F., Aa40
Gill, J., Ba54
Gill, M.A.V., Dd6
Gilchrist, G., Gg1
Gillingham, J.B., Fi24
Ginns, M., Ii33
Girouard, M., Hg14
Gleason, M.R., Fb11
Gleeson, J., Ii25
Glover, J., Bb11
Glover, M., Gi27
Glynn, Sean, Ia19
Godber, J., Bb100
Godfrey, E.S., Ff12
Goff, M., Gi48
Golden, J., Aa76
Goldsmith, V.F., Ab29
Gollin, A., Hb39
Gooch, J., Hj23
Goodburn, R., Ca66
Goode, C.T., Hf32
Goodey, C., Hf84
Goodhart, P., Ic14
Goodman, J.F.B., If59
Goold, D., Ii49
Gootzeit, M.J., Gi8
Gornall, T., He14, 15
Gough, J.W., Fj13
Gourvish, T.R., Gf10
Graham, A.H., Hb67
Graham, B.J., Lg6
Graham, G.S., Gh16
Graham, N.H., Bd10
Graham, R.A., Id6
Graham-Campbell, J., Ca3
Grampp, W.D., Hf78
Gransden, A., Ac7; Ei89
Grant, A., Kb12
Grant, I., Ii14, 15
Grant, N., Bb3
Graves, E.B., Aa41
Graves, R.P., Ia20
Gray, Adrian, Hf35
Gray, Alexander, Gi49

147

Merrington, W.R., Hk13
Merton Jones, A.C., If30
Metcalf, D.M., Ab16; Dd3
Mews, S., Id6, 8
Meyer, B.H., Fk44
Meyer, J., Aa44
Meyers, R., Id31
Meyvaert, P., De7
Michell, R., Hg4
Middlebrook, M., Ii41
Middleton, G.E., Hk4
Middleton, N., Ba11
Middleton, T., Bb105
Miers, S., Gf30
Milburn, G.E., He12, 21
Miles, T.J., Ei54
Mill, J.S., Hb63
Miller, D., Ig9
Miller, Edward, Ef3
Miller, Ellice, Hi4
Miller, F.M., If41
Miller, M., Cb3; Db3; Jb2
Millett, B., Li10
Millett, M., Ca21
Mills, D., Bb110
Mills, D.R., Hg22
Millward, R., If40
Milsom, S.F.C., Ec15
Minchinton, W.E., Hj8
Miner, E., Fk51
Miners, H., Bb106
Minsky, H.P., If1
Mishra, R., Ih1
Mitchell, J.F., Ab3
Mitchell, W.R., Hf62
Mockler, A., Ii38
Moggridge, D.E., If26
Money, E., Ib16
Money, J., Gi59
Moody, T.W., La1, 2
Moon, P., Id20
Moorby, R.L., Hf68
Moore, C.N., Ca20; Lb6
Moore, D., Ga9
Moore, D.C., Gb11
Moore, J.T., Fj12
Moore, P., Jh3

Moran, J., Ei124
More, Sir T., Fk50
Morgan, A., Aa54
Morgan, D., Hc10
Morgan, F.C., Aa16
Morgan, K.O., Hb70
Morgan, P., Fk57
Morgan, P.T.J., Fe4
Morgan, R., Aa25
Morgan, V., Bb112
Morley, P., Ff34
Morrah, P., Fi25
Morrill, J.S., Fb3, c13
Morris, C., Fa3
Morris, J., Ea4, 5
Morris, J.A., Bb107
Morris, M., If42
Morris, R.J., Hk29
Morrison, A., Bd6
Morriss, R.A., Gh43
Morton, A.L., Fj8
Mosley, N., Ha4
Mould, D.D.C.P., Li4
Mountfield, D., Gf13
Mowat, R.J.C., Ca47
Munby, A.N.L., Hl63
Munby, J., Ca6, 22
Munson, J.E.B., Hi17
Murphy, M., Mb10
Murray, I.G., Fg32
Musset, L., Db1
Mussett, N.J., Hf62
Musson, A.E., Hb6, f7, 47, h8
Musty, J., Ca45
Myall, D.G.A., Hf68
Myres, N.J.L., Df4

Napoleoni, C., Gi14
Nash, A., Hl5
Nash, D., Cb14
Nathanson, A.J., Ff6
Nau, L.T., Ei45
Naughton, K.S., Eg8
Neal, W.K., Gh44
Neale, K., Hg15
Neave, D., Gh31
Nelson, J.P., Bb44

151

Patterson, A.T., Bb67
Paul, L.D., Ji7
Pawling, C., If44
Pawson, E., Gf31
Payne, E.A., Ge21
Peacock, S.E., Hc4
Pearce, B., Ib12
Pearce, C., Hb5
Pearsall, D., Ei100
Pearsall, R., Hg59
Peaston, A.E., Ge22
Peate, I.C., Jg6
Peck, L.L., Fc29
Peeke, C., Ge4
Pedersen, J.S., Hi7
Pelling, H., Ib38
Pemble, J., Gh45
Peña, N., Ed3
Penny, N.B., Gb7; Hl53
Pepper, J.V., Fk14
Percival, A., Fk40
Percival, R., Fk40
Percy, F.H.G., Bb54
Perkin, H.J., Hg9; Ia25
Perkins, E.J., Gf15
Perkins, J.A., Hf50
Peroni, R., Hg35
Perry, G., Ij8, 9
Petchey, M.R., Ei63
Petrie, C.A., Hg49
Pettit, S.F., Mi5
Petty, G.R., Db5
Petty, S., Db5
Pevsner, N., Bb75
Philip, I.G., Bc7
Phillips, D., Hf63
Phillips, E.J., Ca10, 33
Phillips, G.A., If6
Phillips, R.J., Hc8
Phythian-Adams, C., Ac9
Pickles, M.F., Gg10
Piggin, S., He25
Pigott, S., Hf45
Pineas, R., Fe2
Pinkerton, J.M., Kc2
Pinnington, J.E., He20
Piper, A.J., Ec24

Pistono, S.P., Ed13, 14
Pitcher, A., Iil
Platt, C., Eg1, j26
Pobal, A., Mg5
Pocock, J.G.A., Ac6; Fj9, 17
Pococke, T., Gh9
Pollard, A.J., Eb3
Pollard, G., Ei3
Pollard, S., Hf75
Ponting, K.G., Gf44
Popham, F.W., Bb120
Port, M.H., Ba64; Hl70
Porter, B., Hd6
Porter, E., Hg16
Porter, J., Hf43
Porter, S., Ab20
Portergill, J., Bb78
Post, J.B., Ec7
Postles, D., Ef12
Potter, K.R., Eb1
Potts, W.T.W., Ba71
Poulton, R., Hb10
Pound, J.F., Fh5
Powell, J.R., Fi8
Powers, B.D., Ii44
Pratt, G.D., Ei52
Pratt, L.R., Id7
Prestwich, M., Ec3
Price, D., Ha9
Pride, E., Hg12
Pridmore, F., Ba1
Pryce-Jones, J.E., Aa73
Prynn, D., Hg23
Pugh, R.B., Ec12, 17; f4
Purdue, A.W., Hb16

Quill, H., Gk8
Quinault, R.E., Hb22
Quinn, D.B., Fd6, 8; La3

Rackham, O., Ba60
Radford, C.A.R., Df7
Rae, T.I., Aa21, 79
Raeburn, A., Hb9
Raftis, J.A., Eg17
Rahtz, P., Df19; Ee18
Raistrick, A., Bb53

Walthew, C.V., Ca5
Walton, J.R., Hl50
Walton, M., Bb8; Fb12
Ward, B., Dc6
Ward, J.M., Gd3
Ward, R., Hc6
Ward, W.R., He23
Ward Dyer, F.J., Hf68
Wardle, D., Ba57
Ware, K., Ge33
Warn, C.R., Hf88
Warner, O., Ba18
Warner, R.B., Li17
Warren, K., Hf20
Warren, W.L., Ac1; Lb9
Warwick, L., Gi27
Wasserstein, B., Id39
Waters, I., Bb18
Waterworth, W.E., Hg20
Watkins, G., Ba45
Watkinson, M., Fg24
Watney, J., Gf62
Watson, A.G., Ei106, 107
Watson, G., Kb5
Watson, G.E., Gd11
Watson, H., If24
Watson, J.W., Gi60
Watson, R., Bb49
Watt, D.C., Ac25; If64
Watts, A.J., Ii31
Watts, U.E., Ac32
Wazink, J.H., Fk56
Weaver, L.T., Bb19, 38
Webb, I., Hl69
Webb, W., Ba49
Webster, C., Fk13
Webster, G., Cb7
Webster, P.V., Ca8
Weeks, J., Hg61
Weigall, D., Fj7
Weinbaum, M., Ec11
Weinberger, J., Fj14
Weiner, A.D., Fk2
Weinroth, H., Id9
Weinstein, M.F., Fb46
Weiss, M., Eb22, 27
Weitzman, A.J., Ga5

Weitzmann, S., Ba11
Welch, M.G., Df4
Welland, D., Hl11
Wells, A.P., Ed8
Wells, C., Ca2
Wells, R., Me2
Wernham, R.B., Fk17
Wertz, S.K., Gi20
West, T., Ba20
Western, H.G., Bb35
Westfall, R.S., Fk5
Westman, B.A. Hanawalt, Ec22, 23
Whale, J., Ib40
Wheare, K.C., Hb13
Wheatcroft, A., Bc10
Whetham, E.H., If32
Whitcut, J., Hi10
White, B.R., Ge7
White, D., Gi61
White, G., Eb4
White, G.P., Ie3
White, L., Gi21
White, R., Je1
White, S.D., Eg2
Whitelock, D., Dc5
Whittet, T.D., Bb43
Whittingham, S., Fk28
Whyte, I.D., Kg3
Wichert, S., Ib44
Widgery, D., Ib4
Wiener, M.J., Hl33
Wigham, E.L., Hb19
Wightman, W.E., Ef2
Wilde, P., Bb128
Wilford, R.A., Ib2
Wilkinson, R.S., Fk20
Wilkinson-Latham, C., Ba22
Willan, T.S., Ff22
Willen, D., Fb28
Williams, B., Ge24
Williams, D., Bb118
Williams, D., Eh13
Williams, D.E., Gg7
Williams, D.H., Je3
Williams, Glanmor, Fe50; Je2
Williams, Glyn, Hg28, 39
Williams, G.A., Ga11

159

SUBJECT INDEX

173

Humanism, Ei31; Fe7, j15, k1, 2, 56; Hl14
Hume, David, Ge27; i19–21, 37
Hungerford family, Ei54
Hunt, D.W.S., Id23; George Ward, Hb3; Richard William, Ei1
Hunter, William, Gi29, k3
Huntingdon, earl of, see Hastings; Selina, countess of, Ge20
Huntingdonshire, Eg13, 17
Husayn (Sharif of Mecca), Id10
Hussey family, Ej1
Huxley, Thomas Henry, Hk8
Huygens, Christiaan, Fk55
Hyde, Edward, earl of Clarendon, Fi27
Hyde Abbey, Bb39
Hywel Dda, kingship of, Jb3

Ickleford (Herts.), Bb35
Ideology, Hl51
Ignotus, Pictor, see Scott
Ilchester (Som.), Bb52
Immigration, Hg25; Ig11
Impeachment, Fc4
Imperialism, Hb68, d6, 12, 15, 17, 24, 27, f27, 102; Id3, f8
Incest, Fb18
Incomes, Gf63; If63; policy, Ib26, f67
Incunabula, Aa51
India, Aa60; Fd8; Ga13, h45; Hd10, 16, e25, 29; Ib10, d4, 21, 32
Indians (American), Ga11
Individualism, Hb63
Indo-China, Id5
Industrialization, Hf1, 46, 47, g35
Industrial: concentration, If68; law, If54–6; relations, Hf51, 66; reform, Hb6; revolution, Ge1, 2, f2, 16; Hd10
Industry, Anglo-Saxon, Df21; Chemical, Hk14; heavy, Hf20, 147; and see Aircraft, Armaments, Building, Coal, Distilling, Engineering, Fishing, Glass,

Hosiery, Iron, Lace, Lead, Lime, Linen, Mining, Papermaking, Pins, Pottery, Salt, Textiles
Infanticide, Fg8
Inflation, If40, 61
Inheritance, Ba65
Inkberrow, monastery of, Dc4
Inns, Bb20; Hg54, 125; of Court, Fe69, k6
Inscriptions, early Christian, Ca34; Roman, Ca10, 24, 26, 33, 51, 66, b5, 9
Inspectors (schools), Hc8
Insurance, Ab45; Ba63; Gf44
International Gothic Style, Ei110
Invasions, Saxon, Ji5, 6
inventions, Hk3
Inventories, Ff15, g37
Invergordon (mutiny), Ii35
investment, Hf8, 56, 64
Ipswich (Suff.), Hg17
Ireland, Aa61, 72; Bb112; Hb2, 28, 56; Ii11; famine in, Hb27; home rule for, Ac28, Hb23, 60; land question, Mb7; problem of, Ma3, b6, 7, 8, h1; Reformation in, Le1, 9–11; social structure of, Lg1; and see Northern Ireland
Irish: abroad, Li15; Anglo-, Mi3; exiles, Mg7; in England, Mg6; parliamentary party, see Parties; Republican Army, Ii11; Mh2
Iron (and steel) industry, Bb42; Ef10, i55, j20; Ff31; Gf25, 52, h13; Hf17, 66; If2, 50
Ironwork, Ca51
Isabella (wife of Edward II), Eb32
Islam, Ei92
Isleworth (Middx.), Bb92
Italy, Ei31; Hl72; Id22; Md1
Itinerary, Cb5
Ivie, John, Fg35
Ivory, Ca44

185

Steam engine, Ba45; Gf54
Steel, *see* Iron
Steel Brothers & Company
  Limited, Hf22
Stendhal (Beyle, Marie Henri),
  Hl40
Stephen (king), Eb1, 4, 19–21,
  e3
Stephens, Anthony, Fk58
Steuart, Sir Henry, Hl22
Stewart, Charles Williams, 3rd
  marquess of Londonderry,
  Hf65; James, earl of Moray,
  Kb11; Robert, viscount
  Castlereagh, Gb2
Stiffkey (Norf.), Ia15
Stilicho, Cb3
Stirling, Db6
Stixwould priory (Lincs.), Eb4
Stockport (Cheshire), Aa5, 6, 7;
  Bb62; Gf32; Hg31
Stokes, Sir Gabriel, Aa56
Stone, Nicholas, Fk15
Storehouses, Ca11
Strafford, earl of, *see* Wentworth
Streetlighting, Fg43
Strike, Hb5, 19, h11; general,
  Ia10, b13, 14, e6, f6–25, 39,
  42–7, 49
Stroudwater, Gf67
Stuart, James, Hk4
Submarines, Ii12, 31
Subsidy rolls, Fc8
Suez Canal, Id25
Suffolk, Bd7; Ca47; Eg5; Fe31
Suffragettes, Hb9, 12; Mb2
Sullivan's Island, Gh1
Sumptuary Laws, Eg10
Sunderland flying boat, Ii34
Sunningdale pact, Mb4
Surnames, Ab26; Eg5
Surrey, Bb90; Gh30, 35
Surveying, Ab9, 48; Bb89
Sussex, Aa10, 57, b18, 22; Bb25,
  d4; Fb4, 37, c15, e19, 45,
  g27, i12; Gh35; Hf35
Sutherland, Gf16; duke of, *see*

Leveson-Gower
Sutton (Yorks.), Ee13
Sutton Hoo (Suffolk), Df6
Swaledale, Bb53
Swansea (Glam.), Gi63; He17; Hf1
Swindon (Wilts.), Ha3, f55; If18
Swords, Df8
Symbolism, Ki4
Symington, William, Gf54
Syria, Ii38

Talbot, Gilbert, 7th earl of
  Shrewsbury, Fg5
Tamlyn, John, Hb36
Tanks, Ii20
Tarbga, battle of, Lb1
Tariffs, Hb39
Taunton, Fg21
Taxation, Ba12; Ec4; Fc8, 21,
  e14, 16, h9; Jg7
Taylor, A.J.P., Ac25; Bc8;
  George, Gf20, 24; Harriet, Hl2;
  John Thomas, Hf75; Joshua,
  Hf75
Teachers, Hi32; Ih6; training of,
  Ij3; *and see* Schools
Technology, Ih9
Tegeingl, Ji3
Telegraphy, Hk19
Television, If51
Temple, Henry John, 3rd Viscount
  Palmerston, Hb30, 76, e20,
  170; Sir William, Fi7; William
  (archbishop of Canterbury),
  Ie2
Temples, Ca15
Temporalities, Fe48
Tenant movement, Mg2
Terrington (Norf.), Fg23
Terrorism, Mh1, 2
Tewkesbury (Glos.), Hf101; Alan
  of, Ei95
Textiles, Aa46; Bb62; Ed11, f9;
  Gf44, 55, g15; Hf47, 75, 101,
  g55, k2; *and see* Knitting,
  Linen
Thames, If24